Also by John Avlon

LINCOLN

and the

FIGHT

for

PEACE

John Avlon

SIMON & SCHUSTER

New York London Toronto Sydney New Delhi

Simon & Schuster
1230 Avenue of the Americas
New York, NY 10020

First Simon & Schuster hardcover edition February 2022

SIMON & SCHUSTER and colophon are registered
trademarks of Simon & Schuster, Inc.

For information about special discounts for bulk purchases,
please contact Simon & Schuster Special Sales at
1-866-506-1949 or business@simonandschuster.com.

The Simon & Schuster Speakers Bureau can bring authors to
your live event. For more information or to book an event, contact
the Simon & Schuster Speakers Bureau at 1-866-248-3049
or visit our website at www.simonspeakers.com.

Manufactured in the United States of America

1   3   5   7   9   10   8   6   4   2

Library of Congress Cataloging-in-Publication Data
Names: Avlon, John P., author.
Title: Lincoln and the fight for peace / John Avlon.
Description: First Simon & Schuster hardcover edition. | New York :
Simon & Schuster, 2022. | Includes bibliographical references and index.
Identifiers: LCCN 2021042304 | ISBN 9781982108120 (hardcover) |
ISBN 9781982108144 (ebook)
Subjects: LCSH: Lincoln, Abraham, 1809–1865—Influence. | Lincoln,
Abraham, 1809–1865—Military leadership. | United States—History—
Civil War, 1861–1865—Peace. | Civil-military relations—United
States—History—19th century.
Classification: LCC E457 .A93 2022 | DDC 973.7092—dc23/eng/20211006
LC record available at https://lccn.loc.gov/2021042304

ISBN 978-1-9821-0812-0
ISBN 978-1-9821-0814-4 (ebook)

To my bride, Margaret
Our beautiful children, Jack & Toula Lou
And my parents, John & Dianne

"Human-nature will not change. In any future great national trial, compared with the men of this, we shall have as weak, and as strong, as silly and as wise, as bad and good. Let us, therefore, study the incidents of this, as philosophy to learn wisdom from, and none of them as wrongs to be revenged."

—*Abraham Lincoln*

Contents

Section IV

Section V

Section VI

LINCOLN

and the

FIGHT

for

PEACE

Introduction

April 4, 1865

Abraham Lincoln walked into the burning Confederate capital, uphill from the river, passing abandoned slave markets on his right, holding his son Tad's hand on the boy's twelfth birthday.

After four years of civil war, the president of the United States was in Richmond. Now he knew all the suffering had not been in vain: liberty and union would defeat slavery and secession.

He did not stride into the city like a conquering hero, flanked by a vast army. Instead, he arrived on a longboat with a small crew including an admiral, a bodyguard, and a dozen sailors, who acted as oarsmen. There was no military escort waiting to greet them as they scraped ashore. They were strangers in a strange land, wandering past burned-out buildings that jutted up like tombstones as smoke billowed against a blue sky.

A low murmur rose among the ruins at the sight of the six-foot-four man in black, slightly stooped, topped by his signature stovepipe hat. It was the sound of rumor turning to revelation. A crowd of liberated slaves gathered around Lincoln. They grabbed at his clothes and fell at his feet. "Don't kneel to me," Lincoln gently rebuked them. "That is not right. You must kneel to God only and thank Him for the liberty you will afterward enjoy."[1]

Thomas Morris Chester, a pioneering black war correspondent for *The Philadelphia Press*, was among the first journalists to see Lincoln enter the rebel capital and he scribbled down the celebration.

"Old men thanked God in a very boisterous manner, and old women shouted upon the pavement as high as they had ever done at a religious revival," he wrote. "There were many whites in the crowd, but they were lost in the great concourse of American citizens of African descent. Those who lived in the finest houses either stood motionless upon their steps or merely peeped through the window blinds."[2]

It seemed that the meek would finally inherit the earth, or at least Richmond.

Death hovered over his shoulder. Surrounded by rowdy crowds, Lincoln's bodyguard thought he spied a sharpshooter in a second-floor window point a rifle at the president and trace his path without firing a shot.[3]

Lincoln and Tad were caught in the eye of a human hurricane, winding up the road toward the marble capitol building on the top of the hill, passing the place where Virginia ratified the U.S. Constitution fewer than eighty years before.

It was an uphill climb and beads of sweat collected on their dust-covered faces. As Lincoln stopped to wipe his brow, an older black man approached the president and took off his hat, placing it over his heart, saying, "May the Good Lord Bless You, President Lincoln." The president responded by removing his own hat and bowed in return.

"It was a bow which upset the forms, laws, customs and ceremonies of centuries," observed Charles Coffin of the *Boston Journal*. "It was a death shock to chivalry, and a mortal wound to caste."[4]

As they passed the notorious Libby Prison, where more than a thousand Union officers had been held in horrific conditions, Lincoln pointed out the brick and iron structure to his son. The crowd shouted, "Tear it down!" but the president raised his hand and quieted them, saying, "No, leave it as a monument."[5] Healing could not occur by simply erasing history. It would require learning the right lessons, so we were not condemned to repeat it.

As they turned a corner in the city center, soldiers from the New York Fiftieth regiment were shocked to bump into their commander in chief, walking with his "long, careless stride," one soldier recalled, "looking about with an interested air" as he casually asked them for directions.[6] They marched him up to the steps of the gray stucco executive mansion, abandoned by Confederate president Jefferson Davis and his family the day before, where Union general Godfrey Weitzel, a twenty-nine-year-old German immigrant, had set up headquarters.

Entering the tall yellow hallway, flanked by plaster Greek statues representing comedy and tragedy, Lincoln was led to the small ceremonial office on the first floor and sank down into the leather chair behind Jefferson Davis's desk. As he leaned back, letting his long legs stretch, he looked out the same window that Davis had gazed through so many times before. His face seemed "care-plowed, tempest-tossed,"[7] but close observers always noticed his "kind, shining" eyes.[8] Lincoln ran a hand through his unruly black hair, and asked for a glass of water.

It was a moment of supreme triumph but there was no hint of triumphalism. General Lee's army had not yet surrendered—that would come five days later at Appomattox Court House. But the Civil War had been won.

The past four years had been defined by political crisis and personal despair: the death of his beloved eleven-year-old son Willie, the death of friends in battle, and the near death of the Union under his watch. His own family had been divided, with Mary's brothers fighting for the Confederacy, while his marriage strained to the breaking point. Seven months earlier, Lincoln believed that he would lose reelection.

Now Lincoln was looking forward: vindicated by the people's vote and determined to stop the cycle of violence, changing his focus from winning the war to winning the peace.

Surrounded by the ghosts of the Confederacy, Lincoln toured the mansion, its tall drawing rooms with crimson wallpaper and cramped living quarters upstairs. He saw military maps that mirrored his own, pinned to the walls of the rebel cabinet room where the stars and stripes now stood.

Lincoln met with his generals around a long dining room table, eager to be briefed on what they had found amid the surviving files of the slave state, while officers toasted with Jefferson Davis's whiskey and Tad dashed around the mansion.

Reflecting his belief that "public opinion is everything," the president wanted to get the feeling of the people in the South and asked to meet with a few prominent Richmond residents. Among them was John A. Campbell, the former U.S. Supreme Court Justice turned

Confederate assistant Secretary of War. They had met two months before at a secret peace conference at Hampton Roads, Virginia, where Lincoln had refused anything short of unconditional surrender. Now Campbell appealed to Lincoln's instinct for mercy and moderation, with the manipulative wit to quote the president's favorite author, Shakespeare: "when lenity and cruelty play for a kingdom, the gentler gamester is the soonest winner."[9]

In this twilight between war and peace, the outcome was certain, but the terms were not yet determined. Lincoln repeated his three "indispensable conditions" for peace: no ceasefire before surrender, the restoration of the Union, and the end of slavery for all time. Everything else was negotiable. Lincoln wanted a hard war to be followed by a soft peace; but there would be no compromise on these core principles.

As he walked out of the Confederate White House, Lincoln stopped on the front steps, flanked by black soldiers in blue uniforms, and spoke to the crowd of freedmen and women. "Although you have been deprived of your God-given rights by your so-called masters, you are now as free as I am . . . for God created all men free, giving to each the same rights of life, liberty and the pursuit of happiness."[10]

Amid riotous cheers, Lincoln left in a carriage led by four horses, waving to the crowd with Tad by his side, rolling toward the capitol building designed by Thomas Jefferson. Its courtyard was a frenzy of jubilation under the watchful eye of Union soldiers, as worthless Confederate bank notes fluttered in the breeze. Lincoln picked up a torn $5 bill and placed it in his wallet as a keepsake.

Down by the docks at sunset, as Lincoln prepared to board a barge that would take him to his ship for the night, General Weitzel asked him for guidance. How should he treat the traitorous rebels and scared citizens now under his command?

Lincoln characteristically offered advice rather than an order: "We must extinguish our resentments if we expect harmony and union. If I were in your place, I'd let 'em up easy, let 'em up easy."[11]

This is the story of Abraham Lincoln's plan to win the peace after winning the war: his vision for national reconciliation and reunification.

Lincoln confronted a problem without precedent. There had never been a civil war fought on such a scale: 384 battles across twenty-six states,[12] leaving three-quarters of a million Americans dead[13]—more than all the country's subsequent wars combined. Laid end-to-end, their coffins would have stretched from New York to Atlanta.[14]

Until that point, civil wars were an afterthought—not even earning a mention in the 1832 military classic *On War* by Carl von Clausewitz.[15] But the slaughter in the world's sole democracy was being closely watched around the world.

European autocrats salivated with "dreams of conquest on the Western continent," in the belief that "self-government has proven itself a failure," a *New York Times* correspondent reported from France.[16] In Britain, a member of the House of Lords boasted that "democracy has been on trial in America and it has failed . . . Separation is inevitable and the establishment of some sort of aristocracy is inevitable!"[17]

Democracy *was* at stake. In combating secession after an election, Lincoln was establishing that "among free men, there can be no successful appeal from the ballot to the bullet."[18] Liberty was on the line as well, with four million enslaved African-Americans held in bondage throughout the South. But Lincoln was also working on the most difficult problem of all: how to stop a civil war. Not just the one hemorrhaging life in his own time, but how to stop a future civil war from igniting from the ashes of the past.

To reunite the nation, he would need to invent a revolutionary new way of winning the peace. Lincoln believed this was "the greatest question ever presented to practical statesmanship,"[19] requiring "the wisdom of a serpent and the gentleness of a dove."[20]

Lincoln's essential insight was that winning the war on the battlefield wasn't enough. In a civil war, you could not simply pound your opponents into submission or salt the fields of the conquered country, like Rome did to Carthage, causing Tacitus to write: "they make a desert and call it peace."[21] After civil war in a democracy, fighting citizens would need to learn to live together again. Lincoln understood that if you do not win the peace, you do not really win the war.

For two years, he had been planning for postwar reconstruction and reconciliation. "In his mind, he was all ready for the civil reorganization of affairs at the South as soon as the war was over," attested General William Tecumseh Sherman. "As soon as the rebel armies laid down their arms, and resumed their civil pursuits, they would at once be guaranteed all their rights as citizens of a common country."[22]

Even amid the pressures of a wartime presidency, Lincoln was thinking long-term, looking beyond the violence of the moment to see the broader canvas of cause and effect, mindful that "the struggle of today is not altogether for today; it is for a vast future also."[23] The fight for peace requires the ability to imagine a future that is not predetermined by the pain of the past—and the leadership to turn that vision into reality.

Working without a historic parallel to guide him, Lincoln established a new model of leadership focused on reconciliation that could make a just and lasting peace possible. He would become the reconciler-in-chief.

Reconciliation is a word deep with meanings. It is the action of restoring harmony and friendship, resolving differences. It can mean confronting contradictions and making a divided system whole and consistent.

In politics, reconciliation is the opposite of resentment and revenge. It is optimistic and practical. The limited literature on what is now formally called "reconciliation-oriented leadership" describes it as reflecting "the ability to control desires for vengeance and retaliation against enemies . . . optimistic assessments of others' capacity for change . . . non-judgmental, non-dogmatic and practical approaches to conflict resolution."[24]

These characteristics were rooted in Lincoln's personality, informing his principles and finding expression in his politics.

He was a man of peace in a time of war, tough-minded but tender-hearted. While spurring his generals to be more aggressive on the battlefield, Lincoln embodied an interpersonal absence of malice. He practiced the politics of the Golden Rule—treating others as he would like to be treated. He did not demonize people he disagreed with, understanding that empathy is a pathway to persuasion. He was uncommonly honest and tried to depolarize bitter debates by using humor, logic, and scripture. Balancing moral courage with moderation, Lincoln believed that decency could be the most practical form of politics. But he also understood that people were more inclined to listen to reason when greeted from a position of strength.

From this foundation, Lincoln developed his prescription for peacemaking: unconditional surrender followed by a magnanimous peace.

Military gains would be secured through political reform to address the root causes of the conflict, economic expansion to offer renewed optimism about a shared future, and cultural reintegration to reunite the nation, with liberty and equality for all.

There have been more than 16,000 books published about Abraham Lincoln, but few—if any—have focused on his role as a peacemaker.[25] This is understandable: he was shot just five days after the surrender of Confederate general Robert E. Lee and did not have a chance to carry out his vision for winning the peace.

But particularly in the last six weeks of his life—between his Second Inaugural Address and his final speech at the war's end—Lincoln articulated a clear vision of the principles that he hoped would guide the United States toward reconciliation and reunification.

Lincoln's personal example in the closing days of the war offers the portrait of a peacemaker. While his assassination would send the country careening off course, his vision would be vindicated long after his death, inspiring future generations in their own quests to secure a just and lasting peace, finding its ultimate expression in the occupations of Germany and Japan and the Marshall Plan after the Second World War. The lessons of his leadership remain relevant today, offering a path away from violent polarization and toward reconciliation in defense of democracy.

The spring of 1865 was a hinge of history, crowded hours of war and peace, beginning with Lincoln's Second Inaugural. It was a secular sermon, a meditation on the war as shared penance for America's original sin of slavery. The redemption of a new birth of freedom—fulfilling the founders' promise in the Declaration of Independence that "all men are created equal"—would require forgiveness and a commitment to rebuilding the bonds of affection between fellow Americans. This was New Testament leadership, offering the promise of national life after so much death.

As the tide of the war turned, Lincoln took a dangerous two-week trip to the front lines, seeing combat up close and comforting wounded Union and Confederate soldiers alike. He huddled with his generals and hammered home the same message: "Let them surrender and go home," Lincoln said. "They will not take up arms again. Let them all go, officers and all, let them have their horses to plow with, and, if you like, their guns to shoot crows with. Treat them liberally. We want these people to return to their allegiance and submit to the laws. Therefore, I say, give them the most liberal and honorable terms."[26]

Ulysses S. Grant's famously generous terms of surrender to Robert E. Lee at Appomattox were a direct expression of Lincoln's wishes on how to achieve the art of peace.

Two nights later, crowds gathered on the torchlit White House lawn expecting to hear a celebratory speech to mark the end of the Civil War. Instead, Lincoln said that the work of reconciliation had just begun and presented a practical explanation of the principles behind Reconstruction. He was willing to be flexible on details but he would not compromise on larger goals, saying: "important principles may, and must, be inflexible."

To that end, Lincoln publicly expressed for the first time his support for giving freedmen the right to vote. In the crowd, a Southern-sympathizing alcoholic actor named John Wilkes Booth hissed "that means nigger citizenship! Now, by God, I'll put him through. That is the last speech he will ever make."[27] And it was.

He was born in the South and moved north and west as a young man, from Kentucky to Indiana to Illinois. His rise was a rebuke to aristocracy: he grew up in a log cabin with a dirt floor, his father was a carpenter and farmer, his mother died when he was nine, buried in a coffin the boy helped build. Abraham never had much formal schooling, but he read ravenously. He worked his way off the family farm, and traveled down the Mississippi on a flatbed boat to New Orleans, where he saw slaves in chains and a slumbering conscience began to awake.

At age twenty-two, Lincoln arrived alone in the river town of New Salem, Illinois, and got a job in the general store in exchange for room and board while he taught himself the law. Neighbors recalled his good humor and uncommon honesty. As a lawyer, he used jokes and stories to disarm opponents and make serious points, a technique he'd learned around the cracker-barrel, reinforced by his favorite books: Aesop's Fables, the Bible, and Shakespeare's plays.

Humor was also a way to "whistle off the shadows," one friend recalled.[28] As a young man, he was a secret poet, alternately passionate and detached, calling off two engagements and enduring at least one dark night when friends hid knives out of fear that he might kill himself. But the thought that he "had done nothing to make any human being remember he had lived"[29] spurred Lincoln past despair. He rallied and married the comely Mary Todd, the mercurial daughter of a prosperous, politically connected Kentucky family.

It would have been easy for an ambitious self-made man to join Illinois's dominant political party and benefit from the Democrats' patronage and power. But Lincoln rejected Andrew Jackson's Southern populists and instead rose to the top of the local Whig Party, a moderate party of merchants and strivers who balanced middle-class morality with a belief in modernization. They backed Henry Clay's "American System" of infrastructure improvements to stitch together frontier communities with roads, canals, and bridges to build a great nation that offered equality of opportunity for all. This was the proper role of government in Lincoln's eyes: to do for people what they could not do for themselves.*[30]

---

* "The legitimate object of government, is to do for a community of people, whatever they need to have done, but can not do, *at all*, or can not, *so well do*, for themselves—in their separate, and individual capacities. In all that the people can individually do as well for themselves, government ought not to interfere." Abraham Lincoln, Fragment on Government, circa July 1, 1854.

As leader of his party in the Illinois state legislature, Lincoln already exhibited his approach to leadership. "He did not try to club men into line," reflected his colleague Shelby Cullom. "It was not a case of force. It was a case of persuasion. People came to support him because they came to believe he was right, and he showed them this was so by his reason."[31]

Lincoln graduated to serve a single term in the House of Representatives from 1847 to 1849. Although he had a grand time getting to know his peers from across the country and learning the arm twisting of congressional politics, Lincoln's time in Washington was undistinguished. His most notable vote came in opposing President James K. Polk's war with Mexico, blasting the glamorization of war as an "attractive rainbow that rises in showers of blood"[32] while warning that America's first entry into empire was unwise. But the Mexican–American War proved popular; anti-war sentiment was not. So Lincoln slunk back to Springfield, with the Whig Party in disarray and decline.

By age forty, Abraham Lincoln felt like a failure. He tried to content himself with providing for his growing family. Hanging a wood shingle outside a second-floor law office in Springfield, he rode the legal circuit, telling stories while meeting with local politicos and newspaper editors. Making real money for the first time, he distracted himself with the always available elixir of laughter and the joy of playing with his children, whom he notably declined to discipline, believing that "love is the chain whereby to lock a child to his parent."[33]

But repercussions from the war with Mexico triggered a political earthquake. The acquisition of new American territory from Texas to California forced the question of slavery's expansion beyond the South. This was the tinderbox the founders feared, threatening to overturn the Northwest Ordinance, which outlawed slavery in new territories. In 1854, Congress pushed through the Kansas–Nebraska Act, putting a veneer of compromise on the expansion of slavery by putting it to a popular vote in new states.

It set off a firestorm that would kill the Whigs, create the most successful third-party in American history, and elevate Abraham Lincoln to the presidency—all within six years.

Lincoln believed the expansion of slavery meant the end of the American experiment. But the Whigs met this moment of crisis with indecision. Split between pro-slavery Southerners and abolitionists in the North, the Whigs were doomed by a muddled message on the great moral issue of their time.

The political landscape was fractured beyond recognition. The Democrats were conservative populists, dedicated to the defense of slavery. The opposition was in evolution. A cacophony of abolitionist parties popped up across New England, from the Liberty Party to the Free Soil Party. But there was a backlash brewing as well: a massive influx of immigrants fueled the rise of the nationalist American Party—better known to history as the Know Nothings. Its members adopted the pose of a secret society as much as a political party, pledging to never support a foreign born or Catholic candidate—reserving special venom for the Irish—and requiring members to say "I know nothing" when asked about their movement. This did not seem ironic until decades later.

Their extremism did not stop them from gaining influence. In a few short years, they elected governors in nine states,[34] eight senators,[35] and seventy-eight members of the House.[36] Several of Lincoln's former Illinois Whig colleagues joined the Know Nothings, but he bucked at the prospect. He'd long been an advocate of new immigrants, eventually buying a silent stake in a German language newspaper.[37]

The flag-waving bigotry troubled him, he wrote his friend Joshua Speed, while stewing on his political homelessness. "I am not a Know-Nothing, that is certain. How could I be? How can anyone who abhors the oppression of negroes be in favor of degrading classes of white men? Our progress in degeneracy appears to me to be pretty rapid. As a nation, we began by declaring that '*all men are created equal.*' We now practically read it 'all men are created equal, *except negroes.*' When the Know-Nothings get control, it will read 'all men are created equal, *except negroes, and foreigners, and catholics.*' When it comes to this, I should prefer emigrating to some country where they make no pretense of loving liberty—to Russia, for instance, where despotism can be taken pure, and without the base alloy of hypocrisy."[38]

Out of this primordial political slime climbed the Republicans. Throughout the upper Midwest, former Whigs were joining with Free Soilers and other abolitionists to oppose the expansion of slavery. In March 1854, one group met in Ripon, Wisconsin, and adopted the name Republican in a nod to the other half of Thomas Jefferson's original Democratic-Republican Party. They held their first convention in July at Jackson, Michigan, with a few dozen citizens standing under an oak tree to escape the heat, and put forward a slate of candidates.

They offered a big tent, including committed abolitionists as well as citizens who simply opposed slavery's expansion, united by a common belief in free labor and the right to rise up the economic ladder. In New York, former Whigs like abolitionist William Seward and the opportunistic newspaper editor Horace Greeley were among the first to rally under the new banner, and Seward wound up winning the Governor's Mansion in Albany that fall. In six months, the Republicans went from a meetinghouse in Wisconsin to control the most powerful and populous state in the Union. Four years later, they took over the House of Representatives.

At first, Lincoln was reluctant to get on the Republican bandwagon, fretting to a friend about his political indecision in 1855: "I think I am a Whig, but others say there are no Whigs, and that I am an abolitionist ... [but] I now do no more than oppose the *extension* of slavery."[39] But he was coaxed into giving a speech at the Republicans' inaugural Illinois convention, receiving cheers that rattled the rafters. Lincoln had found his political home.

When pressed to describe the differences between the fledgling Republican and Democratic parties, he said: "The [Democrats] of today hold the *liberty* of one man to be absolutely nothing when in conflict with another man's right of *property*. Republicans, on the contrary, are for both the *man* and the *dollar*; but in cases of conflict, the man *before* the dollar."[40]

Worthwhile political combat requires a great cause and an opponent who gets the blood up. Lincoln found that in his home state: Senator Stephen Douglas, a self-satisfied rotundity who had once courted Mary and authored the infamous Kansas–Nebraska Act that expanded slavery. He decided to challenge Douglas for reelection in 1858. Douglas was already famous, dubbed "the Little Giant." Lincoln was an unknown, single-issue candidate, representing an upstart political party. Overconfident, Douglas agreed to a series of debates across the state.

This was political pugilism at the highest level—a lanky country lawyer against the Little Giant. "'A house divided against itself cannot stand,'" Lincoln declared at the kickoff of his campaign, riffing off the Book of Matthew. "I believe this Government cannot endure permanently half *slave* and half *free*. I do not expect the Union to be *dissolved*—I do not expect the house to *fall*—but I do expect it will cease to be divided. It will become *all* one thing or *all* the other."[41]

One of the cynical arguments Lincoln confronted was Stephen Douglas's alleged agnosticism on slavery. Douglas said he was exhausted by the defining debate of the day, declaring, "I don't care whether it be voted up or down."[42] It was a matter of economics for the people of the states to decide—and who could be against that in a democracy?

This dodge let Douglas off the hook for backing slavery's expansion while appearing to be supremely rational on the subject. But his affected indifference offended the earnest Lincoln, who slammed Douglas's "absence of moral sense about the question" and accused him of trying "to bring public opinion to the point of utter indifference whether men so brutalized are enslaved or not."[43] He declared war on apathy because it enabled the expansion of evil. Democracy requires a degree of moral imagination regarding how politics and policy affect other people, even if you are not directly affected.

Douglas's pose also diminished democracy's moral authority: "I hate it because it deprives our republican example of its just influence in the world," Lincoln argued, "enables the enemies of free institutions, with plausibility, to taunt us as hypocrites—causes the real friends of freedom to doubt our sincerity . . . [by] insisting that there is no right principle of action but self-interest."[44]

Lincoln won the debates but lost the Senate race. Nonetheless, he became nationally known as his inspired arguments rocketed across the country via telegraph and newspapers. He cemented his reputation with a speech at New York City's Cooper Union in February 1860, in which he thundered: "Let us have faith that right makes might."[45]

The speech electrified the audience. A correspondent for the *New-York Tribune*, George Haven Putnam, started out feeling pity for the "angular and awkward" man whose clothes were "ill-fitting, badly wrinkled, as if they'd been jammed carelessly in a trunk." But those impressions faded as Lincoln got into the groove of his speech and "his face lighted as with an inward fire; the whole man was transfigured." Soon, Putnam said, "I was on my feet with the rest, yelling like a wild

Indian . . . It was a great speech. When I came out of the hall, my face glowing with excitement and my frame all aquiver, a friend, with his eyes aglow, asked me what I thought of Abe Lincoln, the rail-splitter. I said, 'He's the greatest man since St. Paul!' And I think so yet."[46]

The 1860 Republican National Convention was held in Chicago, Lincoln's political backyard. The rail-splitter proved to be a compelling compromise candidate: he was seen as more moderate and honest than New York governor William Seward, and crucially he was from the West—a fresh face from a rising region of the nation. He was nominated on the third ballot.

The Lincoln campaign became a crusade, with young men marching as members of "Wide Awake" clubs, a new generation politically awakened and echoing Revolutionary era militias. Their lanterns were emblazoned with a single open eye while their signs featured the beardless face of Lincoln, who did not leave Springfield to campaign, consistent with the custom.

It was a four-way presidential race. The Democrats were divided, with Stephen Douglas representing Northern Democrats while the forty-year-old incumbent vice president, John C. Breckinridge, was the nominee of secessionist Southern Democrats. To this mix was added a former Whig, John Bell, running under the banner of the Constitutional Union party, promising to preserve both the Union and slavery.

Republicans had momentum and math on their side. In November, Lincoln swept the North and Midwest as well as the states on the Pacific coast. But he was blocked from appearing on the ballot in the Deep South and, despite a decisive electoral victory, Lincoln carried just 39 percent of the popular vote. Regardless, the rise of the Republicans was a political revolution. They had won not only the presidency but both houses of Congress.

After the election, Lincoln said, "let us neither express, nor cherish, any harsh feeling towards any citizen who, by his vote, has differed from us. Let us at all times remember that all American citizens are brothers of a common country."[47] But Southern Democrats refused to accept his legitimacy. The mere fact of Abraham Lincoln's ascension was enough to spark secession and bring on a Civil War.

The story of how a small band of slave-owning extremists was able to hijack American politics, divide the country, and start the Civil War might surprise you.

Secession was not a broad popular movement at first. While white supremacy was ingrained in society, only a small percentage of Southerners actually owned slaves—some 316,000 slave owners out of 5.6 million Southern whites, according to the 1860 census.[48] Southern politicians never dared to put the decision to break apart the Union to a popular vote, because in most Southern states, they likely would have lost.

In 1860, the secessionist candidate Breckinridge lost Virginia, Kentucky, and Tennessee, and failed to win a majority of votes in Georgia and Louisiana. Even after Lincoln's election, political conventions from four states in the Deep South—Mississippi, Alabama, Georgia, and Louisiana—refused to give their citizens a chance to vote on secession. Lincoln hoped that this was evidence of a slumbering pro-Union sentiment among Southerners, arguing in his first message to Congress: "It may well be questioned whether there is to-day a majority of the legally qualified voters of any State, except, perhaps, South Carolina, in favor of disunion."[49]

But Lincoln acknowledged that these separatists "have been drugging the public mind of their section for more than thirty years."[50] They were elites posing as populists, driven by fear of demographic change.

Building a "blood and soil" appeal to racial and regional identity, their anxiety grew as the nation grew. The international slave trade to the United States had been officially banned since 1808. Spain abolished slavery in 1811, followed by Britain in 1833. With the tide turning against them, increasingly isolated and outnumbered, slave states rigged congressional rules to give them disproportionate influence in the belief that real representative democracy would be a death sentence. After all, by 1860 there were 40 percent more slaves than whites in South Carolina.[51] White elites needed to keep control by any means necessary.

Sometimes this meant cloaking their interests in grand constitutional arguments about states' rights. Increasingly, on the floor of Congress, it meant threats of violence while playing the victim—a tactic known as "aggressive defensiveness."

They tried to intimidate their opposition into silence as a way of masking their own declining electoral power. There were more than seventy violent clashes between Southern and Northern members of Congress in the thirty years before the Civil War, as historian Joanne Freeman details in her book *The Field of Blood*.[52] But the real purpose of this violence was to create the illusion that safeguarding slavery was a reasonable alternative to conflict. In the South, they succeeded in framing the debate as a choice between Southern honor and Yankee domination.

They were buying and selling human beings, separating families, enforcing order with shackles and whips. But slaveholders didn't feel evil. They saw themselves as misunderstood bulwarks of civilization. They complained that Northern abolitionists were the real aggressors, causing some to double down on their defense of slavery. As Andrew Jackson's vice president John C. Calhoun argued in 1838, "in reaction . . . many in the South once believed that [slavery] was a moral and political evil; that folly and delusion are gone; we see it now in its true light, and regard it as the most safe and stable basis for free institutions in the world."[53] They claimed that their state's right to slavery was a question of liberty. Twisting logic even further, they argued secession was a form of patriotism because they put loyalty to their state ahead of the nation. They felt judged by outsiders who did not understand their way of life. They reacted to this perceived hate with hate.

The 1859 attack of abolitionist John Brown on Harpers Ferry gave bloody evidence for the South's feeling of persecution by fanatics. His execution gave abolitionists a martyr. But Lincoln took a reasonable tone even at this: "Old John Brown has been executed for treason against a State," he said. "We cannot object, even though he agreed with us in thinking slavery wrong. That cannot excuse violence, bloodshed and treason. It could avail him nothing that he might think himself right."[54]

During the 1860 election, Southern Democrats tried to paint

Lincoln as an extremist who stood for the unconstitutional abolition of slavery through executive power. Lincoln said, and the record showed, that he only opposed the expansion of slavery as a means of keeping the nation united, though he opposed slavery personally.

But negative partisanship—demonizing the opposition to distract from your party's less defensible positions—can be persuasive. Lincoln and the Republicans were routinely attacked as a motley crew of radicals, captured in one widely circulated Currier and Ives print showing Lincoln being carried on a rail into a lunatic asylum, followed by a parade of crudely caricatured special interests.

In the cartoon, a man with long-flowing locks says, "I represent the free love element, and expect to have free license," while a man walking arm in arm with him states, "I want religion abolished." Behind them, a dandified racist representation of a black man in a top hat proclaims in dialect, "De white man hah no rights dat cullud pussons am bound to 'spect" (an inversion of an infamous statement made by Supreme Court Chief Justice Roger Taney). Next in line, a spinster states, "I want women's rights enforced, and man reduced in subjugation to her authority," while a drunk grasping a bottle behind her says, "I want everybody to have a share of everybody else's property," finally followed by a staggering, barefoot ne'er-do-well yelling, "I want a hotel established by government where people that ain't inclined to work can board free of expense and be found in rum and tobacco."[55]

This 150-year-old political cartoon captured enduring stereotypes used to tar progressives as a parade of sexual libertines, atheists, feminists, and socialists. The fact that these stereotypes existed well before African-Americans or women had won the right to vote, or a social safety net actually existed, shows how these deep-seated fears have been mobilized in political campaigns for more than a century.

Slave-owning Southerners threatened secession if Republicans won the election as a way to intimidate undecided voters. Lincoln mocked this threat by comparing it to a highway robber who "holds a pistol to my ear, and mutters through his teeth, 'Stand and deliver, or I shall kill you, and then you will be a murderer!'"[56] It was illogical but it was not a bluff. They believed the election was a matter of life or death. This set the psychological preconditions for civil war.

Within a week of Lincoln winning the presidency, South Carolina's senators resigned their seats as their state legislature approved money to raise ten thousand soldiers. They refused to acknowledge Lincoln's legitimacy. This was soon followed by the Georgia legislature voting to appropriate $1 million to purchase guns and artillery.

The lame-duck Democrat president James Buchanan's response was to blame the Republicans. In his final December message to Congress, Buchanan denounced the "intemperate interference of the Northern people with the question of slavery."[57] His attempts at appeasement did not work.

The week before Christmas, a South Carolina secession convention unanimously voted to leave the United States. On December 30, the federal arsenal in Charleston was seized by local forces. In January, emboldened by this action, Mississippi, Florida, Alabama, Georgia, and Louisiana seceded from the Union in closed partisan conventions, refusing to put the question to a popular vote.

On February 18, Mississippi's former U.S. senator Jefferson Davis was inaugurated president of the Confederate States of America in Montgomery, Alabama, with an alternative constitution that explicitly invoked both God and slavery. Vice President Alexander Stephens of Georgia frankly declared that their new government's "cornerstone rests upon the great truth that the negro is not equal to the white man."[58] In contrast to the promise of the Declaration of Independence, the Confederacy was based on the idea that all men were *not* created equal.

Two weeks later, Lincoln gave his inaugural address in Washington under threat of assassination and insurrection. He tried to appeal to the common bonds between his dissatisfied countrymen and gave the world a glimpse of the poetry of democracy in his closing sentences: "We are not enemies, but friends. We must not be enemies. Though passion may have strained it must not break our bonds of affection. The mystic chords of memory, stretching from every battlefield and patriot grave to every living heart and hearthstone all over this broad land, will yet swell the chorus of the Union, when again touched, as surely they will be, by the better angels of our nature."[59]

At 4:30 in the morning on April 12, South Carolina fired on Fort

Sumter in Charleston Harbor. Lincoln mobilized state militias under federal control in response. He was always careful to accuse "seceder politicians" for the outbreak of war rather than the majority of Southerners. He would not engage in group blame, even as he insisted that there was no right to secession in the Constitution and, therefore, his oath required taking action, where his predecessor, President Buchanan, had allowed the problem to metastasize through indecision.

For Confederates, violence accelerated polarization, providing the push they needed to mobilize the South amid the rapid accumulation of resentments. "Blood grows hot, and blood is spilled," Lincoln wrote. "Revenge and retaliation follow."[60] Every dead soldier added to the thirst for revenge. Tribalism overwhelmed reason as Southerners felt compelled to take sides with their neighbors against the North, deepening divisions until many saw the only alternative to be total victory, a cleansing Armageddon.

And so the war came. The people pushing the virtue of violence said it would all be over quickly. They were wrong.

Four years before, Abraham Lincoln had been a washed-up, one-term congressman: a man without a party or a political future. He had no meaningful military or executive experience. Nothing in his life seemed to prepare him to lead a great nation through the Civil War.

As a new president from a new party, Lincoln was often disrespected and demonized. Newspapers called him "weak and wishy-washy," an "imbecile in matter, disgusting in manner" and an "obscene Illinois ape."[61] Democrats derided him as a tyrant, a fool, and "King Abraham Africanus I." More surprising were the insults hurled from fellow Republicans. Secretary of the Treasury Salmon P. Chase groused that Lincoln was "not earnest enough, not anti-slavery enough, not radical enough."[62] Michigan senator Zachariah Chandler dismissed Lincoln as "timid, vacillating and inefficient,"[63] while Ohio's party founder William Dickson complained he had "no will, no courage, no executive capacity."[64]

Despite all the attacks, he did not obsess over critics. Lincoln believed that "truth is generally the best vindication against slander."[65]

And he genially accepted that his decisions would be judged by their results:"Time will show whether I am right or whether they are right and I am content to abide the decision of time."[66]

As the verdict came in at the end of his first term, *The New York Times* compared Lincoln to George Washington, citing his "great calmness of temper, great firmness of purpose, supreme moral principle and intense patriotism,"[67] while the poet and statesman James Russell Lowell praised him for demonstrating that "profound common sense is the best genius for statesmanship."[68]

What accounts for this transformation from an untested prairie lawyer to a wise wartime president? Lincoln's leadership style flowed from the essential qualities of his personality: empathy, honesty, humor, and humility.

He was the opposite of a demagogue, those leaders who reflexively divide the world into us against them. His motto was "fairness to all"[69] and his favorite Biblical quote was "let us judge not, lest we be judged." Even in heated political debates he said, "I do not question the patriotism . . . or assail the motives of any man."[70]

He possessed the moral imagination to see himself in others, telling listeners that he was antislavery and anti-secession—not anti-South. "I think I have no prejudice against the Southern people," he said. "They are just what we would be in their situation."[71]

Lincoln empathized with his opponents as a means of reasoning with them, understanding that democracy depends upon persuasion. "It is an old and true maxim that a drop of honey catches more flies than a gallon of gall," he said. "So with men, if you would win a man to your cause, first convince him that you are his sincere friend. Therein is a drop of honey that catches his heart, which say what you will, is the great high road to his reason . . . On the contrary, assume to dictate to his judgment, or to command his action, or to mark him as one to be shunned and despised, he will retreat within himself, close all avenues to his head and his heart."[72]

He did not demonize opponents, even as they called for his death. Lincoln instructed ambassadors to "indulge in no expressions of harshness or disrespect or even impatience concerning the seceding states . . . their citizens throughout all political misunderstandings and alienations, still are and always must be kindred and countrymen."[73] Even in private, he declined to attack Confederate president Jefferson Davis and General Robert E. Lee in personal terms, preferring to call them by the familiar, if dismissive, "Jeffey D" and "Bobby Lee."[74] The Civil War was a family feud between brothers, not eternal enemies.

Critics often mistook his kindness for weakness. "I am charged with making too many mistakes on the side of mercy,"[75] he admitted. He disliked interpersonal conflict and a disarming number of colleagues commented on his "childlike" heart. To the dismay of Secretary of War Edwin Stanton, Lincoln issued 343 pardons over the course of his presidency, but he refused to stop the execution of a slave-trader[76] or anyone whose offense was rooted in cruelty.* His administration issued the first modern laws of war in an attempt to stop it from sliding entirely into barbarism. But Lincoln combined his kindness with an iron-willed determination to win, telegraphing Grant in 1864 to "hold on with a bulldog grip, and chew and choke as much as possible."[77]

Even his enemies admitted he was honest. It was a core quality that could not be credibly denied. "He was wise and he was honest," Jefferson Davis confessed toward the end of his life.[78] Stephen Douglas conceded that "he is as honest as he is shrewd."[79] His wife, Mary, declared him "too honest for this world"[80] while criticizing his tolerance for political rivals in his cabinet. His reputation for honesty created trust, giving him credibility when negotiating with adversaries.

His honesty was leavened with humor—a disarming combination. Lincoln's jokes were reprinted in newspapers across the country, enhancing his popularity and reputation for backwoods common sense.

He enjoyed his own jokes at least as much as listeners, with an ironic twinkle in his eye and an infectious laugh that one friend compared to a wild horse's neigh.[81] He was a gifted mimic, a talent that

---

* Though he still receives criticism for the mass execution of thirty-eight Sioux warriors after the Dakota Uprising, less remembered is that Lincoln commuted the sentences of 264 warriors who had been sentenced to death in the same attack after reviewing their charges, over the objection of Minnesota's Republican senator.

lives next door to mockery, but he learned to avoid making other people the butt of his jokes.

"Lincoln had two characters," an old Illinois friend, Judge Henry Enoch Dummer, reflected. "One of purity—& the other as it were an insane love in telling dirty and smutty stories—a good story of that kind has a point with the sting to it."[82]

His storytelling served a purpose. Lincoln often spoke in parables, understanding that stories were the most effective means of communicating to a broad audience. "They say I tell a great many stories; I reckon I do," Lincoln admitted. "But I have found in the course of a long run of experience that common people, take them as they run, are more easily influenced and informed through the medium of broad illustration than in any other way."[83]

But he came under criticism for his constant storytelling, which could seem wildly inappropriate from a wartime president. Lincoln explained, "It is not the story itself, but the purpose, or effect, that interests me," he said. "I often avoid a long and useless discussion by others or a laborious explanation on my own part by a short story that illustrates my point of view. So, too, the sharpness of a refusal or the edge of a rebuke may be blunted by an appropriate story, so as to save wounded feelings."[84]

A deeper truth was revealed when Lincoln's old friend, Illinois congressman Isaac N. Arnold, visited the White House after the Union defeat at Fredericksburg in 1862. He was shocked to find Lincoln reading aloud from one of his favorite humorists, Artemus Ward, and laughing. Perplexed and irritated, Arnold asked Lincoln how he could laugh after such a bloody setback in battle. Then "the President threw down the Artemus Ward book, tears streamed down his cheeks, his physical frame quivered as he burst forth, 'Mr. Arnold, if I could not get momentary respite from the crushing burden I am constantly carrying, my heart would break!'"[85] Humor was self-medication and Lincoln's joking demeanor was often a mask.

To be a peacemaker, it helps to be humble. Lincoln understood that arrogance could lead to overextension and a misjudgment of one man's capacity to control events. Humility takes into account human nature and human frailty.

Lincoln's humility was genuine, even as it coexisted uneasily with his undeniable ambition and subterranean self-confidence. In the White House, aides called him "The Tycoon," an inside joke about the political empire he'd crafted out of whole cloth. But in person, he was unpretentious, indifferent to food and drink, with untamed hair, wrinkled clothes, and a careless black bow tie, described by one visitor as looking like "a rural tourist in the White House." He was a work-horse who worked late into the night and rarely slept, replenishing his energy with conversation, playtime with his children, and trips to the theater. He loved comedies and tragedies—reflecting the duality of his personality—and he appreciated the convivial isolation of the theater, where he could be among the people and by himself simultaneously.

"He was sometimes jolly and genial, and again at other times absorbed and abstracted," attested Illinois senator Orville Browning.[86] Lincoln had the charisma of someone comfortable in his skin and a collaborative leadership style that set a tone and direction and then got out of the way, pulling rank only to spur action, while managing talents who were often outright insubordinate. "Though decided and pronounced in his convictions, he was tolerant towards those who differed from him and patient under reproach," attested Frederick Douglass.[87] He did not let pride overwhelm reason and, mindful of people's strengths and weaknesses, judged their utility at a given task.

Lincoln's humility deepened because of his faith. He was not an orthodox believer or a member of any particular denomination, but he evolved from an irreverent youthful "free-thinker" to read the Bible regularly. On the road to his inauguration, he described himself as "an humble instrument in the hands of the Almighty, and of this, his almost chosen people."[88] His faith grew under the pressures of the presidency, compounded by the bottomless grief of losing his beloved eleven-year-old son Willie to typhoid fever in the White House. He was sometimes seen reading the Book of Job for comfort and resolve, emerging oddly cheerful from the story of righteous suffering as part of God's plan.[89] At the limits of reason, we find either faith or despair.

These core personal qualities shaped his political beliefs—and fundamentally informed his vision for winning the peace.

Lincoln was a temperamentally moderate man, a reconciler in a time of radicals and reactionaries. As a young man, he warned that "as a nation of freemen, we must live through all time, or die by suicide."[90] As an adult, he'd seen the country torn apart as the parties split along regional and ideological lines, loudly denying the others' legitimacy. Distrust and dysfunction were followed by division and destruction.

As president, Lincoln asked Americans to rise "far above personal and partisan politics."[91] To his fellow Republicans he said, "even though much provoked, let us do nothing through passion and ill temper."[92]

"His soul was too great for the narrow, selfish views of partisanship,"[93] said Mary's friend and dressmaker, Elizabeth Keckley. He was impatient with absolutism. "There are few things *wholly* evil, or *wholly* good," he said, "almost every thing, especially of governmental policy, is an inseparable compound of the two."[94]

Political terms get scrambled across the centuries. In Lincoln's time, the words *liberal, conservative,* and *moderate* had different meanings from our current definitions.

The 1828 Webster's Dictionary defined *liberal* as "of a free heart . . . Not selfish, narrow or contracted . . . embracing other interests than one's own." *Conservative* did not have an explicitly political definition at the time but was considered a matter of "having power to preserve in a safe or entire state." *Moderate* was defined as "restrained in passion, ardor or temper; not violent; as *moderate* men of both parties . . . Not extreme in opinion" and "placed between extremes . . . as reformation of a *moderate* kind."[95]

Judging by the meaning of the terms in his time, Lincoln used moderate means to achieve liberal goals on abolition. He wanted to reunite and rededicate the Union, rather than struggling to simply conserve it as it was. As the journalist and Secretary of the Senate John W. Forney said, "Lincoln is the most truly progressive man of the age because he always moves in conjunction with propitious circumstances, not waiting to be dragged by the force of events or wasting strength in premature struggles with them."[96] His gradualism had a grandeur to it because it was connected to a broader vision of how to achieve sustainable change.

"His approach to social improvement was that of a political realist who knew that for every radical action there was the real threat of a conservative counterreaction and that thoroughgoing changes could prove self-defeating," concurs historian Richard Carwardine. "Lincoln formulated both his emancipation and his Reconstruction policies convinced not only that they were true to the Founders' values, but that they offered the best means of making progress and maintaining the momentum of change."[97]

Moral courage made his moderation a powerful force for progress. Lincoln told Noah Brooks that "he thought himself a great coward physically and was sure that he should make a poor soldier" who would "drop his gun and run" at the first sign of danger. He was half-joking, Brooks believed, but then Lincoln added in complete serious-ness: "Moral cowardice is something which I think I never had."[98]

Moral courage and moderation are often considered at odds. But Lincoln was not a moderate in the sense of someone who instinc-tively splits the difference or compromises principles for short-term political gain. Stephen Douglas was a moderate in that mold: his Kansas–Nebraska Act that extended slavery was considered a com-promise bill. But Lincoln refused to compromise with the expansion of slavery.

Nonetheless, he faced constant complaints from abolitionists who were in a position to place their activism ahead of broader respon-sibilities. "Viewed from the genuine abolition ground, Mr. Lincoln seemed tardy, cold, dull, and indifferent," Frederick Douglass reflected. "But measuring him by the sentiment of his country, a sentiment he was bound as a statesman to consult, he was swift, zealous, radical, and determined."[99]

"I hope to 'stand firm' enough to not go backward," Lincoln told one Republican senator, "and yet not go forward fast enough to wreck the country's cause."[100] His gradualism on ending slavery at the outset of the war helped keep the border states—Missouri, Kentucky, Delaware, and Maryland—from sliding over to the Confederacy. But even after the Emancipation Proclamation, he kept pushing for border state legislative amendments to eradicate slavery through legal means.

As evidence of his strategy's success, Lincoln kept a newspaper clipping marking Missouri's vote for abolition folded up in his wal-let until the day he died: "Slavery is dead in Missouri," the editorial read. "But the radicals are not satisfied with the death of slavery. Just like the boy who pounded the dead snake, they want to 'make it *deader'* . . . Because the president did not yield to the demands of the radicals that seemed intolerant and obtrusive, he is charged by hundreds of furious journalists with deserting 'the cause of freedom.' The charge is unfounded and absurd . . . He is not disposed to encourage excesses that might damage the good cause itself."[101]

Boiled down to its essence, Lincoln's political instincts were rooted in the Golden Rule as articulated in the Sermon on the Mount: "Do unto others as you would have them do unto you." Politics predicated upon the Golden Rule might sound naïve. This is simple wisdom, rooted in the most basic enlightened self-interest. But some of the thorniest political debates become clearer when held up to this lens: the fight for equal rights is, at its core, about treating other people as you would like to be treated.

When Lincoln wrote, "As I would not be a slave, so I would not be a master. This expresses my idea of democracy,"[102] or said, "I never knew a man who wished himself to be a slave. Consider if you know any *good* thing that no man desires for himself,"[103] he was using the Golden Rule's combination of common sense and moral imagination to dislodge deeply ingrained prejudice.

Lincoln's vision for winning the peace was likewise rooted in the politics of the Golden Rule: he wanted to treat the South fairly after unconditional surrender. This was not some abstraction—he and Mary still had family and friends in the seceded states. He had not forgotten their common humanity, even if at times they denied his. Leading by example, they invited Mary's sister Emilie to stay at the White House after her Confederate general husband was killed at the battle of Chickamauga. He hoped that a policy of magnanimous peace would help ease resentments and create a more stable basis for reconciliation.

But magnanimity needed to be combined with strength to succeed, just as the olive branches in the eagle's talon on the Great Seal of the United States were balanced by a cluster of arrows. He knew that wars must be decisively won and their gains consolidated through "wise management"—an interconnected approach involving political reform, economic expansion, and cultural reintegration.

After surrender, "Civil government must be re-established,"

Lincoln warned. "There must be courts, and the law, and order, or society would be broken up, the disbanded armies would turn into robber bands and guerillas."[104] The destruction of old institutions required the rapid rebuilding of new ones.

Once the rule of law was established, political reforms would be needed to rededicate the South to representative democracy, while addressing the root causes of the conflict: abolishing slavery and renouncing secession. He successfully fought for the passage of the Thirteenth Amendment to secure the end of slavery in the Constitution and insisted that it be ratified by Southern states as a condition of their readmittance to the Union. While he promised amnesty for rank-and-file rebel soldiers, he hoped it would be balanced by black voting rights. While he wanted to bar Confederate leaders from running for elected office, he opposed transplanted Northerners from running to represent the South in Congress, "elected, as it would be understood (and perhaps really so), at the point of the bayonet."[105]

The best way to get over old history is to make new history. To move beyond the stubborn North–South divide, Lincoln wanted to move the nation's attention westward, where he believed there was opportunity for unlimited economic expansion. He was fascinated by the future, obsessed with new technology like the telegraph, and remains the only president to ever successfully file for a patent (a contraption to get boats over rocky river shoals). Aided immeasurably by a Republican-controlled Congress that could act on its agenda free from obstruction by Southern Democrats, Lincoln signed a series of laws that would determine the future economic trajectory of the United States and connect the nation coast to coast.

The most dramatic expression was legislation supporting construction of the first transcontinental railroad, which Lincoln signed during the darkest days of the war in 1862.[106] That same year, he also signed the Homestead Act, encouraging the settlement of western lands by pioneers granted 160-acre plots for an $18 filing fee, stating that "every man should have the means and the opportunity of bettering his condition."[107] He established land-grant colleges "to promote the liberal and practical education of the industrial classes,"[108] which spawned more than a hundred universities, including Texas

A&M, MIT, Cornell, and a dozen historically black colleges across the United States.

He even had a plan for how to usefully disperse soldiers on both sides after the war in ways that would increase wealth and pay down the national debt. He wanted to incentivize gold and silver mining in the West, believing our resources to be "practically inexhaustible," with enough wealth to make America "the treasury of the world."[109] He saw this westward expansion as a solution for another problem: the flood of postwar labor in which supply would outpace demand. Despite the presence of freed slaves into the labor pool, he did not want to curtail immigration, whose ranks more than doubled during the war.

While economic development was his goal in a continent that was still mostly wilderness, Lincoln laid the groundwork for the national park system by signing the Yosemite Grant Act, which preserved California's Yosemite Valley "for public use, resort, and recreation for all time."[110] Lincoln was pro-business, pro-labor, pro-immigration, and pro-conservation—and saw those positions as complementary, not contradictory.

Lincoln believed political reform and economic expansion would help achieve the most difficult dimension of his plan to win the peace: cultural reintegration.

The country had been divided politically, economically, and culturally by slavery, and the South had defined itself in opposition to the rest of the nation for decades. Reconciliation aimed to reintegrate a slavery-free South back into the Union. Government policy could create the conditions, but the proving ground was personal. That's why Lincoln wanted to harness the power of local communities by giving them a role in their own Reconstruction—despite the objections of many fellow Republicans—while also protecting the most vulnerable.

To ease the transition, Lincoln established the Freedmen's Bureau to help feed and educate former slaves, giving them the opportunity to purchase confiscated land and put them on a path toward self-sufficiency. Lincoln hoped that time—and fair enforcement of laws—would allow blacks and whites to "gradually live themselves out of their old relation to each other."[111]

Lincoln wanted to steer the nation toward what peace negotiator

John Paul Lederach calls "a horizon of reconciliation." It is a distant goal, but its presence within sight gives the journey a sense of purpose and direction. While Lincoln did not think that he alone could control events, he understood the power of his personal example as president. His words mattered in creating a unifying national narrative that could renew commitment to the common good. His actions mattered even more and so, in public and in private, Lincoln not only spoke the words of reconciliation, he attempted to embody it.

But none of this mattered unless there was victory on the battlefield and in politics. If Lincoln did not win reelection in 1864, slavery would be preserved and the Union destroyed forever.

There had never been an election held in the middle of a civil war. It seemed like madness to many of his advisers, but Lincoln rejected their suggestions about suspending the election.

After years of stalemate and slaughter, Republicans were pessimistic about the president's chances. Party chairman Henry J. Raymond groused, "We don't stand a ghost of a chance in November."[112] In his darkest moments, Lincoln agreed.

On August 23, 1864, Lincoln wrote a strange, despairing letter and sealed it before passing it around to his cabinet for their signature. Inside was a prophecy of defeat from the president: "This morning and for some days past, it seems exceedingly probable that the Administration will not be reelected."[113]

But on the same day that Lincoln predicted his political doom, Admiral David G. Farragut took command of the harbor in Mobile, Alabama. A bigger boost came on September 2, when General Sherman captured Atlanta after a five-week siege. The news reached the press at precisely the right time to change the feeling in the streets before the election. As the New York diarist George Templeton Strong wrote: "Thank God the fall of Atlanta is fully confirmed . . . it's importance, both moral and military, is immense."[114]

Democrats were running former Union general George McClellan on a "peace platform" that proposed a truce with the South while keeping slavery intact. The *New-York Tribune* accused Democrats of being "ready to barter the integrity of the Union for the sake of political power."[115] Confederates certainly saw a Democratic victory as a win for their cause and tried to influence the outcome accordingly. The *Charleston Courier* wrote in September of "the intimate connection existing between the armies of the Confederacy and the peace men in the United States . . . Our success in battle ensures the success of McClellan. Our failure will inevitably lead to his defeat."[116]

Lincoln believed in playing offense in politics as well as on the battlefield. In an unprecedented step, in 1864 Lincoln rebranded the Republican Party as the National Union Party to help the country unite beyond party lines by "moving toward a unified center position," as historian John C. Waugh later wrote, "where Lincoln believed the votes were."[117]

To emphasize this shift, Lincoln tacitly agreed to ditch his loyal but distant vice president, Hannibal Hamlin, who had spent much of the war holed up in his native Maine. The necessary balance of the ticket was no longer West and East; it was North and South. In his place, Tennessee military governor Andrew Johnson was nominated.

On paper, this made perfect sense. Pugnacious and populist, Johnson had been the only Southern U.S. senator who refused to resign when his state seceded, making him a hero in the North. Lincoln felt comfort in the fact that they had known each other as young congressmen more than fifteen years before. Now as a "war Democrat," Johnson's rage toward secessionists—declaring that "treason must be made odious"—made him a darling of radical Republicans, despite the fact that he'd recently been a slaveholder. Everyone agreed that he could help secure votes in the border states as well as among disaffected Democrats.

The 1864 election was an existential test for American democracy. "It has always been the fate of republics hitherto to be destroyed by faction. Party-spirit has overpowered patriotism," *Harper's Weekly* wrote in its pre-election editorial. "It has been, therefore, feared by many of the best and wisest men that we should encounter the same peril and succumb to the same fate. That fear is now about to be confirmed or dissipated forever."[118]

As the sun rose on election day, Lincoln was feeling quietly confident. But he "felt no elation and no sense of triumph over his opponents," he confided to his secretaries John Nicolay and John Hay as they waited for returns. Instead, he felt regret over the intensity of the political battles he'd been forced to wage over his career. "It is singular that I, who am not a vindictive man, should always, except once, have been before the people for election in canvasses marked for their bitterness."[119] His absence of malice was evident even on the verge of victory.

That night, Lincoln and his key aides gathered in the telegraph office of the War Department. To cut the tension, Lincoln read aloud from a book by the humorist Petroleum V. Nasby. As results started to tick in over electric wire, Lincoln's boyhood state of Indiana came in first in his favor, followed soon by Massachusetts and then Pennsylvania, which the president noted approvingly, saying, "As goes Pennsylvania, so goes the Union."[120] By midnight, a Lincoln victory seemed assured. A late supper was delivered and a grateful president shoveled fried oysters onto his team's awaiting plates.[121]

Lincoln won in a landslide of 221 to 21 electoral votes, carrying all but three states: McClellan's New Jersey, Lincoln's native Kentucky, and the border state of Delaware. The states that Lincoln added to the Union during his first term—West Virginia, Kansas, and Nevada—all landed in his column.

Perhaps the greatest endorsement of Lincoln's wartime leadership came when an astounding 78 percent of troops in the field voted for him over their former general, McClellan.[122] He'd expanded the political map, winning 355,000 more votes than four years before.[123]

After 2 a.m., Lincoln walked back to the White House, greeted by serenading supporters. The next night, a formal victory celebration was held on the White House lawn: "If the rebellion could force us to forego or postpone a national election it might fairly claim to have already conquered and ruined us," Lincoln said from a second-floor window as Tad ran around behind him. Instead, the results "demonstrated that a people's government can sustain a national election, in the midst of a great civil war. Until now it has not been known to the world that this was a possibility."[124]

The election was over but the battles would not end. Lincoln recognized that his liberal vision of Southern Reconstruction put him on a collision course with many Republican allies. "I am for conciliation:

they seem to be governed by resentment," Lincoln said. "They believe we can be made one people by force and vengeance. I think we are not likely to bring about unity by hatred and persecution."[125]

Lincoln never lost faith that America could overcome its violent divisions. "When the storm shall be past," Lincoln said, the world "shall find us still Americans; no less devoted to the continued Union and prosperity of the country than heretofore."[126]

He never got to see the promised land he pointed us toward. No American president had been assassinated before Good Friday 1865. It was a soul shock to the nation that upended Lincoln's message of mercy.

On Easter Sunday in Philadelphia, the Reverend Phillips Brooks tried to comfort his congregation by saying, "If there were one day on which one could rejoice to echo the martyrdom of Christ, it would be on that day that martyrdom was perfected."[127] Down the street, at the Mikveh Israel Synagogue, Rabbi Sabato Morais eulogized Lincoln by praising his commitment to the Golden Rule: "It is the maxim he illustrated in the immortal document of emancipation . . . what he exemplified by his numerous acts of clemency toward the unworthy."[128] On the outskirts of Chicago, a four-and-a-half-year-old future Nobel Peace Prize winner named Jane Addams came home to see her father crying for the first time in her life, saying, "The greatest man in the world has died."[129]

While some Southerners celebrated, others recognized that they had lost an unlikely advocate. Even Jefferson Davis admitted years later that Lincoln had been a "great man." "If Mr. Lincoln had lived, the South would have had a President that understood her condition, and he would have been of more benefit to her than any other man could possibly have been," Davis said. "His death was a great misfortune to the South."[130]

As Winston Churchill would later write, "The death of Lincoln deprived the Union of the guiding hand which alone could have solved the problems of reconstruction and added to the triumph of armies those lasting victories which are gained over the hearts of men."[131]

He is still known to schoolchildren as a stick-figure with a stovepipe hat and beard. At first, Lincoln's story fits in a grade-school sentence: He is the president who was born in a log cabin, won the Civil War, and freed the slaves. Over time, the caricature deepens into a portrait. New layers reveal themselves as they become relevant to our own struggles, containing the promise that Lincoln can show us how to lead and how to live.

He is an American archetype: the farm boy who hears a call to adventure and forges a path where there was none, dogged by self-doubt but guided by a sense of destiny. He is both a good and a great man, struggling against the odds for a cause bigger than himself. He comes to lead the nation at a moment of maximum danger, inspiring his fellow citizens with words and actions, suffering through a fiery trial but delivering the country safely to the other side.

This is the classic hero's journey, reflected in American history. Leo Tolstoy, the author of *War and Peace*, pronounced him "a Christ in miniature, a saint of humanity."[132] In Japan at the turn of the last century, a book called "Tales of Lincoln" pronounced him "the kindest man among the great men, and the greatest man among the kind men."[133] When one intrepid reporter trudged to a remote area of the Caucasus mountain range in the early 1900s, he was asked by the youth of the village to tell them more about "the greatest ruler of the world . . . He was so great that he even forgave the crimes of his greatest enemies and shook brotherly hands with those who had plotted against him. His name was Lincoln and the country in which he lived is called America."[134]

It was the interconnection of Lincoln's character and his vision of reconciliation that inspired people around the world, placing him in the first rank of humanity's heroes.

There's an understandable temptation to ask what Lincoln would have done if he had lived. But what Lincoln left us is enough. We can connect the dots from his speeches and statements to gain a clear sense of his plan for winning the peace, even though it was a work in progress. We know that when America swerved off Lincoln's path under Andrew Johnson, it proved disastrous. When the next president, Ulysses S. Grant, tried to apply Lincoln's principles, the United States gave African-American men the right to vote and defeated the first incarnation of the Ku Klux Klan. But when Lincoln's vision of Reconstruction was finally abandoned in a corrupt bargain that embraced national reunification at the expense of racial justice, America's failure to fully win the peace resulted in segregation for almost a century.

Generations of Americans scarred by the Civil War and inspired by Lincoln—from Woodrow Wilson to Harry S. Truman, both Confederate descendants—kept searching for how to achieve a just and lasting peace.

President Wilson attempted to secure "a peace among equals" after the First World War. But he deviated from Lincoln's principle of unconditional surrender before an armistice—and capitulated to other allied powers' desire for punishing reparations—setting the stage for the rise of Adolf Hitler.

When Harry Truman abruptly inherited the presidency in the final months of the Second World War, he followed Lincoln's prescription of unconditional surrender and a magnanimous peace more faithfully, if intuitively, culminating in the success of the Marshall Plan.

Lincoln's vision was ultimately vindicated by experience and became a hallmark of American exceptionalism after the Second World War: we build our defeated enemies back up on a foundation of liberal democracy to stop the cycle of violence.

As General Lucius Clay, the architect of the postwar rebuilding of Germany—son of a three-term senator from Georgia, born thirty-three years after the Civil War—explained when asked what guided his successful reconstruction efforts: "I tried to think of the kind of occupation the South would have had if Abraham Lincoln had lived."[135]

Section I

With Malice
Toward None

"To do all which may achieve and cherish a just, and a lasting peace, among ourselves, and with all nations."

—*Abraham Lincoln*

A beam of light cut through the clouds as the president began to speak.

Abraham Lincoln stood on wood scaffolding at the foot of the newly completed Capitol dome, surrounded by family, friends, and rivals—as well as the man who would kill him in forty-one days.

Lincoln held in his hands a 701-word meditation on war and peace, race and reconciliation, sin and redemption. It would become the most famous inaugural address ever delivered and kick off the most consequential six weeks in American history.

The day had begun with a hailstorm from the south.[1] Just before dawn, fierce winds tore through the nation's capital, uprooting trees and threatening to crack the windows of the House of Representatives, as congressmen scrambled to complete their business before the session expired.

As the sun rose, the storm subsided. A crowd of forty thousand people trudged through ankle-deep mud on the unpaved streets of Washington that Saturday, March 4, to witness the inauguration of the only president reelected since Andrew Jackson.

For the first time, the inaugural attendees were both white and black, at Lincoln's invitation—"the negro as a citizen and soldier," noted the *New-York Tribune*, "no longer as a slave and chattel."[2]

Black soldiers had helped turn the tide of the war, a fatal insult to the white supremacy of the Confederacy. Now, even as Union armies threatened the rebel capital of the South, soldiers on leave with their families intermingled with former slaves looking to build a new life. Black men and women stood side by side with white soldiers, party loyalists, and office seekers as well as the society women of Washington, whose clothes were in "a wretched plight; crinoline smashed, skirts bedaubed . . . streaked with mud from end to end."[3] No one seemed to mind. Having survived the war, the carnival of democracy carried its own momentum.

Lincoln bailed on the inaugural parade. The poet-turned-wartime-nurse Walt Whitman saw him traveling "on sharp trot"[4] alone in his carriage ahead of the festivities to get a start on signing bills. The parade went on with Mary Lincoln traveling in her husband's place in the procession, which included white-bearded veterans from the War of 1812 and members of the Good Will and Perseverance fire companies from Philadelphia, who accompanied their fire engines with one-thousand-foot hoses, evidently a source of some civic pride. A working model of the ironclad USS *Monitor* was pulled by white horses, adorned by a blue banner on its bow reading "The Union: Our Home" and stopping every so often to thrill the crowd with gunfire from its turret.[5]

As the clock ticked toward noon, the crowd clustered around the eastern steps of the Capitol, its dome now taller than the surrounding church steeples. Lincoln had insisted that construction continue during the war, despite objections about the cost, to serve as a sign of the Union's confidence in victory. The dome was now capped with a statue of a woman known as "Armed Freedom," standing atop a globe marked with the national motto *e pluribus unum*: "out of many, one."

As the brisk drums of marching bands punctuated the cheerful rumble, inside the Capitol building, the official ceremony was off to a strange start.

Lincoln's new vice president, Tennessee Democrat Andrew Johnson, showed up to the ceremony drunk after trying to cure a hangover and the lingering effects of typhoid fever with tumblers of whiskey. This proved unwise.

"He was plainly intoxicated and delivered a stump speech unworthy of the occasion," raged Ohio senator John Sherman, brother of Union general William Tecumseh Sherman. Maudlin and mumbling, Johnson teetered onstage and railed against class discrimination, declaring himself proud be a "plebian" and recounting his humble origins as a tailor for more than ten minutes.[6] Before being pulled from the stage, Johnson capped his performance by holding a Bible aloft and kissing it with an audible smack of the lips. The secretary of the Navy whispered that Johnson was either "drunk or crazy."[7] In coming days, *The New York World* would jibe that Caligula's horse had more dignity than the new vice president.[8]

Lincoln endured the spectacle by closing his eyes after a time and then quietly asking the master of ceremonies to make sure the vice president did not speak to the public waiting outside.

When the doors of the Capitol swung open and the procession moved out into the open air, the crowd cheered. Scottish-born photographer Alexander Gardner captured the chaotic scene in blurred black and white: a packed stage with the president standing at the center, elevated some ten feet above the crowd, as citizens fanned out along the Capitol steps, crammed on to every elevated space as well as the east lawn, with armed infantrymen stationed at the edges of the crowd, including a black battalion.

Surrounding the towering figure of Lincoln were the key characters of his civil war drama: there was Mary, proud in a purple velvet dress alongside their beloved youngest son Tad, accompanied by "Madame Elizabeth" Keckley, the first family's seamstress and friend, a biracial business owner just a decade away from having purchased her freedom from slavery. Her only son, George, had been killed in the war. Behind the president were radical Republicans, reactionary Democrats, and members of his cabinet, including the hawk-nosed Secretary of State William Seward, Secretary of the Navy Gideon Welles in his terrible toupee, and the imperious Secretary of War Edwin Stanton, who stared out at the crowd from behind tiny spectacles and a mammoth beard.

Close to the stage was Frederick Douglass, the celebrated ex-slave who'd become the most famous orator in America, and Noah Brooks, a California newspaperman who was preparing to join the administration as Lincoln's personal secretary. Up the marble steps to Lincoln's left was John Wilkes Booth, wearing a jaunty top hat, while some of his coconspirators lined up below Lincoln with arms crossed near the scaffolding's edge.

At noon, Abraham Lincoln walked up to the front of the stage, tall and gaunt, dressed in a new black Brooks Brothers suit and an overcoat with an embroidered lining that read "One Nation, One Destiny."[9] He was now down to 160 pounds, and his dusky outdoorsman's skin looked like cracked leather. He'd been closely shaved for the occasion, leaving a swath of his cheeks clean, turning his famous beard into a broad goatee.

Standing over a round iron table on which sat a glass of water, Lincoln took a pair of steel-rimmed spectacles from his pocket and held a single piece of paper in both hands. The text of his Second Inaugural Address was cut and pasted in two columns, separating each sentence into its own paragraph, making it easier to read with an orator's sense of rhythm and emphasis.

As waves of wild applause cascaded across the audience, consider what Lincoln might have seen from the stage: a sea of Union blue, white and black faces, capped with American flags. He could not have missed the statue of George Washington staring back at him, directly in his line of sight.

He'd grown up idolizing Washington, seeing "something more than common" in the struggle for American independence, "something that held out a great promise to all the people of the world for all time to come."[10] Before leaving his home in Springfield, Illinois, Lincoln had told his neighbors gathered at the train station that he had a "task before me greater than rested on Washington."[11] In less than a century, the nation had been born and now it was fighting for its life.

Lincoln raised his arm to quiet the crowd and then stepped into sunlight.

"Just then the sun, which had been obscured all day, burst forth in its unclouded meridian splendor and flooded the spectacle with glory and light," reported Noah Brooks. "Every heart beat quicker at the unexpected omen."[12]

The effect was unmistakable, the kind of coincidence that seemed to have the hand of God in it, as the crowd gasped and cheered. "The clouds parted, and a ray of sunshine streamed from the heavens to fall upon and gild his face," remembered Elizabeth Keckley.[13] Even Lincoln noticed, later telling friends that he was just superstitious enough to take it as a good omen. It seemed a sign of spring, hope after a season of hate.

"Fellow citizens . . ." Lincoln began in his reedy Kentucky tenor, projecting over the crowd with what the correspondent for *Harper's Weekly* described as "a certain grand and quaint vigor, unprecedented in modern politics."[14]

Lincoln rose to the presidency on his reputation for inspiring oratory, wielding memorable phrases with moral clarity. His was an American style, conversational and logical, free from fancy rhetorical flourishes. But he was not a natural speaker, often starting out with awkwardness but warming up as passion and purpose flowed through his body, his blue-gray eyes twinkling as he forgot himself and focused on persuading his audience.

He'd given fewer public addresses in recent years, reluctant to speak off the cuff, aware of the weight of a president's words, especially during wartime. But he was a master of the craft and he deployed all his skill in this Second Inaugural, using his favorite devices: short words, rhyme and repetition, humor and biblical allusion; building to a climactic close that encapsulated his core beliefs into a single resounding sentence.

He began by subverting the typical speech structure. Instead of starting with a defining opening line, a statement of purpose, he offered up the first sentence in a spirit of soaring dullness, undercutting expectations: "At this second appearing to take the oath of the Presidential office there is less occasion for an extended address than there was at the first."

Four years before, the country had been on the brink of civil war. They had struggled and suffered together. Throughout the war "public declarations have been constantly called forth on every point and phase of the great contest," he said. As a practical matter, "little that is new could be presented." He was getting formalities out of the way to focus on essentials.

Even as they gathered, the war raged. Lincoln knew that the strength of the Southern armies was waning, but some newspapers still spoke overconfidently of Confederate capabilities, with *The Economist* opining that they "have still large armies in the field; they have still the ablest generals of the Republic in their ranks."[15] Regardless of rumors, everything depended on military success. "The progress of our arms, upon which all else chiefly depends . . . is, I trust, reasonably satisfactory and encouraging to all. With high hope for the future, no prediction in regard to it is ventured."

There was no triumphalism in the president's address. Lincoln was not speaking as president of the North, but of the whole nation.

He had never recognized the South's right to secede. He tried reasoning with the slaveholding states, using the native tools of a lawyer and politician. He hoped to appeal to a silent majority of pro–Union Southerners. But reason had failed.

"Both parties deprecated war," Lincoln said, "but one of them would make war rather than let the nation survive; and the other would accept war rather than let it perish." Applause broke out in the crowd. Lincoln paused for a moment and then said, simply: "And the war came."

There was a spare, staccato beat to the speech. Roughly three quarters of the words were just one syllable. He used small words for big ideas. Lincoln wanted to speak in a way the common man could understand—but he never talked down to them.

There had been attempts to dress up the cause of the war in high-minded language. Some said the war was just politics by other means, part of an extended debate over states' rights. Confederate president Jefferson Davis tried to argue that the slaveholders' secession was motivated by love of liberty.

Lincoln had always been frustrated by this counterfeit use of language and earlier sketched out a fable to prove his point: "The shepherd drives the wolf from the sheep's throat, for which the sheep thanks the shepherd as a *liberator*, while the wolf denounces him for the same act as the destroyer of liberty, especially as the sheep was a black one. Plainly the sheep and the wolf are not agreed upon a definition of the word liberty." But as the war progressed toward abolishing slavery, Lincoln said, "the wolf's dictionary has been repudiated." [16]

Other slave owners reached for a twisted moral defense. Prominent Southern preachers cherry-picked passages to make the case that slavery was biblically ordained.[17] In their telling, rejection of slavery was a rejection of God. Others insisted the war was primarily an economic issue, a big government attempt to destroy the Southern way of life and seize private property.

Lincoln was done indulging this nonsense. He removed any doubt about the true cause of the war: "One-eighth of the whole population were colored slaves, not distributed generally over the Union, but localized in the Southern part of it. These slaves constituted a peculiar and powerful interest. All knew that this interest was somehow the cause of the war . . ." Truth needed to precede reconciliation.

When the war began, Lincoln simply wanted to stop secession and slavery's spread. He was now determined to redeem something lasting from all the suffering and end slavery for all time.

He'd been strategic in his evangelism for emancipation, leading the public, but never from too far ahead. His Emancipation Proclamation, announced in the fall of 1862 and issued the following New Year's Day, freed slaves in the seceded states. The fact that it was a limited wartime executive order did not reflect a lack of will, as some abolitionists charged, but a recognition of legal and political reality: the proclamation could have been reversed by some future president or overturned by the Supreme Court. Political opponents in the North attacked it as a radical rededication of the war to end slavery rather than simply preserve the Union, spurring a backlash in the midterm elections, with Democrats gaining seats while sweeping out the Republican speaker of the house. But public opinion turned in its wake.

"It is extraordinary how completely the idea of gradual emancipation has been dissipated from the public mind everywhere by the progress of events," editorialized *The New York Times* in 1864. "There seems to be an almost unanimous agreement that immediate emancipation is the wisest and in fact the only practical method."[18] Channeling that momentum, Lincoln successfully pressed for the passage of the Thirteenth Amendment in January 1865, now heading to the states for ratification to make good on the proclamation's promise of "forever free."

But for all Lincoln's determination to impose legal logic on the war, he'd been brought to his knees over the conflict. He would quote the Bible four times in this inaugural. One of the mysteries and misuses of faith was the spectacle of God being invoked on both sides of the conflict: "Both read the same Bible and pray to the same God, and each invokes His aid against the other."

This set up the closest thing the Second Inaugural offered to a laugh line: "It may seem strange that any men should dare to ask a just God's assistance in wringing their bread from the sweat of other men's faces . . ."

The audience chuckled at this dig, but the next phrase "let us judge not, that we be not judged"—a favorite quotation from the Sermon on the Mount—came in like a phantom counterpunch. Though there was no moral equivalence between the two sides, Lincoln would not let the North rest easy with any sense of moral superiority.

Healing the war's wounds would require humility. "The prayers of both could not be answered. That of neither has been answered fully. The Almighty has His own purposes."

Now Lincoln picked up his pace, offering rhyme and repetition, the first such flourish in the speech: "Fondly do we hope, fervently do we pray, that this mighty scourge of war may speedily pass away."

But that was a wish. "Yet, if God wills that it continue until all the wealth piled by the bondsman's two hundred and fifty years of unrequited toil shall be sunk, and until every drop of blood drawn with the lash shall be paid by another drawn with the sword, as was said three thousand years ago, so still it must be said 'the judgments of the Lord are true and righteous altogether.'"

Invoking the Old Testament, this compressed America's original sin into one sentence. The war was collective punishment for centuries of blood, sweat, and tears shed by slaves on American soil.

Lincoln did not speak of "Southern slavery" but American slavery. The North had enabled slavery by purchasing cotton and rice from the South. At the Constitutional Convention, the founders had agreed to preserve it—barring any ban on the slave trade until 1808—to secure the support of Southern states, without ever mentioning slavery by name in the document, "hid away," Lincoln had said, "just as an afflicted man hides away a wen or a cancer, which he dares not cut out at once, lest he bleed to death." Now the cutting had begun. We would pay our debt in blood.

America was suffering at the hand of a remote and inscrutable God whose cosmic ledger was evidently not yet balanced. None of us were fully in control—including the president—because the war, and its outcome, was God's will. But that did not mean we, the living, were powerless. Because of His distance, it was still up to individuals to try and build a better world.

The black Americans in the audience understood Lincoln's aims and began to punctuate his lines with a call and response of "Bless the Lord."

Even after four years of Civil War, Lincoln refused to divide the country into "us against them." Instead, the words *we* and *all* suffused the speech to re-create a sense of common destiny. Collective suffering might be followed by mutual forgiveness and transformation: "in giving freedom to the slave," as Lincoln had said, "we assure freedom to the free."

No one knew the end was near. Lincoln had been speaking for just six minutes in an era where speeches were considered popular entertainment and great orations could last for hours. But Lincoln's concise, clear writing was always his greatest literary strength—even when it contained a touch of the transcendental, reflecting his belief that the written word was humanity's greatest invention because it enables "us to converse with the dead, the absent and the unborn, at all distances of time and space."[19]

Now, in that spirit, he made a sharp final turn from the Old to the New Testament, offering an enduring call to our better angels.

"With malice toward none; with charity for all; with firmness in the right as God gives us to see the right, let us strive on to finish the work we are in; to bind up the nation's wounds, to care for him who shall have borne the battle, and for his widow, and his orphan—to do all which may achieve and cherish a just, and a lasting peace, among ourselves, and with all nations."

These seventy-four words—both a final paragraph and a final sentence—were the culmination of the speech and his career, presenting a vision of victory driven by mercy rather than vengeance, offering a road map toward reconciliation and reunification. These were the words that would endure.

"With malice toward none; with charity for all" became perhaps the most beloved lines Lincoln ever wrote, reprinted on banners and souvenirs.

Malice is a dusty word that has been long out of circulation, but it means the intent to do evil, or even ill will. "What I deal with is too vast for malicious dealings,"[20] Lincoln had written a military governor, asking him to put political schemes aside for the greater good.

Kindness is the absence of malice, in Lincoln's formulation: "I have endured a great deal of ridicule without much malice," he wrote in 1863, "and have received a great deal of kindness, not quite free from ridicule."[21]

The word *charity* today contains a whiff of condescension to some. But it comes from a translation of the ancient Greek word *agape*— meaning a universal love—used by early Christians. So the famous sentence could have read, "With malice toward none; with love for all."

Lincoln's use reflected both meanings of charity—a resolve to help those in need, inspired by a universal love between fellow human beings. It reflected his inner disposition, according to Frederick Douglass, who described Lincoln as "the embodiment of human charity, whose heart, though strong, was as tender as the heart of childhood; who always tempered justice with mercy; so sought to supplant the sword with the counsel of reason, to suppress passion by kindness and moderation."[22]

Wielding mercy to transform conflict would require asking for grace—"with firmness in the right, as God gives us to see the right"— tempering the determination to do justice with humility, balancing faith with the skepticism that understands no person can exclusively know the will of God.

But these lofty sentiments needed to be grounded in hard work to achieve earthly results. It required a rhetorical rolling up of sleeves to bring us back to shared responsibilities: "let us strive on to finish the work we are in."

Consciously or not, Lincoln was tracing lines from the Book of Isaiah, a prophet of peace during a time of civil war: "Come now and let us reason together ... Learn to do good; Seek justice, Rebuke the oppressor; Defend the fatherless, Plead for the widow."[23]

Carrying this flow forward, there came an unexpected, subtle nod to specific policy—"to care for him who shall have borne the battle and for his widow and his orphan." There were towns where an entire generation of men were missing. The war's damage required sustained support for the wounded warriors as well as the wives and children of the dead. This had been a government obligation since the Revolutionary War. What was new, if only implied, was the inclusion of black families in this social contract.

The massacre of black troops at Fort Pillow in Tennessee by Confederate general Nathan Bedford Forrest—who noted with satisfaction that "the river was dyed with the blood of the slaughtered for 200 yards"[24] before going on to command the Ku Klux Klan—led to an outcry in the North. The wife of Fort Pillow's white commanding officer petitioned the president to recognize the rights of African-American widows to equal treatment under the law. Lincoln successfully pressed Congress to fix this injustice.

It was all building up to the crystalizing last clause: "to achieve and cherish a just and a lasting peace, among ourselves and with all nations."

Lincoln had his eyes on something more enduring than simply justice or even peace. Justice alone could be punishing, as it was often with God's will. Peace could be the absence of conflict, an end to hostilities that might preserve slavery, making the lost lives meaningless and the war likely to reignite at a later date. A just peace must follow a just war. That is why there must be a fight for peace: waged with an intensity that rivals war.

This was the president as a prophet of reconciliation, a man who combined opposites all his life, urging his bloodied nation to transcend all the dualities that divided it: North and South, black and white, free and unfree—carrying forward recognition of our common humanity into the wider world, evidence of a cosmic democracy, so that the promise of the United States might be redeemed and serve as a beacon of universal freedom.

Then, with a pause and a nod, Lincoln stepped back and the spell was broken—the inaugural address was over. Cannons fired and bands played. Some in the crowd were still finding their seats.

Lincoln took the oath of office from the newly appointed chief justice, Salmon P. Chase, former secretary of the treasury and Ohio

abolitionist who'd been conniving to snatch the Republican nomina-
tion from Lincoln less than a year before. But by appointing him chief
justice after the death of pickled bigot Roger Taney—who'd written·
the infamous Dred Scott decision, which denied African-American
citizenship—Lincoln had shown an absence of malice, removing a
political rival while ensuring the court would favor emancipation-
related cases going forward.

With his right hand resting on the family Bible, Lincoln took
the oath, for the first time adding the words, "So Help Me God." He
then leaned down to kiss its pages, which were opened to the Book
of Isaiah, 5:27–28—an invocation of energetic purpose—outlined in
the president's hand.

> None shall be weary nor stumble among them; none shall
> slumber nor sleep; neither shall the girdle of their loins be
> loosed, nor the latchet of their shoes be broken: Whose arrows
> are sharp, and all their bows bent, their horses' hoofs shall be
> counted like flint, and their wheels like a whirlwind.

He raised his head to a new round of applause as cannons thundered
in celebration and the band struck up "Hail to the Chief."

In the crowd, Frederick Douglass applauded "in gladness and
thanksgiving,"[25] gratified by the president's description of the war
as divine retribution for the sin of slavery. But he also observed the
widely different reactions to the speech among the crowd, attribut-
ing that to the fact that it "sounded more like a sermon than a state
paper . . . There seemed at the time to be in the man's soul, the united
souls of all Hebrew Prophets."[26]

Illinois congressman Isaac Arnold also reached for biblical com-
parisons: "Since the days of Christ's sermon on the mount, where is
the speech of emperor, king, or ruler, which can compare with this?"
he wrote. "No other state paper in American annals, not even Washington's Farewell Address, has made so deep an impression upon the
people."[27]

But contemporary critics found plenty to grouse about. *The New
York Herald* dismissed it as a "little speech of 'glittering generalities'
used only to fill the program."[28] The Southern-sympathizing *New York*

World was reflexively offended by Lincoln's words, calling it "odious libel" to compare blood that "trickled from the lacerated backs of the negros" with the "bloodiest war in history."[29] Even the friendly *New York Times* puzzled that "it was not strictly an inaugural address . . . it was more like a valedictory."[30] But the *Boston Evening Transcript* saw something different: "No similar document has ever been published to the world," they wrote. "The President was lifted above the level upon which political rulers usually stand and felt himself 'in the very presence of the very mystery of Providence.'"[31]

There were handshakes all around as Lincoln began to make his way back inside the Capitol, as the inauguration crowds streamed back into the muddy streets of Washington. Newly erected telegraph lines connecting New York and San Francisco allowed the speech to speed across the continent.

Lincoln departed in a carriage back to the executive mansion with Tad at his side. Mary followed in a second carriage, waving to the crowds. There was a public reception scheduled and he greeted the party with a certain dread. Walt Whitman attended the festivities and saw the president in "white kid gloves and a claw-hammer coat . . . looking very disconsolate and as if he would give anything to be somewhere else."[32]

The White House was swarmed but the open-door policy did not extend to every American. Frederick Douglass found himself blocked by two policemen at the door, denied entry on the basis of race. He insisted to the two toughs that he was sure that President Lincoln would welcome him, as he had been "impressed with his entire freedom from popular prejudice against the colored race."[33] When Douglass saw a friendly face, he asked that a message be passed on to the president.

Minutes later, the White House doors swung open for Frederick Douglass. As he made his way toward the president in the throbbing hallways, "amid a scene of elegance such as in this country I had never before witnessed," Douglass saw Lincoln standing, "like a mountain pine high above all others."[34]

When the president spotted him, Lincoln spoke with a loud voice intended to make an impression, "Here comes my friend, Douglass," and reached out for a hearty handshake. "Douglass, I saw you in the crowd today listening to my inaugural address," Lincoln said. "There is no man's opinion that I value more than yours; what do you think of it?" When Douglass demurred, saying there were thousands waiting to shake his hand, Lincoln insisted. Douglass replied with grand simplicity, "Mr. Lincoln, that was a sacred effort."[35]

In the long line behind him were the usual mix of office seekers, glad-handers, and sycophants, but there were also soldiers who came to pay their respects and found respect returned. Lieutenant John James Gosper, who lost his right leg in battle, was accompanied by his nurse, Ada Smith, and as the pair approached the president with the lieutenant leaning on one crutch, Lincoln spotted them and passed others to say, "God bless you my boy." As they moved on, the lieutenant whispered to Ada, "I'd lose another leg for a man like that."[36]

The wild celebration went on until 11 p.m. and took its toll on the White House. Drunken revelers stole souvenirs, cutting off pieces of a heavy red velvet curtain for a memento and generally lifting anything that wasn't locked down. It looked "as if a regiment of rebel troops had been quartered there with permission to forage," recalled bodyguard William Crook.[37] The president was distressed at this evidence of democratic excess: "Why should they do it? How can they?"[38]

As his second term began, with all of Lincoln's hope and foreboding, he took some comfort from knowing that he had preached the need for a just and lasting peace. He was playing for history's stakes and understood his vision would not be "immediately popular," as Lincoln wrote New York Republican leader Thurlow Weed. "Men are not flattered by being shown that there has been a difference of purpose between the Almighty and them. To deny it, however, in this case, is to deny that there is a God governing the world. It is a truth which I thought needed to be told."[39]

Section II

Unconditional Surrender

Lincoln at War

"It is an issue which can only be tried by war and decided by victory."[1]

—*Abraham Lincoln*

L incoln was a man of peace, but he was no pacifist. He was a wartime president for all but the last five days of his 1,500-day presidency. Now, at the start of his second term, he was at the peak of his political power. With Congress leaving town on recess until December, Lincoln would have the freedom to end the war and slavery on his own terms. To achieve those goals, he would insist on unconditional surrender.

Throughout the war, there were protests demanding peace, even if it meant the perpetuation of slavery. He had been called a dictator and a "widow-maker" as exhaustion threatened to overwhelm the nation's resolve. "The country was struck with one of those bewilderments which dethrone reason for the moment," Frederick Douglass said regarding the summer of 1864. "The impression had gone abroad that the President's antislavery policy was about the only thing which prevented a peaceful settlement with the Rebels."[2] This was a fantasy.

"No man desires peace more ardently than I," Lincoln wrote. "Still I am yet unprepared to give up the Union for a peace which, so achieved, could not be of much duration."[3] That meant eradicating the root cause of the war—slavery—and ensuring that the rebels accepted decisive defeat.

Lincoln's own military experience consisted of a brief stint as captain of a volunteer Illinois militia in the Black Hawk War of 1832. He'd seen no combat and jokingly described his service as containing only "a good many bloody struggles with mosquitoes."[4] To a friend,

Democratic congressman Daniel Voorhees, Lincoln revealed his feelings of military inadequacy: "Doesn't it strike you as queer that I, who
couldn't cut the head off a chicken, and who was sick at the sight of
blood, should be cast into the middle of a great war, with blood flow-
ing all around me?"[5]

As an untested commander-in-chief, Lincoln borrowed books on
military strategy from the Library of Congress and soon developed
what he described as a "general idea of the war." "We have the greater
numbers and the enemy has the greater facility concentrating forces
upon the points of collision," he said, leading to the conclusion that
the North should put the rebels on defense by attacking "with supe-
rior forces at different points at the same time."[6]

He had no time to lose. Lincoln inherited an anemic army of
16,000 soldiers—with one-third the officer corps resigning to join
the Confederacy—and increased it to more than 400,000 within a
year. The military budget grew from $28 million to $781 million by
1864.[7] He blockaded Southern ports, instituted the first compulsory
draft of soldiers, imposed the first federal income tax to help pay for
the war, and signed the Emancipation Proclamation.

Usually mindful of Constitutional constraints, Lincoln nonetheless took the step of suspending habeas corpus, undercutting civil liberties with the explanation that the Constitution specifically stated it
could only be done "when, in cases of rebellion or invasion, the public
safety may require it"—precisely the circumstances the nation faced.
After initial hopes that he could persuade Union sympathizers in the
South to abandon the war, Lincoln concluded that negotiation was
futile and declared secession "an issue which can only be tried by war
and decided by victory."[8]

This reluctant convert to total war occasionally lost his cool at
the complaints of those who wanted a softer conflict. "What would
you do in my position?" he sarcastically asked one critic. "Would you
drop the war where it is, or would you prosecute it in the future with
elder-stalk squirts, charged with rose-water? Would you deal lighter
blows rather than heavier ones? Would you give up the contest leaving every available means unapplied? . . . I shall do all I can to save the
government, which is my sworn duty as well as my personal inclina-
tion."[9]

The civilian commander was often more hawkish than his generals, who seemed reluctant to take the fight to the rebels instead of merely repelling their attacks and aiming for Richmond. After replacing the aged but legendary General Winfield Scott with the young but arrogant General George McClellan, the president was frustrated by his constant requests for reinforcements and jibed that the Army of the Potomac should be known as "McClellan's bodyguard." He pressed one successor, General Joseph Hooker (whose strenuous social life helped popularize prostitutes' enduring nickname) to "beware of rashness, but with energy, and sleepless vigilance, go forward and give us victories."[10] The victories did not materialize and Hooker was demoted after five months.

Perhaps Lincoln's greatest military disappointment occurred after the pivotal victory at Gettysburg in 1863, when General George Meade pushed Lee's army from Union soil but failed to pursue the enemy. Lincoln was furious, venting in a letter he never sent: "I do not believe you appreciate the magnitude of the misfortune involved in Lee's escape. He was within your easy grasp, and to have closed upon him would, in connection with our other late successes, have ended the war. As it is, the war will be prolonged indefinitely . . . Your golden opportunity is gone, and I am distressed immeasurably because of it."[11]

But in the spring of 1864, Lincoln finally found his man.

His soldiers called him "Unconditional Surrender Grant" after the terms he insisted on at the fall of Fort Donelson in Tennessee. Providentially, the nickname mirrored Ulysses S. Grant's initials. But it also marked the continuity between Grant's approach to war and Lincoln's wishes. "The great thing about Grant is his perfect coolness and persistency of purpose," Lincoln said, "and he has the grip of a bulldog. When he once gets his teeth in, nothing can shake him off!"[12]

He was strong but small with a sturdy build, tobacco brown beard, cool blue eyes, and an ever-present ruby-tipped cigar. Grant had been a middling West Point graduate, and a veteran of the war with Mexico. But he'd given up on a military career before the Civil War came, with its terrible opportunity to rise, writing his father "whatever may have been my political opinions before . . . there are but two parties now, Traitors and Patriots."[13]

War suited him. Grant first proved his mettle as a general on the western front, taking Vicksburg and securing the Mississippi. There was a taciturn burn in him, a smoldering aggression that never tipped into hotheadedness. He could focus under fire with a determined self-assurance that inspired his men. The "confidence he had, of ultimately winning, was contagious," wrote his military secretary Adam Badeau. "No man could be long downcast when near him."[14]

When confronted by a panicked officer worried about a rumored Confederate attack, Grant said, "I am heartily tired of learning what Lee is going to do. Some of you always seem to think he is suddenly going to turn a double somersault and land in our rear and on both of our flanks at the same time. Go back to your command and try to think what we are going to do ourselves, instead of what Lee is going to do."[15]

Critics complained that Grant was a butcher of men, given to bouts of binge drinking. Upon hearing this, Lincoln allegedly said if he could find out what brand of whiskey Grant drank, he would send a barrel of it to all his other generals.

But Lincoln's desire for an aggressive battlefield strategy did not mean that he was willing to accept the excesses of total war. He presided over the creation of the first modern laws of war, issuing General Orders No. 100 in spring 1863, just as the Civil War was turning to its bloodiest chapter. These laws provided the outlines of what it meant to conduct a just war and endured to inform the Geneva Conventions as well as the Nuremberg Trials.

There had been exhaustive analyses of military strategy, from Sun Tzu to von Clausewitz. But a battlefield code of conduct remained unwritten. That changed when Lincoln met Francis Lieber, a Prussian immigrant and former soldier in the Napoleonic Wars who arrived in the United States to teach law and political science at the University of South Carolina. He moved north in 1857 to take a professorship at Columbia University. When the war broke out, his family embodied the divide, with sons fighting on both sides.

"To save the country," Lieber believed, "is paramount to all other considerations."[16] Like Lincoln, he wanted to extend rules of war to the rebels while making it clear that this did not imply a recognition of their government. Lieber also disdained peace activists, believing that "the more vigorously wars are pursued the better it is for humanity. Sharp wars are brief."[17] But there needed to be some agreed code of conduct that could stop civilization from slipping into complete barbarism.

Lieber set out a series of rules designed to make war slightly more humane, writing that "men who take up arms against one another in public war do not cease on this account to be moral beings, responsible to one another, and to God."[18] His rules detailed prohibitions on executions, the use of poison, and assassinations. He proposed protections for prisoners and a distinction between soldiers and civilians. He also singled out acts committed out of a desire for revenge or those characterized by excessive cruelty. He called them war crimes.

Contrary to critics' claims, Lincoln and Lieber's prohibition on war crimes was not naïve but practical. Extreme actions could prove counterproductive by spurring fury and fear of what might happen at the end of the war. The actions of an army that abided by rules of war sent a decidedly different message about what peace could hold for those who accepted defeat.

By December 1864, the tide of the war had turned, secured by battlefield victories and Lincoln's decisive reelection. Confederates were left defending Richmond, as desertions piled up and supply lines were strangled. There were more captured Confederates in Union prisons than were left serving in Lee's army.

Lincoln turned to the congressional battlefield, determined to destroy slavery through a constitutional amendment that he pushed through Congress in January 1865. He felt urgency to pass the amendment before the war's end because he did not trust the country would have the political will to do so once peace set in.

Lincoln called the Thirteenth Amendment "a King's cure for all the evils"[19] because it enshrined the Emancipation Proclamation— a wartime executive order—in the Constitution, removing the possibility of peacetime or partisan retreat. He used all his powers of political persuasion to achieve its passage, offering patronage jobs to border state representatives as well as Democrats who'd lost their seats in the last election. While Lincoln saw politics from a national perspective, he did not consider himself above its rough and tumble. He understood what motivated congressmen and used the powers of the presidency to move them. He was content to achieve transformational goals through transactional means.

On the last day of January, the Amendment passed the House with just three votes more than the necessary two-thirds, sparking an eruption of cheers from the gallery and tears of joy on the floor of Congress. While state ratification was still required, the Thirteenth Amendment was the political expression of unconditional surrender: there would be no retreat from the end of slavery.

Three days after this victory, Lincoln left Washington for a secret meeting with Confederate leaders on the *River Queen*, his presidential steamship, anchored outside Hampton Roads, Virginia. It was the first time that a U.S. president conducted a wartime peace conference in person.

The rivers were full of ice floes that February, so Lincoln traveled to Annapolis by train and walked past the Maryland statehouse as they debated ratification of the Thirteenth Amendment. There he boarded a steamer to join Secretary of State Seward at Hampton Roads. The rebel delegation had been escorted through Union lines because of Grant's belief that they were sincere in wanting to talk peace. They were regarded as the most reasonable Confederates and rumored to be disaffected with Jefferson Davis: Confederate vice president Alexander Stephens, former Supreme Court Justice John A. Campbell, and Confederate senator Robert Hunter, accompanied by a slave. Upon arrival, they were plied with champagne, whiskey, and a sumptuous dinner in a display of personal respect as well as the North's plentiful provisions. Lincoln joined them the next morning.

Sitting down in the saloon of the *River Queen*, winter sun streaming through the skylight above, Lincoln was in an expansive mood as Seward and the Confederates smoked cigars on the leather banquette. "He seemed to be in a splendid humor," recalled Stephens, "very talkative and pleasant with all of the commissioners."[20] Lincoln had served in Congress with Stephens as a fellow Whig and the two traded jibes about Stephens's elfin size, while the Confederate vice president recalled that the talkative Lincoln had once been known as the representative from the great state of "All Noise."[21]

This display of friendliness was both genuine and strategic. Lincoln was breaking the interpersonal ice, showing that he meant it when he'd said in his first inaugural that "we must not be enemies, but friends." But in negotiations, he combined empathy with assertiveness.

Lincoln wanted to be clear about his bottom line: "The restoration of the Union is a sine qua non with me. I will listen to no proposal that does not include an immediate restoration of the National Authority."[22] As he'd said many times, the South could have peace any time it wanted by simply laying down their arms, recommitting to their one common country, and accepting the end of slavery. His position had only been strengthened by reelection.

The Confederate delegates countered with an odd dodge, proposing that the North and South could unite against a common enemy by declaring an armistice and then riding into Mexico together to dislodge the French-backed Emperor Maximilian in a muscular defense of the Monroe Doctrine.[23] Afterward, they could negotiate the details of peace.

Lincoln thought the idea was absurd and rejected it on two basic principles.

First, he would not agree to any armistice before the Confederate's unconditional surrender. A ceasefire is not a peace agreement. Mercy would follow their acceptance of defeat.

Second, he pointed out there could be no declaration of war with Mexico without consent of Congress—and any armistice treaty would require recognizing the Confederacy as an independent nation. This he would never do. They were not citizens of two countries but "our one common country."

The Confederates hotly objected, saying that Lincoln was demanding "an unconditional submission to the laws of authority of the United States—the sort of submission which the slave yields to the master." This was an ironic, repeated riff among Confederates and their sympathizers: fear that the North would make the South slaves—either to federal power or to black Americans. It was evidence of a deeper anxiety, with one Copperhead congressman describing the Civil War as being "for the freedom of the blacks and the enslavement of the whites."[24]

Seward waved away their concern along with the smoke from his cigar, pointing out that Lincoln was only requiring acceptance of key terms before any cessation of violence. All other details could be determined in negotiations. "We are not conquerors," Seward said, "further than we require obedience to the laws."

But Senator Hunter was in full froth: "What you are saying, Mr. President, is that we of the South have committed treason, that we have forfeited our rights, and that we are proper subjects for the hangman. Is that what your words imply?"[25]

"Yes," Lincoln calmly acknowledged. "That is about the size of it."[26]

His disarming honesty turned scowls into wry smiles. Senator Hunter admitted they were not worried about harsh treatment from Lincoln, despite the expected charges of treason, which traditionally carried penalty of death: "We have about concluded that we will not be hanged as long as you are President—so long as we behave ourselves."[27]

They knew him to be a reasonable man. Judge Campbell asked how Lincoln proposed to enact Reconstruction, assuming that the South agreed to peace. Lincoln replied he would do his best to ensure fair treatment at the end of the war, pointing out that he had the sole power to pardon and restore property and would do so with the "utmost liberality." But he cautioned that the lampposts around Washington might feel differently—a subtle nod to the feelings of vengeance that raged in his party and could erupt if his kindness were taken for granted.

"Whatever may have been the view of your people before the war, they must be convinced now, that slavery is doomed," Lincoln said.[28] He put forward another proposal—suggesting that Stephens go home to Georgia and get the governor to recall all state troops from the war, convene the state legislature to ratify the Thirteenth Amendment "prospectively"—taking effect in five years.[29] In effect, Lincoln was offering the South a path to reenter the Union with time to adjust to the new reality of emancipation.

Lincoln was improvising now, offering different paths within the context of unconditional surrender on his indispensable conditions.

Seward seemed momentarily seasick when Lincoln offered another inducement: $400 million in exchange for voluntary emancipation.

He said the money would be paid to slave owners in exchange for their human property, half upon agreement and the other half after the ratification of the Thirteenth Amendment by the readmitted Southern states. Lincoln calculated that the cost of perpetuating the war through August was far in excess of that number. This would save money and lives while offering compensation rather than confiscation.

But while Lincoln searched for alternative paths to an acceptable peace, the Confederates rejected Lincoln's refusal to recognize the existence of their self-declared country. Senator Hunter reached for precedent in England's Civil War, arguing that even King Charles I had negotiated with members of Parliament who took up arms against him.

Lincoln just laughed it off and said, "I do not profess to be posted in history. On all such matters, I'll turn you over to Seward. All I distinctly recollect about the case of Charles the First is that he lost his head in the end."[30]

Even in their weakened state, Confederates could not accept a denial of their sovereignty because it would admit their effort was illegitimate from the start. This was an unbridgeable divide driven by pride, resolvable only by victory and defeat.

As Lincoln stood up to leave in the waning light of the winter afternoon, he said somewhat sadly to Stephens, "Well, there has been nothing we could do for our country. Is there anything I can do for you personally?" The Confederate vice president paused for a second and then asked if his nephew, Lieutenant John A. Stephens, might be released from a prisoner of war camp on the banks of Lake Erie, where he'd been held for more than a year. Lincoln wrote down his name and said he'd be glad to do it as long as an imprisoned Union officer was released in return. This personal kindness chased the bitter with the sweet.

The Hampton Roads peace conference lasted only four hours. But it was not a failure. Lincoln walked away demonstrating that he was in control of the war's outcome and yet still willing to meet with Confederates to consider peace proposals.

When Lincoln informed Congress of the aborted conference, he was praised by radical Republicans and peace Democrats alike. *The*

New York Herald declared that he had proven himself to be "one of the shrewdest diplomats of the day . . . a giant among pygmies."[31] The *Washington Chronicle* said that far from being a failed negotiation, its impact "will be to unite the North and divide the South."[32]

Feelings of unity in Washington were short-lived. Under the Capitol dome, politics remained a battlefield. The fight was over who would control Reconstruction, and Congress was not inclined to surrender that power to the president.

Lincoln set forth his first public declaration of Reconstruction policy in a December 1863 "proclamation of amnesty and reconstruction." It was a wartime executive order designed to undercut the South's resolve by offering a full pardon from charges of treason to rank-and-file rebels who swore to "henceforth faithfully support, protect and defend the Constitution of the United States and the Union of States." If upheld, the proclamation promised "the restoration of all rights of property, except as to slaves."

The president went further, proposing a specific formula to "reinaugurate loyal state governments" by requiring that only 10 percent of the voters in the state swear an oath of allegiance before an election could be held to establish a new state constitution that abolished slavery. This would kick off the process of readmission into the Union with elected representatives to Congress.

This 10 percent plan infuriated many radical Republicans, who felt it was far too low a threshold to secure a change in the hearts and minds of secessionist southerners. But as historian LaWanda Cox explained, it was intended to be "not a policy of leniency but one of expediency, a means to precipitate an antislavery minority government."[33]

Crucial to Lincoln's vision of Reconstruction was his explicit prohibition on giving amnesty to Confederate leaders. This included any Confederate cabinet members or government official, any Confederate officer above the rank of colonel, as well as any former member of the U.S. Congress or judge who resigned their positions to join the rebellion. To this list was added anyone who treated captured black or white Union soldiers with less dignity than proscribed to prisoners of war in the Lieber Code.

Lincoln wanted mercy extended to the misled common man. But he was determined to prohibit senior Confederates from reestablishing their power in a reconstructed South on the basis of a simple oath.

Lincoln was characteristically caught in the middle of the political crossfire. Self-described "Radical Republicans" pushed for more punishment on the South, with the powerful Pennsylvania representative Thaddeus Stevens declaring, "I would seize every foot of land, and every dollar of their property."[34] So-called Peace Democrats wanted not reconstruction of the South, but restoration of the old elites. Louisiana was now the unexpected focus of their fight.

Lincoln had long been fixated on Louisiana as a laboratory for Reconstruction. New Orleans and the surrounding parishes fell under Union control in 1862. Lincoln had visited New Orleans as a young man on a flatboat trip down the Mississippi River and knew it contained a large and educated Creole population. In the summer of 1863, Lincoln wrote a private letter to General Nathaniel Banks, commander of New Orleans, outlining his vision for a reconstituted government. Lincoln stated that he hoped the new state constitution would abolish slavery. But he went further, urging Louisiana "to adopt some practical system by which the two races could gradually live themselves out of their old relation to each other, and both come out better prepared for the new. Education for young blacks should be included in the plan."[35] This was directional guidance, not a specific prescription, but it reflected Lincoln's evolutionary vision of multiracial democracy.

But by February 1865, the Big Easy had become a big problem. Louisiana had delivered on a new state constitution that abolished slavery, consistent with Lincoln's 10 percent plan. This entitled them to elect members of Congress. But seating those representatives required congressional approval.

This ran into a roadblock erected by a strange alliance of radical Republicans and reactionary Democrats, who had very different reasons for opposing the president. Radicals believed Lincoln had not gone far enough to secure black voting rights. Reactionaries felt he'd gone too far in pushing for the Thirteenth Amendment. Both sides wanted to assert congressional primacy over Reconstruction. Louisiana was the first real chance they had to flex their muscle.

Irritated by this obstruction, Lincoln lost his considerable cool in a cabinet meeting, declaring, "I am to be bullied by Congress, am I? If I do, I'll be durned."[36] These flashes of anger exposed how much he struggled to discipline his underlying emotions, what secretary William Stoddard called "the storm that is continually stirred up within him by the treacheries, cowardices, villainies and stupidities, which, almost daily and hourly, he is compelled to see and understand and wrestle with and overcome."[37]

Making matters worse was the chief instigator: Massachusetts senator Charles Sumner. He'd been a legend in abolitionist circles since he was almost beaten to death on the floor of Congress by South Carolina congressman Preston Brooks in 1856. Severely wounded, Sumner survived to become a living martyr to the cause.

He was less likeable in person than in legend. Sumner was a self-styled member of the intellectual elite, a proud Harvard man who dressed in the latest fashions, wearing spats and patterned cravats that complemented his wide sideburns. This peacocking could inspire contempt; the writer Thomas Carlyle thought him nothing but "wind and vanity."[38] Sumner liked gossip, flattery, and moral superiority—but not evidently the company of young women. Nonetheless, he was a rare favorite of Mary Lincoln and as a result, he spent considerable time in the Lincolns' social circle, which served a useful political purpose for the president.

But when Sumner stopped the seating of Louisiana's Republican congressional delegation, aligning with proslavery senators, Lincoln took the betrayal personally. It was part of a pattern: Sumner had refused to support a railroad concession to secure the vote of a New Jersey Democratic congressman to pass the Thirteenth Amendment. "I can do nothing with Mr. Sumner in these matters," a frustrated Lincoln told White House secretary John G. Nicolay.[39]

Their differences reflected the gap between legislators' ideology and the president's executive responsibility. When a leading radical, Senator Benjamin Wade, demanded that Lincoln replace a general, the president asked who should replace him. "Anybody!" came the furious reply. "Anybody will do for you," Lincoln said, "but I must have *somebody*."[40]

Lincoln worried that overzealous radical Republicans could destabilize the postwar reunification of the nation. Lincoln's secretary John Hay privately called these radicals "Jacobins," after the guillotine enthusiasts of the French Revolution, because they often held progress hostage in the name of ideological purity. Lincoln tussled with the more extreme elements of his party when necessary—but their differences were often more a matter of style and speed rather than substance.

He tried to convince Congress to rise above the partisan divides, saying, "I would have preferred to meet you upon a level one step higher than any party platform . . . I am sure that from such more elevated position, we could do better battle for the country we all love, than from those lower ones, where through force of habit, the prejudices of the past and selfish hopes of the future, we are sure to expend much of our ingenuity and strength, in finding fault with, and aiming blows at, each other."[41]

But even in wartime, polarization had its own remorseless logic, and the president's appeals often fell on deaf ears. Lincoln tried to hide his frustration. To maintain a friendship of considerable political advantage, Lincoln still selected Senator Sumner to be an official escort for Mary at his second inaugural ball.

It was held two days after the inauguration, in the block-long Patent Office Building, which now houses the National Portrait Gallery. During most of the war, it had served as a military hospital, with wounded soldiers' cots resting on marble floors, surrounded by tiny models of modern invention. But on the night of March 6, the sickbeds were moved out to make room for a ballroom with a bandstand primed for what a *New York Times* correspondent called the "graceful mazes of the dance."[42]

Gaslight chandeliers lined the center of the great hall, flanked by giant American flags. Long tables were crammed with a decadent spread, featuring oyster stew and terrapin soup, platters of pheasant, and plates of lobster, as well as dishes that have since disappeared from American menus like pickled oysters, calf's foot jelly, and beef à la mode. But dessert was the main event: ornamental pyramids of macaroons, oranges, and caramel candies; fourteen different kinds of cakes and pastries; as well as troughs of ice cream, including the then-popular flavors of burnt almond, white coffee, and maraschino cherry.[43]

War-time economizing was, for a night, forgotten. The first lady, who planned the menu, would enjoy the pomp and circumstance one last time.

The attendees arrived at 9 p.m., showing tickets good for one man and two women. Dancing to a string band had already begun when the Lincolns arrived an hour and a half late. Lincoln ambled in alongside the speaker of the house, Schuyler Colfax, while Mrs. Lincoln followed on the arm of Charles Sumner.

They greeted the crowds, with Lincoln enduring another interminable round of handshakes before the first couple, accompanied by their eldest son, Robert, in his military uniform, were escorted to blue and gold sofas arranged on a dais in the middle of the room.

The pageantry could not disguise his real feelings. "Mr. Lincoln was evidently trying to throw off care for the time," *The New York Times* correspondent noted, "but with rather ill success, and looked very old; yet he seemed pleased and gratified."[44]

He was steeling himself for new storms. "His mind was seriously affected in contemplation of the new responsibilities which would devolve upon him," reflected Interior Secretary John Palmer Usher, "conscious that changes were about to occur which would impose upon him new duties in which he might possibly find himself in conflict with many of the public men who had supported the government in the war."[45]

Amid the pressures of war and peace, the petty aspects of the presidency were wearing on him, particularly the constant jockeying for presidential appointments in his second term. Lincoln's visits to the theater were always occasions for escape, but lately he'd been attending German opera in the hopes that he'd meet no office seekers for at least three hours.

Newspaper editorials urged the reelected president to take a break. The *New-York Tribune* warned, "If the president is to outlive the term in which he has just entered, a radical retrenchment must be promptly effected in the current exactions on his time and energies . . . all who know him from 1860 must have observed his air of fatigue, exhaustion and languor—so different from his old hearty, careless jovial manner . . . his death or a permanent disability now would be a calamity."[46]

Black in Blue and Gray

On March 13, 1865, telegraphs buzzed with the news that Lincoln had fallen so ill that he had to conduct a cabinet meeting from his nine-foot bed in the White House.

Lincoln was sick, but the Confederacy was on its deathbed. That day, Confederate president Jefferson Davis reluctantly signed legislation allowing the conscription of black soldiers. Absurdly, any slave who fought for the slave state would be offered their freedom.

Confederate general Howell Cobb—a onetime U.S. Secretary of the Treasury—blasted the "pernicious idea" in a letter to the secretary of war, stating without any evident irony, that "if slaves will make good soldiers then our whole theory of slavery is wrong."[1]

It was more than a recognition that slavery was fatally flawed. It was an admission that the war would soon come to an end. Desperation had cut Lee's army to the bone. In January, Lee warned about the "alarming frequency of desertion,"[2] after fifty-six soldiers abandoned him over three days, blaming "insufficiency of food and non-payment of troops."

While Confederate troops were withering, the Union Army received powerful reinforcements in the form of 180,000 black soldiers,[3] helping to deliver battlefield victories while upending prejudices in the process. Lincoln cheered them on, believing that the "bare sight of fifty thousand armed and drilled black soldiers upon the banks of the Mississippi would end the rebellion at once."[4]

In the South, the figure of the black Yankee soldier was indeed greeted with fear and fury. Their very existence—strong and armed, proud in uniform—was an insult to the idea of white supremacy. That's why the most brutal reprisals—execution and re-enslavement—were reserved for black Union soldiers at the hands of the Confederates. In response, Lincoln issued an Order of Retaliation:"For every soldier of the United States killed in violation of the laws of war, a rebel soldier should be executed; and for every one enslaved by the enemy or sold into slavery, a rebel soldier shall be placed at hard labor on the public works and continued at such labor until the other shall be released."[5]

Lincoln had initially resisted calls to conscript black soldiers, worrying that it would push border states like Kentucky into the Confederacy. But characteristically, Lincoln evolved.

After all, African-Americans had long served as sailors in the Navy, and during the war a few field commanders enlisted escaped slaves. In Louisiana, where there had been a tradition of black militias, General Benjamin Butler formed the Corps d'Afrique—the first full-black regiment in U.S. history. In October 1862, the First Kansas became the first black regiment to see combat, pushing back a Confederate force twice its number at the Battle of Island Mound in Missouri.[6] Their commander, Captain William D. Matthews, a free black businessman, recruited his troops with a stirring call to action:"Now is our time to strike. Our own exertions and our own muscle must make us men. If we fight, we shall be respected. I see that a well-licked man respects the one who thrashes him."[7]

African-American communities across the country had been agitating to get in the fight. Thomas Morris Chester had been among them. A highly educated son of Harrisburg, Pennsylvania, he disdained American discrimination and became a vocal advocate for colonizing Liberia—a scheme Lincoln supported as well at the time. Upon arriving in Monrovia, Chester served as editor of the *Star of Liberia* newspaper. The outbreak of Civil War brought him back home to recruit a local black militia, determined to confront "desperate men who are struggling to destroy free institutions on this continent" as well as "secession sympathizers in the North, who have been industriously attempting to reason themselves into the belief that black men will not fight."[8] But his proposed militia ran into resistance from Pennsylvania's governor, despite Confederate incursions into the state. Instead,

Chester joined *The Philadelphia Press,* where he would chronicle black regiments' success on the road to Richmond.

On New Year's Day 1863, Lincoln federalized the effort in the eighth paragraph of the Emancipation Proclamation, declaring that formerly enslaved people "of suitable condition, will be received into the armed service of the United States." In May, the Department of War established a bureau for United States Colored Troops. This was a revolution within a revolution.

Lincoln urged his commanders to take advantage of the new standard, writing General Grant that voluntarily conscripting freed slaves "is a resource which, if vigorously applied now, will soon close this contest. It works doubly, weakening the enemy and strengthening us."[9]

Combat validated the wisdom of the decision. In June 1863, at the Battle of Milliken's Bend in Louisiana, when far larger Confederate forces attacked an integrated band of Union troops and were repelled, white soldiers' minds were changed. "The bravery of the blacks at Milliken's Bend completely revolutionized the sentiment of the army with regard to the employment of Negro troops," one Union officer wrote. "I heard prominent officers who formerly had sneered at the idea of the Negros fighting, express themselves after that, as heartily in favor of it."[10]

After fighting side by side, experience overcame prejudice. By the end of the war, twenty-five African-American soldiers would be awarded the Medal of Honor for their heroism.[11]

Lincoln also understood that the presence of black troops fighting for their freedom set a powerful example that would echo on long after the war's end. In a letter read aloud to a crowd in Springfield, Lincoln wrote: "You say you will not fight to free negroes. Some of them seem willing to fight for you.... [After the war] there will be some black men who can remember that, with silent tongue, and clenched teeth, and steady eye, and well-poised bayonet, they have helped mankind on to this great consummation; while, I fear, there will be some white ones, unable to forget that, with malignant heart, and deceitful speech, they have strove to hinder it."[12]

The Confederate attempt to conscript slaves was on Lincoln's mind when he gave a brief speech to the 140th Indiana Infantry Regiment from the balcony of the National Hotel on St. Patrick's Day.

"I have always thought that all men should be free; but if any should be slaves it should be first those who desire it for themselves, and secondly those who desire it for others. Whenever I hear anyone arguing for slavery, I feel a strong impulse to see it tried on him personally."[13] The soldiers cheered.

Lincoln believed that the presence of black troops in blue would help change the culture of the country in years to come. As he planned for a liberal Reconstruction, their heroism gave Lincoln leverage to push forward another idea that had seemed radical only months before.

In a letter to General James Wadsworth, Lincoln asked whether "universal amnesty should not be accompanied with universal suffrage." He then answered his own question: "I cannot see, if universal amnesty is granted, how, under the circumstances, I can avoid exacting in return universal suffrage, or, at least, suffrage on the basis of intelligence and military service."[14]

In Lincoln's search for symmetry, any gestures toward reconciliation for Southern soldiers would need to be fairly paired with not just emancipation but voting rights—beginning with the black Union soldiers who had fought for freedom.

Father Abraham
on the Front Lines

City Point, Virginia, was a small town with a big name when black Union troops captured it in May 1864. Within months, the sleepy hamlet at the confluence of the James and Appomattox rivers was transformed into one of the busiest ports in the world—and the final Union army headquarters of the war.

It was a start-up city, with more than 280 buildings and 150,000 troops, visited by dozens of ships a day,[1] providing abundant supplies behind enemy lines. It was strategically positioned just east of Petersburg, the key supply center for General Lee's army, a railroad hub and the linchpin for defending the Confederate capital, twenty-four miles to the north. If Petersburg fell, Richmond would follow.

In June, the nine-month siege of Petersburg began under Grant's command. Both armies settled in for a long struggle, digging more than thirty miles of waterlogged trenches in a bloody stalemate between fortifications the soldiers called "Fort Hell" and "Fort Damnation."[2]

Grant was planning a final spring assault when news of the president's illness reached City Point in March 1865. His wife, Julia, suggested he invite the president to visit. Grant dismissed the idea with a trace of self-consciousness, saying, "If President Lincoln wishes to come down, he will not wait to be asked. It's not my place to invite him."

To break the tie, they turned to Lincoln's eldest son, the newly commissioned Captain Robert Lincoln, who had joined Grant's staff at the president's request after finishing his studies at Harvard. Robert came down on Julia's side, saying that his parents would come if they felt they were not intruding. Grant then walked to the telegraph office and fired off a simple, friendly invitation: "Can you not visit City Point for a day or two? I would like very much to see you and I think the rest would do you good." Lincoln lost little time in replying: "Your kind invitation received. Had already thought of going immediately after the next rain. Will go sooner if any reason for it."[3] He wanted to get out of Washington.

That night at the White House, the Navy presented the president with its recommended ship to make the perilous voyage to the front—the USS *Bat*, the fastest boat in the Union fleet, a captured blockade runner built in Liverpool. Lincoln gamely deferred to their judgment: what was good enough for the crew was fine for him. "I'm only a fresh-water sailor," he said, referring to his days on the Mississippi, "and I guess I'll have to trust you salt-water folks when afloat."[4]

The next day, Lincoln apologetically called the commander of the *Bat,* Captain John S. Barnes, back to the White House to say that Mrs. Lincoln would be joining the trip. The *Bat* was unsuitable for female company—it was too streamlined for speed to be refurnished for comfort. And so the *River Queen* was drafted back into action.

She was a white, side-wheeled steamship that functioned as an aquatic Air Force One during the final months of the war. The *River Queen* was massive—stretching 181 feet, the equivalent of half a football field—and fast, with 650 horsepower.[5] There were two decks in the back and one in front, with an outdoor promenade. Though originally built as a luxury steamship to handle travel between beach communities on the East Coast, it seemed to anticipate its presidential charge with two carved eagles against an American flag–draped shield on the side of either water wheel.

At 1 p.m. on March 23, the presidential party boarded the *River Queen* and departed for City Point, with the *Bat* accompanying for security. They could not be too careful. Five months before, her sister ship, the *Greyhound,* had been blown to bits by a cast-iron bomb covered in tar to look like a massive piece of coal that concealed fifteen pounds of gun powder. The danger would not be over once they arrived. In the summer of '64, Confederate saboteurs planted a time bomb on a munitions barge at City Point, leveling buildings with a deafening blast, spraying shrapnel throughout the camp and killing 184 men.[6]

Southern desperation fueled threats of assassination. Lincoln kept a file of death threats in his desk, viewing them with a bemused fatalism. "Why would anyone want to massacre me?"[7] he half-joked.

"He never exhibited the slightest concern for his personal safety," noted Captain Barnes. "He lived and moved as freely and unconcernedly as the least conspicuous citizen."[8] Nonetheless, the president's traveling party included two armed guards—William Crook and Charles Penrose—as well as Mary, her maid, and Tad.

Tad gained his nickname as a baby because his father decided he looked like a tadpole, with an outsized head and tiny body. He had a cleft palate that caused him to lisp and he called his dad "Papa-Day"—a child's conflation of "Papa Dear."

Tad was doted on without discipline after the death of his big brother Willie. Now he was Willie's age and the beloved boy was joyous, bubbling over with affectionate hugs, disarming questions, and wild whoops. He loved racing his pet goats down the halls of the White House in a miniature chariot while wearing a small blue Army uniform and parading around a pardoned pet turkey named Jack. Tad had carte blanche to crash cabinet meetings, often fell asleep in front of the president's office fireplace, and would occasionally plead the cases of people he met in the waiting rooms. But he possessed a compassionate common sense that delighted his father, providing welcome breaks from the burdens and formalities of office.

"I believe he was the best companion Mr. Lincoln ever had," attested William Crook, "one who always understood him and whom he always understood."[9]

As they pushed off from the Seventh Street wharf in the afternoon, Tad darted below to explore the ship's inner workings while energetically introducing himself to the crew.

Lincoln remained on deck, alone, staring out into the waters of the Potomac, until they passed Alexandria. Then he went inside to join the rest of the traveling party, where he enjoyed sea stories by the boat's captain, who'd spent a lifetime navigating the mid-Atlantic.

The president's steady demeanor could not save him from seasickness that night, as the boat tossed in the stormy waters of Chesapeake Bay, a plight compounded by the ill effects of toxic water aboard the ship. It was no wonder that sailors enjoyed rum; it was often safer to drink than water—Lincoln's preferred beverage, which he liked to call "Adam's Ale." When offered champagne to settle his stomach on an earlier stormy voyage, he declined, saying, "I have seen too many men sea-sick on land from drinking that stuff."

But he was feeling better when morning came, eating a breakfast of grilled fish with his family while Mary recounted a nightmare in which she'd seen the White House on fire. When the *River Queen* docked at Fort Monroe for resupply, the first lady nervously telegraphed the White House to find that her fears were unfounded.

City Point glowed on high bluffs above the James River when they arrived after sunset on March 24. General Grant was there to greet the presidential party and Lincoln escorted Julia Grant by the arm into the *River Queen's* interior cabin, where Mary was waiting on the plush banquettes. Then the two men excused themselves to meet in private about the state of the war.

Grant was a man of few words but many cigars. Nonetheless, he allowed himself to speak optimistically about the siege of Petersburg and the coming collapse of Richmond. He also had a surprise for Lincoln: within hours, the leading generals of the Union army would gather at City Point—William Tecumseh Sherman and cavalry commander Philip Sheridan, along with generals E. O. C. Ord and George Meade as well as Admiral David Dixon Porter—for a meeting with their commander-in-chief before a final spring offensive that would bring the Confederate army to its knees.

This accelerated Lincoln's timetable. He had calculated that the war would last until at least midsummer. Lincoln was cautious after having his hopes dashed by generals who did not capitalize on victories to destroy Lee's army. But this evening, he emerged beaming from his meeting with Grant.

Spring mornings are often foggy and cool in Virginia, but the clouds soon burn off to reveal a blue sky. So it was as Lincoln stared out from the breakfast table aboard the *River Queen* with Tad. The family was reunited when Robert came aboard in uniform bearing news of a predawn rebel raid on Fort Stedman—a "little rumpus" as Lincoln described it—a few miles up the line.

Far more than a "little rumpus," it was Robert E. Lee's last, desperate attempt to turn the tide of the war. At 4 a.m., Confederate troops under the command of Major-General John B. Gordon—a future governor of Georgia and U.S. senator—stormed across the no-man's-land at one of its narrowest points to capture Fort Stedman while Union soldiers were sleeping.

The Confederate plans fell apart as they found themselves under fire from three directions, with a Union counterassault led by Brigadier General John Hartranft. Reinforcements failed to materialize, and after four hours of furious fighting in what one soldier called "a ring of fire and death," the Confederates had lost 3,500 soldiers—killed or wounded or taken prisoner—while the Union lost 1,100 from a far larger standing army.[10] By 8 a.m., General Lee ordered a retreat.

The fierce fighting occurred a mile from where the president was sleeping. With victory secure, Grant agreed to resume Lincoln's scheduled review of the troops.

Lincoln was given a small black pony named Jeff Davis to ride. The two made a ridiculous pair, with the stretched president making the horse look like a Shetland, with his long legs almost trailing the ground, betraying a flash of white socks between his black trousers and boots. Lincoln freely acknowledged the absurdity with laughter at his own expense.

Once reaching the Union headquarters, Lincoln shook hands with the officers. Colonel Theodore Lyman observed the president closely, if somewhat unkindly, in a letter home.

"The President is, I think, the ugliest man I ever put my eyes on," he wrote to his wife. "On the other hand, he has the look of sense of wonderful shrewdness, while the heavy eyelids give him a mark of almost genius. He strikes me, too, as a very honest and kindly man and, with all his vulgarity, I see no trace of low passions in his face. On the whole, he is such a mixture of all sorts, as only America brings forth. He is as much like a highly benevolent Satyr as anything I can think of . . . as humanity runs, I am content to have him at the head of affairs." [11]

Outside the officers' tent, recently captured Confederates sat in the sun with "matted hair, tangled beards and slouched hats." Lincoln studied them sympathetically. One of the prisoners saw the president riding by, "seemingly not the least concerned and as if nothing had happened"[12] despite the morning's raid, and he knew the war would soon be over.

As Lincoln rode on horseback alongside Grant and Meade, word spread among the Union troops and they started wildly waving their battle flags and beating their drums for the man they called Father Abraham. "I never before heard such cheering," recalled one soldier from Wisconsin. "The President was kept busy lifting his hat and bowing. He rode so close to the lines that we could see his smile and hear his 'Thank you, my brave boys.'"[13]

They were suddenly interrupted by the sound of artillery. Seeking shelter at nearby Fort Wadsworth, Lincoln and Tad watched a Union attack on an entrenched rebel position in the woods ahead. Taking General Meade aside, the president asked if the location was safe for his son. With Meade's assurance, they remained there for two hours, as Lincoln held Tad's hand and explained the battle unfolding before them.

The exhilaration of being on the front lines faded when Lincoln returned to the train station to see the depot filled with the dead and wounded. Lincoln was silent, "but his whole face showing sympathetic feeling for the suffering about him," Barnes recalled. After boarding the train, Lincoln said that "he had seen enough of the horrors of war, that he hoped this would be the beginning of the end, and that there would be no more bloodshed or ruin of homes."[14]

That night, Lincoln sat around a campfire with Grant and his senior staff, light and shadows dancing across his face. He spoke about the hardships of the war: the spiraling death toll, the growing national debt, and the malicious meddling of foreign nations like England, which had to be contained with difficult diplomacy lest they give the South international legitimacy, expanding the scope of the Civil War. He praised the Union soldiers and Northern citizens for their steadfast support in this unprecedented crisis. Then Grant asked, "Mr. President, did you at any time doubt the final success of the cause?"[15]

"Never for a moment," Lincoln said, staring into the fire for a second, then looking up to make eye contact and slapping his knee for emphasis.

Lincoln and the Kittens

Abraham Lincoln found solace in telegraph offices. They were a refuge from the grasping demands of the presidency. Amid the electric spark and tap-tapping, Lincoln loved getting the latest information from what he called "lightning messages," and firing off replies. He could read and write without interruption, but with the added comfort of junior officers to share jokes with when the spirit moved him. It was an ideal arena for Lincoln's instinct to be alone in small crowds.

Bookending his days at City Point's telegraph office, Lincoln relaxed by leaning back in his chair, "with his long legs twisted and coiled as if he hardly knew what to do with them," recalled Grant's aide Adam Badeau, "and talked, apparently with the greatest freedom . . . All through the rough exterior of conversation, the abundant jokes, the plain, homespun talk,—as plain as his face, but as full of power and meaning."

On the morning of March 26, Lincoln broke into a broad smile as he reviewed correspondence from Secretary of War Stanton. "Well, the serious Stanton is actually becoming facetious," he said. "Just listen to what he says in his dispatch: 'The rebel rooster looks a little worse, as he could not hold the fence. . . . I hope you can remember General Harrison's advice to his men at Tippecanoe, that they can "see as well a little farther off."'"[1]

As laughter subsided, Lincoln spied three kittens murmuring at his feet. Their mother had died, soldiers explained, and they had been adopted by the men of the telegraph office.

Lincoln stooped down to gently pick them up, one by one, and place them in his lap, petting them while quietly consoling, "you poor little creatures, what brought you into this camp of warriors? . . . Thank God you are cats, and can't understand the terrible strife that is going on."[2] Then he said to the commander of the Telegraph Corps, Colonel Theodore Bowers, "I hope you will see that these poor little motherless waifs are given plenty of milk and treated kindly."[3]

Whenever Lincoln returned to the telegraph office at City Point, soldiers would find the president petting the kittens and cleaning their eyes with his handkerchief.

"It was a curious sight at an army headquarters," recalled Grant's aide-de-camp Horace Porter, "to see the hand that had affixed the signature to the Emancipation Proclamation, and had signed the commissions of all the heroic men who served the cause of the Union, from the general-in-chief to the lowest lieutenant, tenderly caressing three stray kittens. It well illustrated the kindness of the man's disposition and showed the childlike simplicity which was mingled with the grandeur of his nature."[4]

The Lincolns were due for an afternoon excursion and they boarded Grant's steamship, the *Malvern*, to visit General Ord's troops fighting on the frontlines. Onboard, the president asked with some concern what would happen if Confederates counterattacked at City Point. But his spirits lightened considerably when the boat reached a bend in the river and he saw Sheridan's cavalry crossing a pontoon bridge, as thousands of soldiers bathed and watered their horses, shouting and laughing.

When they heard the president was aboard, the soldiers cheered the commander-in-chief. Lincoln went up on deck and, grinning widely, as Barnes described, "waved his high hat as if saluting friends in his native town and seemed as happy as a schoolboy."[5]

After lunch, Lincoln reviewed the troops, starting with the black soldiers of the XXV Corps, commanded by Major General Godfrey Weitzel. He then climbed on Grant's steed, Cincinnati, and rode two miles with General Ord. Mary Lincoln and Julia Grant followed in an open carriage along the bumpy "corduroy roads" made passable by laying logs across muddy passages.

That's when the trouble began. Lincoln insisted that the review get underway, not wanting to inconvenience the waiting soldiers. Mary Ord, the general's young wife and an accomplished equestrian, decided to accompany the president and her husband through the review while Mrs. Lincoln was still in transit. This set off an angry panic in the first lady, who suspected a flirtatious insult in the form of Mary Ord.

"What does that woman mean by riding by the side of the President? And ahead of me?" she vented to Julia Grant and Captain Barnes, who accompanied them in the carriage. "Does she suppose that he wants *her* by the side of him?"[6]

A fusillade of insults fired from the first lady's lips, heightened by the anxiety that the soldiers would think Mary Ord was the president's wife—or worse, that she aspired to a similarly intimate position.

When Julia tried to calm her and explain that no insult was meant, the first lady turned on her companion. "I suppose you think you'll get to the White House yourself," she snapped, referring to Washington rumors that already saw Grant as a future president. When Julia protested she had no such ambitions, Mary pushed further with haughty disdain and a barbed compliment: "You'd better take it if you can get it. 'Tis very nice."[7]

As the troop review got underway, Grant's six-year-old son Jesse remembered the spectacle decades later: "The horse President Lincoln rode walked calmly, almost as though conscious that his burden must be carried with anxious care, while the President sat stiffly erect, the reins hanging slack from his hands. Father was but forty-two years old then, but I had always looked upon him as the largest and, next to my Grandfather Dent, the oldest man in the world. But beside President Lincoln, father looked small and for the first time I saw him as a young man. In a tightly buttoned frock coat and wearing a high hat, Mr. Lincoln appeared enormously tall, much taller than when standing. And to me, the boy watching . . . the unsmiling, worn, but kindly face, the tall black-coated form, riding before that colorful throng, gave me a feeling of awe that time has not effaced."[8]

But the majesty of the moment was lost to Mary. She arrived with

the troop review already underway, adding insult to her imagined in-
jury. She unloaded on Mary Ord in front of the officers, "called her vile
names . . . and asked what she meant to be following up the President."[9]
Overwhelmed and embarrassed, Mary Ord broke down in tears.

Lincoln remained blissfully unaware of the incident until later that
evening. He was in high spirits on the ride back. After dinner, the
president called for a military band to strike up an unexpected dance
for the assembled officers and their wives. As a young man, Lincoln
joked that he "danced in the worst way" and did not partake in the
festivities, but hung back in the aft cabin talking war and peace with
General Grant.

Mary took his absence as an opportunity to reignite the fight.
Surrounded by officers and their wives, the first lady demanded that
General Ord be removed from command as punishment for his wife's
alleged insult.

The commotion grew so loud that Grant and Lincoln were summoned from their meeting and tried to intercede, with the general
defending Ord while the president looked on with mortification, trying to calm his wife without confronting her in public.

He absorbed the humiliation "as Christ might have done; with an
expression of pain and sadness that cut one to the heart, but with supreme calmness and dignity," recalled Adam Badeau. "He called her
mother, with his old-time plainness; he pleaded with his eyes and tones
and endeavored to explain or palliate the offenses of others 'til she
turned on him like a tigress; and then he walked away, hiding that noble,
ugly face that we might not catch the full expression of its misery."[10]

After a collective breath, the party rolled on in the Lincolns' absence. The occasionally explosive tensions in the Lincolns' marriage
were not a well-kept secret. The first lady had been known to criticize
her husband in public, and one quarrel overheard in the White House
involved Mary holding her husband's pants hostage before a cabinet
meeting.[11] This seemed, sadly, par for the course.

Around midnight, Captain Barnes was woken up by an orderly
asking that he report to the president's quarters. When he arrived, he
found himself in the wreckage of a domestic dispute.

Mary launched into a recitation of grievances as her husband looked on apologetically, his face "an expression of sadness that seemed the accentuation of melancholy which at times so marked his features."[12] The president interjected that he had not even taken notice of Mrs. Ord's presence while the first lady tried to get Captain Barnes to back up her account.

Placed in the uncomfortable role of marriage counselor to the first family, Barnes stuck to the facts and explained that no offense had been meant. Lincoln thanked him and then escorted him to the door to bid him good night.

Years later, Barnes stated that the constant strain of fights with the first lady was the source of "the vein of sadness which ran through the naturally cheerful disposition of the greatest and noblest man this country has produced."[13] As to Mary Lincoln, Barnes compassionately commented, "she was at no time well; the mental strain on her was great, betrayed by extreme nervousness approaching hysteria, causing misapprehensions, extreme sensitivity as to slights, or want of politeness or consideration. I had the greatest sympathy for her, and for Mr. Lincoln, who I am sure felt deep anxiety for her. His manner toward her was always that of the most affectionate solicitude, so marked, so gentle and unaffected that no one could see them together without being impressed by it."[14]

Morning dawned, with its promise of new beginnings, and Lincoln, an instinctive conciliator, made a point at breakfast to smooth over any embarrassment by sharing the latest dispatches from the secretary of war with Captain Barnes.

A morning meeting with the generals restored Lincoln's sunniness, and then the *River Queen* departed upriver to a strategic vista and military hospital at a place known as the Point of Rocks.

Lincoln visited with wounded officers who had been under the care of Clara Barton, founder of the Red Cross. These hospital visits often left him drained and depressed, but today he could revive his spirits with a walk in the woods alongside Mary and Tad, bringing a picnic lunch they enjoyed near an ancient oak with a sign on it that read, "Woodsman, spare this tree."[15] It was, according to legend, the place where Pocahontas saved the life of Captain John Smith, in an early bit of romantic American history.

They walked another half mile to a high signal tower. Lincoln climbed a series of ladders 175 feet in the air, offering commanding views of the surrounding countryside. He could see the white tents of General Lee's Army of Northern Virginia, two miles to the west.

In the Confederate camp, there were no sprawling supply lines and food was scarce. Newspapers reported runaway inflation throughout the South, with flour at $1,500 per barrel, coffee at $50, and eggs $35 per dozen,[16] making everyday life behind Confederate lines a struggle to survive.

In contrast, the bustle and abundance in City Point was a testament to the North's industrial might. Every day, new ships came bearing supplies and reinforcements. The Union had only grown more prosperous and more populous during the war, while the South's share of national wealth was cut in half as battles scarred the rural region.

City Point was readying for the arrival of General William Tecumseh Sherman for a final war council.

"War is hell,"[17] Sherman famously said, and he believed the more brutal it was, the sooner it would be over. Sherman's greatest asset was his audacity. His second greatest asset was his friendship with a fellow West Point ne'er-do-well, Ulysses S. Grant. As Sherman later said, in one of the most enduring expressions of brotherly love, "I stood by Grant when he was drunk. He stood by me when I was crazy. And now we stand together always."[18]

When Sherman arrived at City Point late that afternoon, Charles Coffin of the *Boston Journal* captured Sherman's appearance as he came ashore with his "commanding forehead . . . sandy whiskers closely cropped. His coat was shabby with constant wear. His trousers were tucked into his military boots. His felt hat was splattered with mud."[19] He and Grant greeted each other on the docks with a warm handshake and talk of progress on the front. They walked together into the camp "both smoking, and as cordial to each other as two school boys,"[20] socialized with Julia in the Grant family cabin, and then paid a brief visit to the president. The next day, they would all meet on the *River Queen* to determine the final steps of the war.

Peacemakers on the
River Queen

T hey were hammering out a national fate"[1]—that's how the poet
and biographer Carl Sandburg described the meeting between
Lincoln, Grant, Sherman, and Porter aboard the *River Queen*.

They were self-made midwestern men who had been dismissed
by many unkind eyes as failures before reaching this pinnacle of respect and influence. They were impatient with self-pity. They trusted
each other. Now they were preparing to win the war—and the peace.

Their meeting would be memorialized in a painting called *The
Peacemakers* by G. P. A. Healy that hangs in the White House, providing inspiration to every president since Harry Truman authorized its
purchase on Lincoln's birthday in 1947.[2] The title comes from the
Sermon on the Mount: "Blessed are the peacemakers: for they shall be
called the children of God."

The canvas shows the four men sitting in a semicircle in the upper
saloon of the *River Queen*. The room is low-ceilinged but otherwise
spacious, with pale blue walls, sea-green curtains, and gilded molding
over a brightly colored Persian rug.

Sherman is on the left, captured in profile as he punctuates a point
to the president, his fingers caught in mid-snap.

Grant looks on from a leather bench, one eyebrow cocked, eyes
betraying a hint of amusement at his loquacious old friend.

Lincoln leans into the conversation, listening intently, legs crossed, while his chin rests in the crook of his right hand, index finger pushing up against his cheekbone, while his left hand clasps the arm of the wooden chair. He is the focus of the frame.

Admiral Porter sits off to the right of the president on a generously upholstered red armchair, lumpish but dignified, with immense whiskers that give him a walrus-like appearance.

A perfectly framed rainbow arches in the window behind Lincoln's head, a symbol of peace that the painter added as a metaphorical flourish when he painted the canvas months after Lincoln's death. Otherwise, the painting was based on interviews with Sherman and Porter, with a diagram of the room supplied to ensure accuracy. "We did not sit at a table nor do I recall having any maps or papers," Sherman recalled, "we merely sat at ease in such chairs as happened to be there."[3]

There is a serenity and sweep to the painting that transcends the constraints of the cabin. It has the feeling of enlightenment itself, the power of thoughtful people working in concert to build a better world.

Lincoln's posture at the meeting was burned into Sherman's memory, the way his gaunt body seemed to bear the full weight of the war. "At rest or listening, his legs and arms seemed to hang almost lifeless, and his face was careworn and haggard," Sherman wrote. But Lincoln's features came alive in conversation, causing his spirit to soar: "the moment he began to talk his face lightened up, his tall form, as it were, unfolded, and he was the very impersonation of good humor and fellowship."[4]

Lincoln's mind was decisive and could command total recall, which Grant characterized as "tenacity of purpose ... all that could be desired in a great statesman. His quickness of perception often astonishes me. Long before the statement of a complicated question is finished his mind will grasp the main points, and he will seem to comprehend the whole subject better than the person who is stating it."[5]

It was a ninety-minute meeting, commencing at noon on March 28. It was an informal war counsel, buoyed by the belief that rebels would soon be defeated but anchored by the knowledge that a single misstep at this moment could prolong the conflict for many more bloody months.

The first topic of business was the state of troop movements and the battle plan to bring an end to the rebellion. Smoking his perpetual cigar, Grant offered updates on Phil Sheridan's march to cut off Lee's remaining supply lines to Petersburg before the final offensive. He intended to end the war then and there.

He knew that was Lincoln's goal as well. "It was President Lincoln's aim to end the whole business," Grant recalled. "He was most anxious about the result. He desired to avoid another year's fighting, fearing the country would break down financially under the terrible strain on its resources ... The entire expense of the government had reached the enormous cost of four millions of dollars a day. It was to put an end to this expense that Lee's capture was necessary."[6]

There was concern that Lee would try to slip away south and join General Joe Johnston in North Carolina, leading to a protracted guerrilla war in the woods. In his memoirs, Grant spoke of the gnawing anxiety that he masked. "I was afraid, every morning, that I would awake from my sleep to hear that Lee had gone, and that nothing was left but a picket line."[7]

This possibility rekindled Lincoln's bitter memories of Lee's escape after Gettysburg. But the brusque Sherman dismissed the notion. "He cannot move without breaking up his army, which, once disbanded, can never again be got together," Sherman said. "I have destroyed the Southern railroads, so that they cannot be used again for a long time."[8]

This drew a questioning glance from Grant. "What is to prevent their laying the rails again?" he asked. "My bummers don't do things by halves," Sherman replied, referring to his foraging corps. "Every rail, after having been placed over a hot fire, has been twisted as crooked as a ram's-horn, and they never can be used again."

"Give yourself no uneasiness," Sherman assured Lincoln, "the Confederacy will collapse in a few days: we hold the line between Goldsboro and Wilmington; we can over-run the South without hindrance; we are masters of the situation and General Johnston must surrender."[9]

"Very well," Lincoln sighed, "but we must make no mistakes ... Offer Johnston the same terms that will be offered Lee; then if he will not accept them, try your plan; but as long as the Confederates lay down their arms, I don't think it matters much how they do it. Don't let us have any more bloodshed than can be avoided. General Grant is in favor of giving General Lee the most favorable terms." So, of course, was he.

The war, all agreed, would soon be over. Lee would be caught in a vise.

But momentum was essential. "If proper terms are offered, and with wise management," Lincoln believed, "these two armies will lay down their arms in a week, and then all the Confederate armies will follow their example. It will be like those rows of brick boys sometimes put up: knock down the first one, and the rest all follow."[10]

Peace was on Lincoln's mind more than war. "Mr. Lincoln exclaimed, more than once, that there had been blood enough shed, and asked us if another battle could not be avoided," Sherman recalled. "I remember well to have said that we could not control that event; that this necessarily rested with our enemy; and I inferred that both Jeff. Davis and General Lee would be forced to fight one more desperate and bloody battle."[11]

Grant echoed this assessment: "Mr. Lincoln asked if it would not be possible to end the matter without a pitched battle, with the attendant losses and suffering; but was informed that that was a matter not within the control of our commanders, and must rest necessarily with the enemy."[12]

Lincoln's vision of peace was still a work in progress, but when Sherman asked the president if he'd developed postwar plans, Lincoln gave clear parameters, telling Sherman to assure the governor of North Carolina that "as soon as the rebel armies laid down their arms, and resumed their civil pursuits, they would at once be guaranteed all their rights as citizens of a common country; and that to avoid anarchy the State governments then in existence, with their civil functionaries, would be recognized by him as the government de facto till Congress could provide others."[13]

There was a grand simplicity behind the inevitable complexity of securing peace. "All he wanted of us was to defeat the opposing armies," Porter recalled, "and to get the men composing the Confederate armies back to their homes, at work on their farms and in their shops."[14]

"Let them all go, officers and all, let them have their horses to plow with, and, if you like, their guns to shoot crows with," Lincoln said. "Treat them liberally. We want these people to return to their allegiance and submit to the laws. Therefore, I say, give them the most liberal and honorable terms."[15]

Lincoln was determined to restore a civil government to the South as quickly as possible, and he hoped generous terms would rekindle trust, turning the page from war to peace. When asked what he wanted to do with Jefferson Davis, Lincoln replied with a story about a man who had taken the total abstinence pledge. When asked by a friend if he'd like a drink, the man requested lemonade instead. But spying a bottle of brandy on the shelf, he suggested that if the lemonade were spiked with the booze, "unbeknown" to him, he would not object. Sherman understood that Lincoln would prefer that Davis escape the country, "unbeknown" to him.[16]

Lincoln's wisdom left a deep impression on the warlike Sherman: "I was more than ever impressed by his kindly nature," Sherman reflected, "his deep and earnest sympathy with the afflictions of the whole people, resulting from the war, and by the march of hostile armies through the South; and that his earnest desire seemed to be to end the war speedily, without more bloodshed or devastation, and to restore all the men of both sections to their homes."[17]

As Sherman left City Point that afternoon on the *Bat* to speed his way back to his men in North Carolina, Lincoln walked with him to the gangplank, leaving the general with the lasting impression that "of all the men I ever met, he seemed to possess more of the elements of greatness, combined with goodness, than any other."[18]

Lincoln's vision was clear and it would directly inform Grant's actions at Appomattox.

But first, Grant had to take Petersburg.

The Ghosts of Petersburg

"There is no doubt that, this morning, the curtain rises upon the last act of this great drama," wrote a reporter for *The New York Times* as he surveyed City Point on the morning of March 29.[1]

Grant was determined to end the nine-month siege that day. One million rounds of ammunition were headed to Ord and Meade's troops at the front as well as fresh horses to reinforce Sheridan's cavalry. Grant was preparing to move his headquarters from the comparative safety of City Point closer to Petersburg.

Lincoln arrived at Grant's small cabin at 8:30 to wish him well. The two men made small talk to ease the tension, with Grant regaling the president with some of the bizarre advice he'd received on how to end the war abruptly. One self-appointed military genius suggested that Grant outfit the army with bayonets a foot longer than the enemy's to ensure that in any clashes between the armies, the Union blades would enter Confederate flesh first and the war would be ended.

Lincoln laughed and said, "Well, there is a good deal of terror in cold steel. I had a chance to test it once myself," and proceeded to tell Grant a tale of walking down an alley as a young man in Louisville at midnight when some thug tried to mug him with a Bowie knife, "that seemed to my stimulated imagination about three feet long. . . . For two or three minutes he flourished his weapon in front of my face, appearing to try to see just how near he could come to cutting my nose off without quite doing it. He could see in the moonlight that I was taking a good deal of interest in the proceeding, and finally he yelled out, as he steadied the knife close to my throat: 'Stranger, kin you lend me five dollars on that?' I never reached in my pocket and got out money so fast in all my life. I handed him a bank-note, and said: 'There's ten, neighbor; now put up your scythe.'"[2]

Lincoln walked Grant's party to their railcar. Ulysses kissed Julia goodbye. Lincoln felt a twinge of family anxiety when he said good-bye to his son Robert, who was traveling with Grant to the front: "Robert, good-bye. God Bless you! Remember to do your duty always."

To Horace Porter, the lines in Lincoln's face "seemed deeper and the rings under his eyes were of a darker hue. It was plain that the weight of responsibility was oppressing him."[3]

As the president shook hands with each person in Grant's party, the general's chief of staff, John Rawlins said, "I hope we shall have better luck now than we have had."

"Well," Lincoln replied, "your luck is my luck and the country's, the luck of all of us . . ." then his voice trailed off as a shadow passed across his face. "Except the poor fellows who were killed. Success won't do them any good. They are the only ones not to be benefited by it."[4]

Restoring the mask of command, Lincoln waved a final goodbye and shouted, "God bless you all. Remember, your success is my success."[5]

As the train rolled away, Grant went to the back of the rail car, lit up another cigar, and with his head encircled in a wreath of smoke, remarked to Rawlins, "The President is one of the few visitors I have had who have not attempted to extract from me a knowledge of my movement, although he is the only one who has a right to know them. He intends to remain at City Point for the present and he will be the most anxious man in the country to hear from us. His heart is wrapped up in our success; but I think we can send him some good news in a day or two."[6]

Now there was nothing for the "most anxious man in the country" to do but wait. Lincoln haunted the telegraph office in the coming days, waiting for Grant's dispatches from the front, distracting himself with brief outings with Admiral Porter and Tad on a tugboat the president affectionately nicknamed "Buggy."

Out on the water and in the spring sunshine, the president seemed to relax, at one point telling Porter that he would look back on those moments as the real vacation of his administration.

Later that day, Lincoln went on a carriage ride with Mary into the countryside, where they came upon an old graveyard on the banks of the James River. It was a peaceful, shaded place with spring flowers blooming around the graves. He took her hand and they walked together amid the weathered white stones and green grass. "Mary," he said, "you are younger than I. You will survive me. When I am gone, lay my remains in some quiet place like this."[7]

As evening fell, he received reports of troops in position, with fighting set to commence. It began to rain in the moonless night, and Lincoln could hear artillery and rifle-fire break out at 10:15. "The sound was very distinct here," he telegraphed Stanton the next morning, "as also were the flashes of the guns upon the clouds." He was not alone in his perceptions; as a chaplain with a New York regiment wrote, it "seemed as if two contending thunderstorms had met."[8]

The rain fell for two days, delaying Grant's long planned offensive. "First a Scotch mist, then unsteady showers," one soldier wrote, "and then a pour, as if the equinox, hurrying through the elements, had kicked over the water-buckets."[9]

The Virginia backroads, always bad, became impassible, with horses and wagons sinking deep into the muck. Grant tried to take it in stride, writing Julia: "This weather is bad for us, but it is consoling to know that it rains on the enemy as well."[10] But amid the downpour, the general fell prey to uncharacteristic self-doubt as his chief of staff argued for a suspension of the long-planned attack on Petersburg.

Phil Sheridan provided a pep talk at a critical moment. He arrived at Grant's tent in the pelting rain and could sense that something was off. A tiny sparkplug of a man, irritable even on a good day, Sheridan excused himself to cool down his temper while warming up his wet body in front of a fire. That's where Grant found him and confessed he was considering a suspension of operations.

Sheridan's response was swift. "I at once begged him not to do so," Sheridan recounted, "telling him that my cavalry was already on the move in spite of the difficulties." Then, drawing himself to seem far bigger than his 5-foot-5-inch height, Sheridan declared: "I tell you, I'm ready to strike out to-morrow and go to smashing things."[11]

That's what Grant needed to hear. He was always apt to believe "those who expect success are almost certain to succeed," according to Adam Badeau, who watched Grant's resolve rekindle by the firelight. The attack would go on.

Lincoln had been away from Washington for more than a week. It was by far the longest trip of his presidency. When asked by the South Carolina–born wife of an officer how long he might remain at City Point, he replied with a story. "Well, I am like the western pioneer who built a log cabin. When he commenced, he didn't know how much timber he would need, and when he had finished, he didn't care how much he'd used up. So you see, I came in doubt among you without any definite plans, and when I go home, I shan't regret a moment I have spent with you."[12]

But Lincoln's absence from Washington was causing gossip. On March 30, Secretary of State Seward came to City Point, bearing paperwork and concern about any peace terms that might be negotiated in his absence. This was part of Lincoln's plan—despite his close relationship with Seward, he did not want to have his cabinet involved in dictating the terms of peace.

Nonetheless, Lincoln allowed for the possibility that he had lingered at City Point for too long, telegraphing Secretary of War Stanton for perspective. Stanton made the case that the president's presence near the front lines could actually hasten the end of the war: "I hope you will stay to see it out, or for a few days at least," Stanton telegraphed back. "I have strong faith that your presence will have great influence in inducing exertions that will bring Richmond; compared to that, no other duty can weigh a feather ... a pause by the army now would do harm; if you are on the ground, there will be no pause."[13]

This practical argument validated Lincoln's instincts. If his presence would encourage aggressiveness out of fear for underperforming in front of the president, then he would stay at City Point.

But he decided to send Mary back to Washington, accompanied

by Seward and General Carl Schurz, a German immigrant abolitionist. Lincoln and Tad would remain, anticipating the end of the war and the child's twelfth birthday. The boy was now the man's closest companion.

Waiting for news from the front, Lincoln lingered at the telegraph office during the day and paced the decks of the *River Queen* at night. He seemed depressed and distracted, weighty with the knowledge that more carnage was ahead. In such melancholy moments, he liked to recite his favorite poem, "Why Should the Spirit of Mortal Be Proud?," particularly its penultimate verse: "Hope and despondency, pleasure and pain/Are mingled together in sunshine and rain/And the smile and the tear, and the song and the dirge/Still follow each other, like surge upon surge."[14]

The sound of distant gunfire over the water stoked his tortured hopes. He could see the flash of the cannon and refused repeated requests to retire below deck.

"Mr. Lincoln would not go to his room," William Crook recalled. "Almost all night he walked up and down the deck, pausing now and then to see if he could see anything. I have never seen such suffering in the face of any man as was in his that night."[15]

Fortune favored the bold on muddy ground. Sheridan's 9,000 troops braved the rain and Confederate rifles to take Dinwiddie Courthouse and pressed on to control the critical junction of Five Forks, cutting off rebel access to their last railroad supply line. In fierce fighting, the casualties came in 10-to-1 at the expense of the Confederates, including the death of General A. P. Hill, shot through the chest. He would be buried—at his request—standing up. When General Lee heard the news, he said, "He is now at rest, and we who are left are the ones to suffer."[16]

Cheers cascaded through Union lines as dispatches confirmed Sheridan's victory. As Grant sent reinforcements to support the cavalry's gains, all knew this was the beginning of the end. With its supply lines cut, Lee's Army of Northern Virginia was living on borrowed time and Richmond could no longer be defended.

That evening, *New York Herald* war correspondent Sylvanus

Cadwallader came to City Point bearing captured Confederate battle flags from Five Forks as gifts from Grant. As the journalist handed the flags to a beaming Lincoln on the lower deck of the *River Queen*, the president held them outstretched in his arms, and said, "Here is something material—something I can see, feel and understand. This means victory. This *is* victory!"[17]

Lincoln invited Cadwallader into the Upper Saloon to describe what he'd seen at the front, poring over large maps spread out onto tables where the troop advances were shown in red and black and duly updated. The president "manifested the joy of a schoolboy as he narrated each bit of good news," Cadwallader recalled.[18]

More good news came for Lincoln after he went to bed. Captain Penrose was reluctant to wake the often-sleepless president, but bearing a dispatch about an impending all-out attack by Union infantry at dawn, Penrose knocked on the door of Lincoln's cabin. "As he stood there in his night shirt that reached barely to his knees and left exposed his long, thin legs that were thickly covered with black hair," Penrose remembered. "He held a candle in one hand, and, while I was reading the dispatches, with the other kept reaching down and scratching his legs. He was mightily pleased with the victory, and putting his hand on my shoulder he said, 'Captain, I should never have forgiven you if you hadn't waked me up to hear such good news.'"[19]

Bad dreams kept him from enjoying the moment. That night, after collapsing back into bed, Lincoln had a nightmare, as he recounted to Mary days later:

> I heard subdued sobs, as if a number of people were weeping ... I went from room to room; no living person was in sight, but the same mournful sounds of distress met me as I passed along. It was light in all the rooms and every object was familiar to me, but where were all the people grieving as though their hearts would break? I was puzzled and alarmed. What could be the meaning of all this? Determined to find the cause of a state of things so mysterious and so shocking, I kept on until I arrived at the East Room [of the White House] which I entered. There I met with a sickening surprise. Before me was a catafalque, on which rested a corpse wrapped

in funeral vestments. Around it were stationed soldiers who were acting as guards; and there was a throng of people, some gazing mournfully upon the corpse, whose face was covered, others weeping pitifully. "Who is dead in the White House?" I demanded of one of the soldiers. "The President," was his answer. "He was killed by an assassin!" Then came a loud burst of grief from the crowd which awoke me from my dream.[20]

The president could sleep no more. In search of news and company, Lincoln entered the telegraph office early that morning. At 6:40 a.m. a dispatch sped across the wires from General Grant: Confederate lines around Petersburg had finally been broken.

It was Sunday, April 2. Jefferson Davis was praying at St. Paul's Church in Richmond when a uniformed messenger briskly walked to his pew in the middle of services carrying a message from General Lee, advising him to evacuate the capital by nightfall. Davis's face turned ashen as panicked whispers cascaded through the pews.

Twenty-four miles away, joy was the order of the day. Military bands banged away at City Point. Lincoln telegraphed Mary, who decided to return to be by her husband's side in this moment of triumph, accompanied by a small crowd of friends.

With regular updates of the army's progress, by evening Lincoln felt justified in sending Grant a message of congratulation. "Allow me to tender to you, and with all of you, the nation's grateful thanks for this additional, and magnificent success. At your kind suggestion, I think I will visit you tomorrow."[21]

With the *River Queen* gone to Norfolk on military matters, Lincoln stood up on the deck of the *Malvern* with Admiral Porter in the moonlight after Tad had gone to bed and displayed his boyish love of crash and bang.

"Can't we make a noise?" he asked the admiral, hoping for a celebratory rattling of Navy guns. The admiral complied and soon the Union ironclads were shelling indiscriminately in the direction of the Confederate navy, with satisfactory flashes upon the dark horizon.

Suddenly, a massive explosion caused Lincoln to leap up from his chair: "I hope to heaven one of our vessels has not blown up!" he exclaimed, afraid that his own indulgence could have cost Union lives.

Porter calmed his commander in chief, noting that to his trained ear, the explosions were at least two miles away. He predicted a succession of such explosions as the Confederates destroyed their own boats to stop them from falling into Union hands.

"Well, our noise has done some good," Lincoln said. "That's a cheap way of getting rid of ironclads. I am certain Richmond is being evacuated, and that Lee has surrendered, or those fellows would not blow up their ironclads."[22]

At that hour in Richmond, railroad boxcars hastily marked with the names of the Confederate cabinet, packed with official papers and gold nuggets, rumbled through the night to Danville as their capital burned behind them.

Early the next morning, Lincoln boarded a train to visit Grant in Petersburg. He wanted to see the town that had been under siege for so long and get a sense of the challenges ahead. Victory on the battlefield would need to be followed by rebuilding.

As he sat in the railcar reading the morning's newspapers with Admiral Porter by his side, three young men tried to forcibly board the train, demanding to see the president. Porter blocked the car door and shoved two of the men to the muddy ground, declaring that he would shoot the next man who tried to set foot on the platform. Soon joined by Tad, Barnes, and Crook, they set off for Petersburg, where Robert would be waiting.

As they neared their destination, the train slowed to let a group of bedraggled young Confederate prisoners cross the tracks. "Poor boys! Poor boys!" Lincoln softly said almost to himself. "If they only knew what we are trying to do for them they would not have fought us, and they would not look as they do."[23]

Greeted by Robert at the station, Lincoln climbed up on a chestnut warhorse and rode through the battle-scarred town along the empty Jerusalem Plank Road.

It was a ghostly scene. They passed a battlefield where the only sound came from flies buzzing over the bodies of Pennsylvania Zouaves strewn across the ground, their Moroccan-inspired uniforms splattered with blood and mud.

The dead lay where they fell—or, in one case, not fallen at all. Lincoln saw the corpse of one Union infantryman still standing up, stuck in thigh-high thick mud, with a bullet hole through his forehead and his rifle still clasped in his hand.[24]

Surveying the scene, a tear ran down Lincoln's cheek as Crook saw "the old lines of sadness" settle again on the president's face.

Steering toward the stars and stripes now flying from the battered courthouse in the town center, Union soldiers broke the spell with hearty cheers when they saw their commander in chief. Sergeant Eugene Beauge of the Forty-Fifth Pennsylvania wrote home of seeing Lincoln "riding at a slow gallop through our division, guiding his horse with one hand, his stove-pipe hat in the other"[25] while Lieutenant James F. Merrill of Seventh Rhode Island remembered that "we rushed along the way to greet him and I never will forget the mournful smile that he gave us."[26]

When they reached Grant's temporary headquarters at 21 Market Street, Lincoln leaped off his horse and strode up to the big red brick building, face beaming and hand outstretched to Grant, who walked off the porch to greet him. "It looked as if instead of merely shaking hands, he would have liked to hug the general," Crook recalled.[27]

"Do you know, general, I had a sort of a sneaking idea all along that you intended to do something like this,"[28] Lincoln said with a grateful grin.

The owner of the home, a local attorney named Thomas Wallace, invited them to sit inside. Lincoln recognized Wallace as an old Whig political ally from his days in Congress. He did not know that Wallace's wife was a cousin of Confederate general A. P. Hill, who had been killed at Five Forks two days before.

Despite being in mourning, the Wallace family tried to be accommodating. As Thomas Morris Chester dryly reported, Wallace seemed to have been "suddenly transformed into a Union man by the magical influence of triumphant bayonets."[29]

But the family must have been relieved when Grant insisted that they sit outside instead to enjoy a degree of privacy. They moved two high-backed wooden chairs out onto the white portico. Lincoln scooted to the edge of the front steps so his long legs could stretch out comfortably.

Inside the Wallace house, Tad was getting jumpy. General George Sharpe produced a plate of sandwiches, saying, "Here young man, I guess you must be hungry." Tad latched on to the plate and began to devour the meal, declaring between mouthfuls, "Yes, I am, that's what's the matter with me!"[30] causing the adults to erupt in laughter.

Outside, the president and the general talked for ninety minutes, about taking Richmond and the terms of surrender for Lee's army.

"The President, of course, was cheerful at the great success which had been achieved, but there was a dash of anxiety mingled with his satisfaction," recalled Adam Badeau. "He foresaw the imminent civil complications that success involved. His great heart was full of charity, however, and he was planning already what merciful magnanimity he could show to those who had resisted and reviled himself and his government so long."[31] Grant had heard these same plans on the *River Queen*, but Lincoln wanted his wishes clear to the man who would carry them out on the battlefield.

Lincoln deferred to his general on military affairs. But he was uncompromising about cordoning off political questions and not allowing their delegation to the military. This was a constitutional imperative as well as a matter of personal preference.

Now Petersburg lay at their feet, a living example of the devastation that the whole nation would inherit when the war ended. Rebuilding would take federal investment. Hearts and minds would hopefully follow. Compounding the unprecedented challenge was a refugee crisis that Lincoln had not seen with his own eyes until that morning.

Slaves spent the previous night hiding in local churches, hoping to survive the final bombardment. They emerged, blinking into the morning sun of a new world as Union troops patrolled the silent streets. Lincoln understood the freedmen could not be abandoned in the South with the expectation that justice would be done.

The fledgling Freedmen's Bureau stood ready to help. Tasked with "control of all subjects relating to refugees and freedmen,"[32] and located within the Department of War, they would shelter, feed, and educate the former slaves with the goal of helping them achieve self-sufficiency.

But economic self-sufficiency depended upon the ownership of land. In January, General Sherman issued Special Field Order No. 15, which confiscated 400,000 acres of coastal land in Georgia and South Carolina from plantation owners and redistributed it to the families of freed slaves in forty-acre plots, giving birth to the enduring slogan "40 acres and a mule." While Lincoln authorized the order, it was explicitly a wartime measure. Lincoln, ever the lawyer, opposed the permanent redistribution of land without due process out of respect for private property. In response, the Freedmen's Bureau proposed allowing slaves to lease forty-acre plots for a period of up to three years, within which time they could buy the land outright as a result of their profits.

These were broad postwar responsibilities that no American army had contemplated before—consolidating gains by securing the peace.

At the moment, there were more immediate concerns. So long the glittering prize, Richmond's fall now seemed to be only a matter of time.

Just a few hours before, unknown to Lincoln and Grant as they sat on the porch, the Department of War received the first telegraph from Richmond in four years.

A fifteen-year-old telegraph operator named Willie Kettles was manning the station when he received the electric *tap-tap-tap* from Richmond announcing that General Weitzel had entered the city at 8 a.m.

Stumbling over himself, the teen sprinted to tell his boss. Soon the news spread throughout the building and jumped the iron fence to civilians as reporters picked up on the buzz and transmitted it to the wider world.

Even Edwin Stanton got carried away with the spirit of celebration: he picked up Willie Kettles and placed him in a windowsill of the War Department as he called out to the cheering crowds below, "This is the boy who received the first message from Richmond!"[33]

"Almost by magic the streets were crowded with hosts of people, talking, laughing, hurrahing and shouting in the fullness of their joy," Noah Brooks reported for the *Sacramento Daily Union.* "Men embraced each other, treated each other, made up old quarrels, marched along the streets arm-in-arm, singing or chatting in that happy sort of abandon which characterizes people when they don't care whether school keeps or not."[34]

In Petersburg, there was stillness. White citizens huddled in their homes as liberated slaves came out of the shadows to greet the soldiers in blue. Across the street from the Wallace house, a reporter spoke with a black woman and pointed out the president, asking if she recognized him. She shook her head slowly. "That is the man who made you free," he said, and a smile grew across her face. "Lord Bless him!" she exclaimed. "Is that Mr. Lincoln?"

As word spread, a crowd of newly freedmen and women gathered in a silent reverie opposite the front porch. Brigadier General Michael R. Morgan recalled the scene, with "the President seated, looking down on a yard full of negroes and they all looking up at him, not a word being spoken on either side."[35]

A little after noon, Lincoln bade Grant goodbye and rode through the scarred streets, stopping to look at the remains of the Dunlop Mansion, which had been riddled with artillery fire during the siege and now stood with its Southern charm shattered: windows smashed, wooden shutters hanging from a single hinge. Lincoln shook his head.

Around the corner, tobacco warehouses still burned from fires set by the Confederates on their way out of the city, sending plumes of sweet-smelling smoke toward the sky.

Scattered bales of golden tobacco were sprawled across the street, gamely snatched up by the Union troops—a spoil of war so small that even Lincoln joined in, picking up a few bales and tying them to his saddle, even though he never smoked or chewed the stuff. Tad also wanted to partake in the pilferage, primarily because he did not want to feel left out of the fun.

There was a spirit of cheerful anarchy cascading among the Union troops. It was evident in the tone taken by the newspaper already being printed up and distributed by soldiers, dubbed "Grant's Petersburg Progress."

The front-page editorial was simply titled "We Are Here" and promised its readers that "Our intentions are strictly honorable. We intend to publish a live paper as long as circumstances will permit; that is, as long as we can steal the paper and get men detailed to set the type . . . We believe in the United States, one and indivisible, in Abraham Lincoln, our adopted father, in U.S. Grant, Captain of the Hosts, and ourselves as the principle sojourners in the Army of the Potomac; and the Freedom of the Contraband, the speedy extinction of the Rebellion and the perdition of Jeff. Davis here and hereafter."[36]

Before leaving the city, Lincoln stopped by the house of Roger A. Pryor, a former congressman turned Confederate general. His wife met the president at the door, declining a meeting on her husband's behalf, explaining that General Lee was still fighting and they could not meet with the head of the opposing army.

Healing the wounds of Civil War would take time. But Lincoln took heart from the example set by a young girl who approached him with a handful of flowers, which he accepted with gratitude.

He waved his hat to the cheering Union troops, who boisterously promised him that they would see to the end of the war on his behalf: "We'll get 'em Abe," they said. "You go home and sleep sound tonight; we boys will put you through!"[37]

An orange sun was beginning to set as Lincoln returned to City Point, full of hope that the end of the war could not be far off.

While Tad went to his cabin, Lincoln walked to the telegraph office, where the best news of the war was waiting for him: Richmond had fallen.

Delighted, Lincoln swung around in his swivel chair and read the telegram aloud.

Then came a second telegraph from Stanton, warning Lincoln to resist the temptation to visit Richmond, asking him "to consider whether you ought to expose the nation to the consequences of any disaster to yourself."[38]

Lincoln immediately dictated a reply: "Thanks for your caution, but I have already been to Petersburg, stayed with Grant for an hour and a half, and returned here. It is certain that Richmond is in our hands and I think I will go there tomorrow. I will take care of myself."[39]

That night, Lincoln paced the decks, eager to begin the next day's adventure. "Thank God that I have lived to see this," he said within earshot of Admiral Porter. "It seems to me that I have been dreaming a horrid dream for four years, and now the nightmare is gone. I want to see Richmond."[40]

A Magnanimous Peace

Lincoln and the Fall of Richmond

"We must extinguish our resentments if we expect harmony and union. If I were in your place, I'd let 'em up easy. Let 'em up easy."

—*Abraham Lincoln*

R ed flames rose over Richmond, sending smoke into the blue-black sky. As Union troops marched toward the fallen Confederate capital just before dawn, they heard a furious galloping and then saw the silhouette of a man outlined by fire, standing tall on the seat of a carriage, legs apart to steady himself as he jerked the reins to bring him faster toward freedom.

"They is running from Richmond," he shouted, like a Paul Revere in reverse. "They is running from Richmond! Glory, Glorrry!"[1]

The fires were set by retreating Confederates, first burning government records in huge bonfires, then setting light to cotton and tobacco warehouses, and finally destroying the city's bridges, sparking a blaze that would consume more than 800 buildings.

Black soldiers were leading the advance into the self-immolated slavocracy. Thomas Morris Chester was embedded with the troops on the early morning of April 3, when the black Fifth Massachusetts Cavalry rode into Richmond, led by Charles Francis Adams, Jr.—the grandson and great-grandson of U.S. presidents—followed by soldiers from the all-black XXV Corps under the command of General Godfrey Weitzel, containing two Medal of Honor recipients, James Daniel Gardiner and Miles James.[2] A son of New York City Irish immigrants, General Thomas Devin led his brigade into the city marching to the beat of the drum corps playing "Battle Cry of Freedom."

It was a diverse army fighting for unity, an American mix of race and class, immigrants and aristocracy, bringing a bloodless end to the bloodiest conflict in our history.

When Union troops entered Richmond shortly after 8 a.m., they found a city reeling from the night's drunken riots. Stores had been looted despite the flames, as desperate citizens risked their lives to cart off wheelbarrows full of bacon and flour. Hundreds of barrels of bourbon tumbled from a second-story distillery, crashing to the ground and pouring downhill like "a miniature whiskey Niagara," one Union soldier recalled, with a current "strong enough to have swept a man off his feet."[3]

As the flames engulfed the Confederate War Department and threatened wealthy homes in the city center, white citizens moved furniture, portraits, and family keepsakes into the city streets to avoid consumption in a fiery collapse. But the streets were no longer a place of safety for the slave-owning class. "It was retributive justice," Thomas Morris Chester wrote, "upon the aiders and abettors of treason to see their property fired by the rebel chiefs and plundered by the people whom they meant to forever enslave."[4]

Former slaves and poor whites lined the sidewalks to cheer the soldiers with shouts of joy: "Slavery's chain done broke at last!!" "Jesus opened the way!" and "I've not seen that flag for four years"— "evidences of the latent patriotism of an oppressed people, which a military despotism has not been able to crush," reported Chester.[5] The scene "was not only grand but sublime. Officers rushed into each other's arms, congratulating them on the peaceful occupation of this citadel. Tears of joy ran down the faces of the more aged,"[6] as the American flag was hoisted above the former Confederate capitol.

Southern citizens had been told to expect rape and looting from the Union troops. Instead, Richmond mayor Joseph Mayo rode out to meet the conquerors and asked for the Yankees' help to put out the blaze and restore order to his fallen city. A black soldier was assigned to stand guard outside the home of the ailing Mrs. Robert E. Lee for her safety.[7]

That morning, Tad Lincoln woke up ready to celebrate his twelfth birthday. With his mother in Washington, he had his Papa-Day almost to himself. It would be an epic day, father and son primed for an adventure together.

Admiral Porter had his own agenda. He wanted to provide the president with a triumphant naval procession into Richmond. Events would not unfold as he intended.

At Porter's order, sailors had spent the night frantically trying to clear mines out of the James River, which twisted northward from City Point to Richmond. It had been rendered impassable by a succession of floating explosives and metal wires drawn across the rapid current, overseen by Confederate defenses like Fort Darling on ninety-foot-high bluffs, which made Union ships easy targets for artillery.

The *Richmond Whig* newspaper had somehow gotten wind of the plan: "We learn that it is not improbable that His Excellency, President Lincoln, will reach the city this afternoon."[8] Assassins had been put on notice via the front page: the president was coming to town.

They pushed off at 9 a.m., with Lincoln sitting on deck in the morning sun eating apples with a paring knife, while Tad scampered below to talk to the sailors and inspect the engines.

The presidential party traveled in a flotilla for security, with Admiral Porter leading on the *Malvern*. Lincoln proceeded on the *River Queen* with Tad, followed by a transport ship called the *Columbus*, which was packed with fresh horses and supplies for the troops in Richmond; Captain Barnes brought up the rear on the *Bat*.

At first, they passed ships whose crews saluted the president on deck with three cheers. "It was a most beautiful sight and one which seemed to impress Mr. Lincoln very pleasantly," Porter remembered. "I never saw him look happier although he glanced rather askance at the ugly torpedoes that now and then showed their heads along their banks where our boats had hauled them out of the way."[9]

But the sunshine and celebration gave way to a more surreal scene as they passed a break in the river known as Bermuda Hundred, clogged with dead horses, artillery shells, and the wreckage of war ships, with one sunken vessel so close to the surface that Lincoln could see its ghostly hull as they passed over.

At Fort Darling, the president's convoy approached a Union minesweeper, the USS *Commodore Perry*, indicating that the removal of explosives had not been cleared upriver toward Richmond. Lincoln and Porter decided to board a barge, with a tugboat named the *Glance* pulling them from a safe distance ahead to guide their progress and absorb any detonation directly without killing the president. Accompanied by twelve sailors and marines manning the tug, Lincoln and Tad were joined by a small crew including Admiral Porter, Captain Penrose, and William Crook.

Bodyguards couldn't have helped with what happened next: the president and his party almost died in a freak accident.

Navigating the narrow channel, the immense water wheel of the *Perry* began to turn and draw the barge carrying the president into its path. The crew began shouting wildly and waving their hands, as warning bells rang out, but the captain had instructed his engineer to ignore any disturbance signals, so he ran to the engine room and gave the order to stop. "It was not an instant too soon," a signal officer on the *Perry* recalled, "had the wheel gone over once more it would have caused the death of most in the barge."[10]

Disaster averted, the shaken party was determined to continue its mission to Richmond. Six miles upriver they met their next test at a place known as Tree Hill, where a massive ship had run aground.

It contained the most decorated man in the Navy, Admiral David Farragut. The hero who had taken New Orleans and Mobile was aboard the *William Allison*, a captured Confederate steamer he hoped to triumphantly present to President Lincoln at City Point.

Farragut had not expected to meet the president here, run aground in shallow water, while Lincoln was rowed toward him in a humble barge. The day's comedy of errors did not offer Lincoln's admirals the chance to show off for their boss. Lincoln asked that the *Glance* assist the *Allison*, but the hapless tug soon found itself grounded as well. As Richmond park ranger and historian Michael D. Gorman dryly notes, "The only two admirals then in the U.S. Navy had both separately grounded their vessels at Tree Hill."[11]

It was a lesson in the dangers of hubris, and this reminded Lincoln of a story. "Admiral, this brings to mind a fellow who once came to me to ask for an appointment as minister abroad," he told Porter. "Finding he could not get that; he came down to some more modest position. Finally, he asked to be made a tide-waiter. When he saw he could not get that, he asked me for an old pair of trousers." Lincoln laughed. "But it is well to be humble."[12]

Porter was suffering from the sin of pride, skulking into the Confederate capital, with sailors pulling against the current, like a Viking party of yore but in a less impressive boat. Luckily, Lincoln was a forgiving man.

There was one final obstacle on the six-hour voyage: no one knew where to land in Richmond and there was no one to ask. The barge betrayed no sign that the president was on board and no one told General Weitzel of the president's new time of arrival. When they arrived at the Port of Richmond at a prominent pier known as Rockett's Landing, there were no soldiers, and the docks, built for larger boats, towered above the barge.

So the crew rowed on in search of a shore to pull the boat onto land, finding a suitable sandbar a few blocks farther, where Shockoe Creek connects with the James River.

There in the shadow of Libby Prison, they saw a few dozen newly liberated slaves at work building a bridge. They stepped on to solid ground, with only the sailors' carbines to protect the president.

It was three in the afternoon on a hot day, with fires still sending smoke into the sky. There was no official greeting party to meet the president on this historic occasion, but there was one lucky and enterprising journalist, Charles Coffin of the *Boston Journal*, who left Petersburg the day before to get to Richmond ahead of Lincoln. After checking in to the Spotswood Hotel, as a few remaining Confederates tried to drown their sorrows at the bar, he took a stroll around the city and happened to see the presidential party soon after they reached the shore with a sandy thud.

"There was no committee of reception, no guard of honor, no grand display of troops, no assembling of an eager multitude to welcome him," Coffin reported. "He entered the city unheralded; six sailors, armed with carbines, stepped upon the shore, followed by the President, who held his little son by the hand, and Admiral Porter;

the officers followed and six more sailors brought up the rear."[13] This was the scoop of a lifetime, as Coffin walked into the enemy capital alongside Lincoln, an eyewitness to history.

A shock of recognition reverberated across the waterfront. One man about sixty years of age noticed the barge pulling into the otherwise empty riverfront and held his hand above his eyes to peer out and recognized the man in the tall black hat. "Bless the Lord," he said, "there is the great messiah . . . and he's come at last to free his children from their bondage!"[14]

"They all dropped work and rushed to the boat to shake hands with their supposed savior," Admiral Porter remembered. "No electric wire could have carried the news of the President's arrival sooner than it was circulated through Richmond. As far as the eye could see the streets were alive with negros and poor whites rushing in our direction, and the crowd increased so fast that I had to surround the President with the sailors with fixed bayonets to keep them off."[15]

As Lincoln held his son's hand in his left, he reached out with his right to shake hands with the adoring crowd, who were reaching out to touch the hem of his garment, a long black overcoat too heavy for the warmth of spring.

As men in the crowd threw themselves at Lincoln's feet, his essential modesty demanded a republican response. "I am but God's humble instrument; but you may rest assured that as long as I shall live no one shall put a shackle on your limbs and you shall have all the rights which God has given to every other free citizen of this Republic."[16]

Proclaiming "love and gratitude" but "no disrespect," one old man explained that "after being so many years in the desert without water, it's mighty pleasant to be looking at last on our spring of life." Then he joined hands with some of the people standing around him and began to sing an old Methodist hymn: "Oh, all ye people clap your hands / And with triumphant voices sing / No force the mighty power withstands / Of God, the universal King."[17]

There was beatitude in Lincoln's demeanor this day, a grace that radiated outward. "His face was lit up with a divine look," Porter remembered. "Though not a handsome man and ungainly in his person, yet in his enthusiasm he seemed the personification of manly beauty, and that sad face of his looked down in kindness."[18]

Still clasping Tad's hand, Lincoln walked uphill, encircled by a dozen sailors in blue cloth caps and baggy pants holding carabines, surrounded by a rowdy crowd, following the road for more than a mile, heading toward the dome of the capitol. Beads of sweat collected on their faces, soon covered with dust and specks of soot.

They walked by buildings with doors broken open and windows shattered; past the slave-trading center of Richmond, with ornate auction houses and slave jails, where families had been separated and sold for a century, past the building where James Madison, John Marshall, and Robert E. Lee's father had ratified the U.S. constitution less than eighty years before.

"Some of the negroes, feeling themselves free to act like men, shouted that the President had arrived," Thomas Morris Chester wrote. "This name having always been applied to Jeff, the inhabitants, coupling it was the prevailing rumor that he had been captured, reported that the arch-traitor was being brought into the city. As the people pressed near, they cried 'Hang him!' 'Hang him!' 'Show him no quarter!' and other similar expressions, which indicated their sentiments as to what should be his fate. But when they learned that it was President Lincoln their joy knew no bounds."[19]

The joy threatened to spill into anarchy. "There was a danger of our being crushed to death," Porter remembered.[20] "It would have been so easy for an assassin to put a knife in his back." While the city was under federal control, there were still no Union soldiers to be seen, no cavalrymen "whom I could send on in advance to announce the arrival of the President of the United States."

The celebration had a sinister tinge. Here was the president, outnumbered and quite possibly outgunned, walking into the heart of the Confederate capital. Any Southern sympathizer might strike out and then disappear into the crowd.

Admiral Porter was acutely aware of the risk: if the president were to be assassinated on his watch, the blood would be on his hands. William Crook, Lincoln's bodyguard, was similarly stressed by the multiplicity of threats, but he took a glass-half-full view looking back upon that march, writing, "It seems to me nothing short of miraculous that some attempt on his life was not made. It is to the everlasting glory of the South that he was permitted to come and go in peace."[21]

Charles Coffin applied an almost anthropological lens on what he was watching unfold around him: "We who have always had our liberty, we cool blooded Anglo-Americans, can have no adequate realization of the ecstasy of that moment on the part of those colored people of Richmond. They were drunk with ecstasy. They leaped into the air, hugged and kissed one another, surged around a little group in a wild delirium of joy."[22]

As they turned on to Franklin Street, they passed the Exchange Hotel, which had been the site of an infamous annual slave sale. The sight of President Lincoln walking past the symbol of tyranny roused the growing crowd. "The men threw up their hats," Thomas Morris Chester wrote. "The women waved their bonnets and handkerchiefs and clapped their hands and sang, 'Glory to God! Glory! Glory! Glory!'—rendering all the praise to god who had heard their wailings in the past, their moanings for wives, husbands, children, and friends sold out of their sight, had given them freedom, and after long years of waiting, had permitted them thus unexpectedly to behold the face of their great benefactor. 'I thank you, dear Jesus, that I behold President Lincoln!' was the exultation of a woman who stood upon the threshold of her humble home, with streaming eyes and clasped hands gave thanks aloud to the savior of men." [23]

While thousands of newly freed blacks clustered around the president, the wealthy whites of Richmond stayed indoors, peeking out at the scene through drawn blinds. There was a sense of menace in the city. Out of the corner of his eye, Crook caught sight of a man in Confederate gray pointing a rifle at Lincoln. The bodyguard stepped in front of the president to take the bullet if need be. He looked over at Lincoln and saw that, "His face was set; it had the calm in it of a brave man when he is ready for whatever may come."[24]

Amid all the chaos and destruction, there were fleeting signs that gave Lincoln hope for reconciliation. He spied a woman near the Spotswood Hotel wearing an American flag draped around her shoulders. In a "spark of good feeling toward the President and the Union,"

Porter recalled, "a young and pretty girl" rushed through the crowd to kiss his hand, saying, "God Bless you, only friend of the South."[25] In another account, Lincoln received a bouquet of flowers from a young girl with a note on it that said, "From Eva to the Liberator of the slaves."[26]

With every step, the crowds seemed to expand, engulfing the presidential party. "They came from cross streets and alleys, from every direction in the city, and so rapidly did they gather they seemed to spring from the very earth,"[27] recalled First Lieutenant George T. Dudley of the Fiftieth New York Engineers.[28]

Around that time, General George Shepley—a former military governor of Louisiana—was settling into the offices of Confederate secretary of state Judah Benjamin when he spied the rowdy crowd from his window and dispatched an aide to see the source of the commotion. He quickly returned to say that it might be the president. "Putting spurs to my horse, I rode immediately to the advancing multitude," Shepley recalled.[29] Lincoln looked up at him and said, "Hullo, General! Is that you? I was walking 'round to find headquarters."

After walking through Richmond for almost an hour, President Lincoln was securely under military escort. It was just after 4 p.m. when he strode up the front steps of the Confederate White House now flanked by Union soldiers and turned around to face the crowd.

He bowed in thanks and then said: "My poor friends . . . you are free—free as air. You can cast off the name of slave and trample upon it; it will come to you no more. Liberty is your birthright. God gave it to you as he gave it to others, and it is a sin that you have been deprived of it for so many years. But you must try to deserve this priceless boon. Let the world see that you merit it, and are able to maintain it by your good works. Don't let your joy carry you into excesses. Learn the laws and obey them; obey God's commandments and thank him for giving you liberty, for to him you owe all things. There, now, let me pass on; I have but little time to spare. I want to see the capital and must return at once to Washington to secure to you that liberty which you seem to prize so highly."[30]

"The people seemed inspired by this acknowledgment," Thomas Morris Chester reported, "and with renewed vigor shouted louder and louder, until it seemed as if the echoes would reach the abode of those patriot spirits who had died without witnessing the sight."[31] This was not just victory, but vindication.

Inside the Confederate White House

Lincoln entered the gray stucco mansion, walked through its yellow entryway, and stepped up the stairs to a room that until hours earlier had served as Jefferson Davis's public office. It was small with a high ceiling, burgundy wallpaper with a floral print, and a framed picture of George Washington. In one corner, a leather chair and large desk looked out past a wrought-iron gate into a square now filled with liberated slaves as smoke rose from the ruins of buildings in the distance.

He spied the chair and said, "This must have been President Davis' chair," before sinking into its leathery expanse. Lincoln looked around the room, and then asked no one in particular, "I wonder if I could get a drink of water."[1]

"I can see the tired look out of those kind blue eyes over which the lids half drooped," remembered Captain Barnes. "It was a supreme moment ... but there was no triumph in his gesture or attitude. He lay back in the chair like a tired man whose nerves had carried him beyond his strength. All he wanted was rest and a drink of water."[2]

Lost in reverie, Lincoln drank down the glass of water. Then, after a beat, he seemed to remember his role, wiped the corner of his mouth with a handkerchief, and bounced up out of the chair, seemingly revived. "Come, let's look at the house," he said with a twinkle in his eye as he and Tad received a tour of the home. It had been left in a hurry: the Davis family's personal effects were still scattered on tabletops and mantels.

On the first floor, there was a formal sitting room and a dark green dining room, where an afternoon meal was being prepared. Officers were already sampling Davis's liquor cabinet, "the ex-president's prime old rye and applejack, of which his former servants politely helped us," one officer fondly recalled.[3] The bottles were passed around in jubilant toasts, with only Lincoln abstaining.

As they climbed to the second floor, they spied the small offices and saw maps still pinned to the walls, showing Confederate troop movements, the counterparts of the maps Lincoln had obsessed over for months. An American flag now stood in the corner where a Confederate flag had rested for years.

When they returned downstairs, General Shepley told Lincoln that a few remaining Confederate leaders requested a meeting to talk peace.

"The President listened patiently and indicated his sense of the magnitude of the propositions submitted for his consideration by great nervousness of manner," William H. Merriman of *The New York Herald* reported from within the mansion, "running his hands through his hair and moving to and fro in the official chair of the late Jefferson Davis."[4]

Considering his options, Lincoln agreed to the meeting, asking General Shepley to "say to them that I will entertain their propositions, with the condition that I will have one friend"—a senior aide at the meeting—"with the same liberty to them."[5]

That "one friend" was still absent from the captured mansion. General Weitzel had not expected the president until late afternoon and planned to meet him at Rockett's Landing. He was at work in the state capitol building when he received hurried word that Lincoln had already arrived. He quickly made his way to the Davis mansion, flush with embarrassment as the president greeted him warmly.

When Lincoln heard that Weitzel's XXV Corps had been among the first to take Richmond, he wryly responded, "Well, the people in Richmond have been wanting black soldiers for some time past, and now they've got them."[6]

They sat down for a "simple, frugal" late lunch, prepared by Davis's servants, as the president received the latest intelligence from Richmond's fiery first day back in the Union. As the dining room filled up with senior officers looking for drinks and face time with the president, Lincoln greeted the ones he did not know with a kindly but diplomatic, "I am happy to see you."

Entering the room, a Union-sympathizing former congressman named John Minor Botts, who'd been imprisoned for his loyalist views, threw his arms around the president and said, "Thank God, I have lived to see this day."[7] The hobnobbing came to an end when Lincoln received word that Judge Campbell was waiting in the reception room.

Judge John Campbell was a familiar figure to Lincoln—a former U.S. Supreme Court Justice who had left the Union to serve as assistant secretary of war for the Confederacy, under John C. Breckinridge, the former vice president of the United States who had been one of Lincoln's opponents in the 1860 election. A native Georgian, Campbell studied at West Point with Jefferson Davis and Robert E. Lee, and was appointed to the Supreme Court at age forty-one by Whig president Millard Fillmore. He was considered a moderate Southerner, in favor of gradual emancipation; supporting states' rights but opposed to secession. Nonetheless, after Fort Sumter, he was the only Supreme Court justice to resign his seat. The four years of war exerted more than the normal gravitational pull of late middle age; he was bald with a shock of wild snowy hair falling over his ears and a cultivated tuft of hair beneath his chin that stuck out above his shirt collar. He was the highest-level Confederate official left in the fallen capital.

When he'd met Lincoln two months earlier at the Hampton Roads peace conference, Campbell tried unsuccessfully to insist on a ceasefire before surrender. Now the balance of power had shifted completely; the Confederacy had no leverage.

Campbell had a sense of Lincoln's approach to peace and reconciliation, and earlier in the day he'd heard those positions echoed by General Shepley, who assured him that "the public authorities would pursue a conduct of liberality and forbearance . . . one not calculated to wound the sensibilities of the people." He understood that "the state would probably be put under a military government but the governor would be selected from the state, and would not be obnoxious."[8]

It's notable that General Shepley's views so closely tracked with President Lincoln's vision. While much of his Republican Party back in Washington wanted vengeance, Lincoln's desire for a liberal peace had been transmitted down to the officer corps through public documents and conversation among the military brass after the sit-down with Grant, Sherman, and Porter on the *River Queen*.

They met in Davis's office, with the door closed to keep out the din of celebration. The judge seemed pale and tired, feeling the weight of the Confederacy's failure. He began the conversation by conceding to the obvious: "The war was over and all that remained to be done was to compose the country."[9] He explained that he did not have authority to negotiate on behalf of the Confederate government. Instead, he was on a mission to convince Lincoln that there were reasonable men in the South who wanted peace and had long harbored doubts about the wisdom of war.

Campbell acknowledged that though there had been "passion, petulance and animosity in the secession movements . . . there was also serious difference of opinion."[10] He argued that Virginia had been temperate compared to states like South Carolina and Georgia; they had not agitated for secession and only took that fateful step when a state of war already existed. Perhaps not coincidentally, Campbell was also describing his own reluctant path to the Confederacy—after all, a person's politics is often a result of projecting their own perspective onto the world around them.

The judge was presenting himself as a practical and penitent man—ready to concede defeat and get to work healing the wounds of war. And, he said, he was not alone in the highest ranks of Virginian society. This appealed to Lincoln's long-slumbering belief that there was a hidden Unionist sentiment in the South he could reason with. Campbell mentioned that his fellow travelers included Virginia governor John Letcher—who tried to broker a peace before the war—and even Robert E. Lee.

Lincoln listened intently and then said that Campbell's "general principles were right; the trouble was how to apply them."[11] But he was frustrated by the absence of any one person empowered to negotiate on the Confederacy's behalf because that meant more unnecessary deaths when the outcome of the war was no longer in doubt. Nonetheless, he appreciated Campbell's approach and said he wanted to talk again and hoped to hear directly from other leading citizens of Richmond. As a result, Lincoln impulsively announced he would stay the night so they could meet again. Officers insisted he could not safely spend the night in the city and so it was decided that they would meet on the *Malvern*—which had belatedly arrived in Richmond—the next morning.

After Campbell's departure, generals Weitzel and Shepley suggested that the president take a formal tour of the city from a horse-drawn carriage. When they stepped outside, Tad was already waiting on its broad seats, happily holding court with the former slaves who clustered around him.

The waiting crowd cheered when they saw Lincoln emerge from the Confederate White House. Then, according to J. J. Hill, a soldier with the black Twenty-Ninth Regiment from Connecticut, Lincoln stopped on the steps and spoke specifically to the freedmen.

"Although you have been deprived of your God-given rights by your so-called masters, you are now as free as I am, and if those that claim to not know that you are free, take the sword and the bayonet and teach them that you are; for God created all men free, giving to each the same rights of life, liberty and the pursuit of happiness."[12] Here, a few blocks from Thomas Jefferson's capitol, Lincoln was explicitly extending the promise of the Declaration of Independence to them as a birthright they had been unjustly denied until now.

He tipped his hat to the crowd as he climbed into the carriage beside Tad, with Admiral Porter joining as William Crook rode alongside. With a brisk trot they were off, escorted through the city streets by a squadron of black cavalry, as many in the crowd ran alongside, kicking up dust and making a joyful noise.

The first stop was the Greek Revival Virginia statehouse, which towered over the city from atop a nearby hill. As they traveled down Grace Street, where some of the wealthiest families lived, the scene was recorded by one of the city's grandes dames, Frances Doswell. She heard the celebratory gunfire that announced Lincoln's arrival and left her dinner table to "go to the window to see him, as we would go look at a wild beast," she recorded in her diary. "The streets were crowded, mostly tho with negroes & they huzzaring hollering: one said 'Jeff Davis did not wait to see his master but he has come at last.'"[13]

On the corner of Grace and Eighth Streets, a notice had been nailed to a tree containing orders from General Shepley: "Any citizen, soldier, or any person whatever, who shall hereafter plunder, destroy, or remove any public or private property of any description whatever, will be arrested and summarily punished ... The soldiers of the command will abstain from any offensive or insulting words or gestures towards the citizens ... the citizens of Richmond are assured that, with the restoration of the flag of the Union, they may expect the restoration of that peace, prosperity, and happiness which they enjoyed under the Union."[14] This was the promise of defeat with dignity.

They passed the unmarked home of legendary Chief Justice John Marshall—whose relative, Charles, was serving as a senior aide in Lee's army—and St. Paul's Episcopal Church, where only two days before Jefferson Davis had received Lee's message urging evacuation.

The president's party turned into the capitol yard with its massive monument to George Washington—depicting the first president on horseback, flanked by famous Virginians including Jefferson, Marshall, George Mason, and Patrick Henry—surrounded by a sea of people. They swarmed around furniture abandoned by wealthy families, who hoped their heirlooms would be safe behind the iron gates surrounding the capitol grounds.

A few yards in the distance, under a protective iron dome, was a statue of Lincoln's youthful hero Henry Clay, who devoted much of his life to averting the civil war that had finally engulfed the nation. During the war, his statue had been stoned by local schoolboys and two fingers broken off his marble hands. Now his statue silently witnessed the war's end.

Lincoln stopped to take in the scene. The capitol of the rebellion had been reclaimed in the name of a second American revolution to make the nation forever free. General Shepley recalled that Lincoln "looked at it all attentively, with a face expressive only of a sort of pathetic wonder. Occasionally, its sadness would alternate with one of his peculiar smiles."[15]

Now the Stars and Stripes flew over the Confederate capitol. In a bit of intentional symmetry, it was the same flag that had been raised over the recaptured port of New Orleans. Watching it wave in the breeze, Lincoln said that if he'd felt in stronger health, he'd have liked to raise the flag with his own two hands.

According to William Crook, the presidential party then entered the capitol and were shown into the abandoned Confederate cabinet room where "the furniture was completely wrecked; the coverings of desks and chairs had been stripped off by relic-hunters, and the chairs were hacked to pieces."[16]

Throughout the building the old order was overturned: state papers and equally worthless Confederate currency were strewn along the marble floors.

That afternoon, in the center of the empty legislature, Thomas Morris Chester was writing a dispatch for the *Philadelphia Press* while sitting at the elevated desk of the speaker of the Confederate House: "so long dedicated to treason, but in the future to be consecrated to loyalty."[17] A Confederate officer saw him and flew into a rage, ordering the black journalist to step down.

Chester looked up, acknowledged the outburst with a nod, and then went back to writing. When the Confederate rushed over to dislodge the reporter, he was met with a black fist that knocked him back, witnessed by two other journalists. The Southerner then ran over to a Union soldier, demanded his sword and was denied. Chester offered to roll up his sleeves and fight further but the man declined, slinking back into the shadows. "I thought I would exercise my rights as a belligerent," Chester said with satisfaction, and returned to his work.[18]

Surrounded by crowds, the presidential party rolled slowly through the smoldering ruins of what had been Richmond's business district, past burnt tobacco and cotton warehouses as well as former newspaper offices. The Confederate treasury building still stood, somehow spared the destruction all around. As Lincoln passed the Spotswood Hotel, one Confederate matron spied the president from a suite on the upper floors and pronounced him "tired and old—and I must say, with due respect to the president of the United States, I thought him the ugliest man I had ever seen."[19] Lincoln got this a lot.

Soon they stopped outside the infamous Libby Prison at the corner of Twentieth and Cary Streets, which Coffin described as "the one building above all others whose every brick, if voice full, could rehearse a tale of woe."[20] Now, in a role reversal, the building housed Confederate prisoners of war. As Chester jauntily recounted: "The Hotel de Libby is now doing a rushing business in the way of accommodating a class of persons who have not heretofore patronized that establishment. It is being rapidly filled with rebel soldiers, detectives, spies, robbers, and every grade of infamy in the calendar of crime. The stars and stripes now wave gracefully over it, and traitors look through the same bars behind which loyal men were so long confined."[21]

Outside, a new order was already asserting itself. Chester saw a former slave owner being guarded by one of his liberated slaves. "Hallo, Jack is that you!" the past master called. "The negro guard looked at him with blank astonishment, not unmingled with disdain, for the familiarity of the address. The rebel captive, determined upon being recognized, said, entreatingly, 'Why, Jack, don't you know me!' 'Yes, I know you very well,' was the sullen reply, 'and if you don't fall back into that line, I will give you this bayonet.'"[22]

Lincoln stared at Libby Prison for some time, taking care to explain to Tad some of the horrors that occurred inside. The crowd's fury bubbled over and they shouted, "Pull it down!" Lincoln quieted them and said, "No, leave it as a monument."

They rolled on through remnants of Richmond's history, past the Old Stone House that served as George Washington's headquarters during the war for independence, past the church where Patrick Henry enflamed imaginations with his revolutionary cry, "Give me Liberty or give me Death!" A contemporary echo—in deed, if not word—existed nearby in the Van Lew mansion, which housed a prominent Unionist family whose daughter Elizabeth had run a spy ring comprised of ex-slaves, some of whom operated out of the Confederate White House.

It was now past 6 o'clock and the springtime sun was beginning to set. The generals urged Lincoln to head to the *Malvern* for a night's rest. As they approached Rockett's Landing, General Weitzel asked the president how he should treat the local Confederate residents.

Staring at the sunset over the James River, Lincoln declined to offer a specific order that might constrict local commanders from using their judgment, but he made his guidance clear. "We must extinguish our resentments if we expect harmony and union. If I were in your place, I'd let 'em up easy. Let 'em up easy."[23]

With that, Lincoln boarded a barge to take him to the *Malvern* with Tad, William Crook, and Admiral Porter. He smiled and waved to the crowd, as one woman shouted, "Don't drown, Master Abe, for God's sake!"

Writing in her diary that night, Richmond matron Judith Mc-Guire wrote: "Almost every house is guarded; and the streets are now perfectly quiet. The moon is shining brightly on our captivity."[24]

In his room at the Spotswood Hotel, Charles Coffin wrote a dispatch for his Boston newspaper that summed up the day's sweep of history and humanity:

> No wonder that President Lincoln, who has a child's heart, felt his soul stirred; that the tears almost came to his eyes as he heard the thanksgivings to God and Jesus, and the blessings uttered for him from thankful hearts. They were true, earnest and heartfelt expressions of gratitude to God. There are thousands of men in Richmond tonight who would lay down their lives for President Lincoln—their great deliverer—their best friend on earth. He came among them unheralded, without pomp or parade. He walked through the streets as if he were only a private citizen and not the head of a mighty nation. He came not as a conqueror—not with bitterness in his heart, but with kindness. He came as a friend, to alleviate sorrow and suffering, to rebuild what has been destroyed.[25]

Conversations with the Enemy

I have always found that mercy bears richer fruits than strict justice,"[1] Lincoln said. Now, he was putting that principle to the test, celebrating his boy's birthday on a gunboat anchored across from a smoldering city full of men who wanted to kill him.

That night, there were two suspicious requests to see the president on the *Malvern* from mysterious figures who disappeared when confronted with specific questions about their orders. The sometimes overly imaginative Admiral Porter later insisted that one of the men was none other than John Wilkes Booth.[2]

Talk of assassination was everywhere in Richmond. Union general Edward H. Ripley met a Confederate torpedo man named William Snyder, who warned that he was privy to a secret plot to murder the president in Richmond or Washington. Snyder said he hoped that Lincoln would be on his guard because he was in "great danger of violence." Alarmed, Ripley asked to meet the president; he received a note back from Lincoln telling him to come by at 9 a.m.

In the morning, Ripley met with Lincoln in the cabin of the *Malvern*, while Tad jumped on the couch and ran the length of the room. As Lincoln listened, he placed his elbows on the table and rested his chin in the cradle of his hands. Ripley recalled "his great melancholy eyes filling the cabin with the mournful light they emitted,"[3] as he begged the president to take greater precautions with his safety.

Lincoln dismissed the threats, saying, "No, General Ripley, it is impossible for me to adopt and follow your suggestions. I deeply appreciate the feeling which has led you to urge them on me, but I must go on as I have begun in the course marked out for me; for I cannot bring myself to believe that any human being lives who would do me any harm"—offering as evidence the previous day's walk through the streets of Richmond when "anyone could have shot me from a second-story window."[4]

Departing the meeting, disappointed, Ripley looked back and saw the face of a man "so worn, emaciated and pallid that he looked more like a disembodied spirit than the successful leader of a great nation in its hour of supreme triumph."[5]

Lincoln's next meeting on the *Malvern* was the main event of the morning—Judge Campbell's return to discuss peace. At Lincoln's request, he had reached out to other prominent Richmond citizens. Most were unreachable, and a few he contacted were unwilling to meet with the president. So he arrived with only the prominent attorney and Confederate consul to Great Britain, Gustavus Myers, in tow.

General Weitzel accompanied them to Rockett's Landing in a military carriage where they discussed the merits of loyalty oaths. Weitzel offered his opinion that they were invitations to perjury because "when men take an oath reluctantly they are not apt to respect it."[6] But the young general wanted to hear the Southerners' opinion. There was a palpable courtesy that he wanted to convey, setting the tone for occupation and reconciliation.

They boarded the *Malvern* at 10 a.m. Lincoln welcomed the men warmly and sat down in the admiral's quarters to discuss possible peace terms.

Lincoln acknowledged that neither Judge Campbell nor Myers had the authority to negotiate on the Confederacy's behalf, but said he hoped that their credibility within the Confederate cabinet could help serve as a bridge to the retreating rebel government, now more than one hundred miles away in Danville.

Lincoln presented a document, written in his own hand the night before, formally reintroducing the conditions he presented at Hampton Roads.

As to peace, I have said before and now repeat that three things are indispensable.

1. The restoration of the national authority throughout all the states.
2. No receding by the executive of the U.S. on the slavery question from the position assumed thereon in the late annual message and in preceding documents.
3. No cessation of hostilities short of an end of the war and the disbanding of all forces hostile to the government. That all propositions coming from those now in hostility to the government, not inconsistent with the foregoing will be respectfully considered and passed upon in a spirit of sincere liberality.[7]

As he read the list, Lincoln offered commentary on each item, like a country lawyer going over a contract.

The first condition was a simple recognition of the sovereignty of the Union. The second was an end to slavery in America for all time, which Campbell and Myers recognized was now a foregone conclusion and accepted without objection.

But the third item was still a matter of contention. "We will not negotiate with men as long as they are fighting against us," Lincoln insisted.[8] "The last election established this as the deliberate determination of the country."

In return for surrender, he was willing to grant almost any reasonable request that could hasten national healing. Lincoln believed that failure to accept these conditions would lead to another war and he "hoped in the Providence of God that there never would be another."[9]

Campbell and Myers were struck by Lincoln's sincerity and civility. In contrast to radical Republicans, Lincoln did not seem interested in revenge. "The President declared his disposition to be lenient towards all persons, however prominent, who had taken part in the struggle," Myers recorded, "and certainly no exhibition was made by him of any feeling of vindictiveness or exultation."[10]

Lincoln also dismissed the importance of retrospective loyalty oaths, believing them to be unenforceable and backward, rather than forward-looking. As he'd said to Stanton, "On principle I dislike an oath which requires a man to swear he *has* not done wrong. It rejects the Christian principle of forgiveness on terms of repentance. I think it is enough if the man does no wrong *hereafter*." But Lincoln said he would be inclined to offer pardons to those who requested them with the qualification that "it would not be proper to offer a pardon to Mr. Davis, whom we familiarly call Jeff Davis—who says he won't have one."[11]

Campbell believed Lincoln felt "genuine sympathy for the bereavement, destitution, impoverishment, waste, and overturn that war had occasioned at the South."[12]

Myers was impressed not just by Lincoln's words but also by the actions of Union troops. Since entering Richmond, they had been guided by a "conciliatory course" that had "powerful effect in allaying the apprehension and producing kindly feelings on the part of the Citizens," while an alternative, more punitive, course would "be productive of irritation and conducive to no good result."[13]

Then Lincoln proposed an idea that would spark controversy on both sides of the divide. According to Campbell, he suggested reconvening the same Virginia state legislature that had voted to secede to vote to restore Virginia to the Union as their sole topic of action, effectively ending the war before the official surrender.

This seems to have been offered on the spur of the moment. Lincoln had not yet mentioned it to any of his military or political advisers. Perhaps Lincoln's instinct for big picture symmetry drew him to the idea; there would be poetic justice if the same Virginia legislature that voted to secede reconvened in the reconquered capitol to vote for the restoration of the Union.

But Lincoln was thinking legally as well as symbolically: the vote would have carried with it the force of state law. This was consistent with his belief in federalism. Beyond the necessities of war, he believed that local people pushing solutions from the ground up rather than the top down provided a far more durable framework for self-government. Southerners would kick back if they felt dictated to or despised, Lincoln believed. They had to be coaxed into taking responsibility for the rebuilding of civil society.

This instinct held some wisdom, but his idea contained a fatal flaw that Lincoln apparently did not anticipate: with this proposal, he ran the risk of legitimizing a rebel legislature.

But Campbell and Myers saw the suggestion as magnanimous. "I believe that his scheme of pacification would have gone as far to the mitigation of the evils which have befallen the country,"[14] Campbell recalled. They agreed to attempt what the president suggested. At that point, wrote Myers, "our interview ended. Throughout, it was conducted with entire civility and good humor."[15] Good humor is not typical of negotiations to end a war—except, perhaps, a war between brothers.

As Campbell and Myers left the *Malvern*, something completely different was awaiting the president.

Standing in the hallway was an old acquaintance, an irascible old Southern Democrat named Duff Green, who came aboard wielding a six-foot-tall wooden walking stick and a long white beard that trailed in the wake of his chin. He was ornery and the guards thought him insane, but Lincoln waved him in. "He always was a little queer," he explained, "I shan't mind him."[16]

It was no secret that the Kentucky-born newspaper editor and Calhoun confidant was a Confederate who'd supplied weapons to the Southern cause. Nonetheless, Lincoln welcomed him with a smile, always happy to see someone from the old days, and mindful of the need to repair relationships now that the war was almost over. Reacquainting himself with the Duff Greens of the world was a form of his public opinion baths—there would be many more like him in the hinterlands.

But Duff Green was in no mood for reconciliation, and he tore into the president with the fury of an old man whom time was passing by.

"Well sir, I hope you are satisfied," Duff said. "You have burned and destroyed our towns and laid waste to our estates. You have caused weeping and wailing throughout the whole South with your hellish acts and your mercenaries have cut the throats of hundreds of Southern people and their blood cries aloud for vengeance. And now, you come to glut your eyes with the sight of the misery you have created.

Like Nero you fiddle while Rome is burning."[17] That, at least, was in Porter's recounting.[18]

According to Crook, the broadside concluded with Green saying, "I do not know how God and your conscience will let you sleep at night after being guilty of the notorious crime of setting the niggers free."[19]

Lincoln's response also diverged in the two men's tellings. According to Porter, Lincoln pushed back forcefully, saying, "No sir, you have cut your own throats and you have unfortunately cut many of our throats in so doing. Our interview is ended, sir. I have received you as a penitent, but I find you an insolent beggar!"[20]

While emotionally satisfying, it doesn't quite square with Lincoln's tendency to avoid interpersonal conflict when possible. More in keeping with Lincoln's personality is Crook's version: "President Lincoln sat through this verbal barrage without showing any emotion and without saying a word. If he was angry about what Green had just said to him, he did not show it. After he finished his outburst, Green calmly told the president, 'I would like, sir, to go to my friends.' Lincoln turned to General Weitzel and said, just as calmly, 'General, please give Mr. Green a pass to go to his friends.'"[21]

And with that, Duff Green departed—a bit player in the big drama, foreshadowing how difficult reconciliation would be.

Lincoln pulled out of Rockett's Landing at noon, seeing the James River in reverse, passing abandoned Confederate fortifications, guns silent, flies buzzing. He saw the Dutch Gap Canal, where 140 Union soldiers had been lost in a futile offensive, then turned a curve and passed Bermuda Hundred, before the water widened.

As they set anchor at City Point, Lincoln saw hundreds of Confederate prisoners aboard a transport barge in the harbor. The rebels crowded on the deck to see him with their bellies newly full of beef and bread.

"There's old Abe," one Confederate shouted, spurring an unusual round of cheers from the prisoners, who seemed almost delighted to be in the presence of the president. Porter recalled that "there was a pleased, puzzled look on the faces of those rude soldiers which seemed to say 'can this benevolent looking man be the demon that we have had described to us, and who has been held in terror over our little children?'" Porter believed that "almost every man of them would have voted for him as President sooner than Jefferson Davis."[22]

"They will never shoulder a musket again in anger," Lincoln said to Porter. These men had been decisively defeated.

Back on land, Lincoln returned to the comforting confines of the telegraph office, catching up on missed correspondence. There was a message from Secretary of State Seward saying that there were matters that required his personal attention piling up at the executive mansion and he offered to bring them to City Point if the president remained there. Lincoln replied that he intended to return within two days, gently dissuading the secretary of state from embarking on the journey.

Lincoln received word that a Confederate general, Rufus Barringer—a brother-in-law of Stonewall Jackson—was biding time as a comparatively pampered prisoner of war inside the Union garrison. Upon hearing the name, Lincoln perked up: "Do you know I have never seen a live rebel general in full uniform,"[23] he said with a bit of mischief. And so Confederate general Rufus Barringer was retrieved from his confines and brought to Lincoln in the telegraph office. Lincoln stood up to shake his hand as a sign of respect.

As he removed his reading glasses and stared down at the general, he said, "Barringer from North Carolina? General, were you ever in Congress?" The captured Confederate general said he had not been. "Well, I thought not," replied Lincoln. "I thought my memory couldn't be so much at fault. But there was a Barringer in Congress with me, and from your state too!"

"That was my brother, sir."

Lincoln beamed, enjoying the rekindled connection. "Do you know that that brother of yours was my chum in Congress? Yes, sir, we sat at the same desk and ate at the same table. He was a Whig and so was I. He was my chum, and I was very fond of him and you're his brother. Well, shake again."[24] The two men sat down in a long conversation that touched on Lincoln's days in Congress and discussed the relative strengths and weaknesses of military leaders in the South and North.

As the Confederate general rose to depart, Lincoln asked, "Do you think I can be of any service to you?" The question was so absurd in its modesty that it caused some of the onlooking Union officers to chuckle. The Confederate general replied, "If anyone can be of service to a poor devil in my situation, I presume you're my man."[25]

Lincoln put his eyeglasses back on and began writing a note, offering commentary as he wrote: "I suppose they will send you to Washington, and there I have no doubt they will put you in the old capital prison. I'm told it isn't a nice sort of place, and I'm afraid you won't find it a very comfortable tavern; but I have a powerful friend in Washington—he's the biggest man in the country—and I believe I have some influence with him when I don't ask too much. I want you to send this card of introduction to him, and if he takes the notation he may put on your parole or let up on you.... Anyway, it's worth trying."[26]

Lincoln completed writing and after blotting it dry handed General Barringer a note for Secretary of War Stanton:

> This is General Barringer of the Southern army. He is the brother of a very dear friend of mine. Can you do anything to make his detention in Washington as comfortable as possible under the circumstances? A. Lincoln.[27]

The Confederate general choked up as he tried to express his gratitude. But after he left the telegraph office, Barringer was heard sobbing outside.

As night fell, Lincoln received news that Seward had been severely injured in a runaway carriage accident. He was struck unconscious for a time but was now resting at his home, suffering a broken shoulder and a fractured jaw. With his closest adviser incapacitated and Stanton requesting his presence back in Washington, Lincoln knew that his two-week trip to the front must come to an end.

But Mary was already on her way to City Point with an entourage including Senator Charles Sumner, the French nobleman Marquis de

Chambrun, her seamstress Elizabeth Keckley, and Interior Secretary James Harlan, accompanied by his wife and his daughter Mary, the love interest and future bride of Robert Lincoln. His return would be delayed by at least a day.

He could not rest. After everyone else was asleep, Lincoln went to check on his son, startling Tad's bunkmate, William Crook, who woke to see "something tall and white and ghostly" standing by his berth. It was Lincoln wearing a long white nightgown, wanting to make sure his boy was sleeping through the night, a comfort needed by the parent as much as the child.

"The old man is pretty angry," he told Crook, referring to the day's earlier confrontation with Duff Green, "but I guess he will get over it."[28] Then he bid him goodnight.

Lincoln enjoyed a rare peaceful morning aboard the *River Queen*, staying on board until the first lady's party arrived at noon.

After greeting them at the docks, Lincoln gave the visitors a guided tour around the *River Queen*, recounting the Hampton Roads Conference and meetings with Grant and Sherman that took place within its wooden quarters. Then he read aloud some of the recent dispatches from Grant, bringing out maps that showed the location of the respective regiments and explaining the general trajectory of battle plans that would force Lee to finally surrender.

"In spite of the manifest success of his policy it was impossible to detect in him the slightest feeling of pride, much less vanity," said the Marquis de Chambrun. "He spoke with the modest accent of a man who realizes that his success has crowned his persistent efforts, and who finds in that very success the end of a terrible responsibility."[29]

After the presidential presentation, Mary asked to visit Richmond. She had been desperately disappointed that Lincoln made the initial trip without her and now wanted to see the conquered city. For the politicos in tow, it was a chance to get a grand triumphant tour of the rebel capital. For Elizabeth Keckley, it was a visit back to the city where she'd grown up a slave, fathered by her mother's owner.

So the *River Queen* was turned to that purpose; despite a round of requests that the president join them, he declined, citing pressing responsibilities. It was an explanation they could not refuse. A few hours after pulling into port, Mary and her party departed for a sightseeing tour, leaving Lincoln to work in peace after waving them off at the dock.

Lincoln headed back toward the telegraph office, where he sent General Weitzel a directive regarding the Virginia legislature. The issue had been eating at him and he decided to officially open the barn door with an order to allow the legislature to meet if they took actions to pursue peace, but to disperse them by force if they fell back into their warring ways. Then he covered his managerial bases by dispatching a note to Grant explaining the idea, tempering expectations. "I do not think it very probable that anything will come of this," Lincoln telegraphed. "Nothing I have done, or probably shall do, is to delay, hinder, or interfere with you in your work."[30] Ending the war with the surrender of Lee was still to be Grant's sole focus.

Now he was in a jolly mood, reciting from memory a favorite story by Artemis Ward about pirates being foiled on Lake Erie, when he was disturbed from his reverie by the news that Vice President Andrew Johnson had taken it upon himself to visit City Point with the portly former New York senator Preston King, without presidential approval.

"Don't let those men come into my presence," Lincoln said, rising up from his chair in an uncharacteristic flash of fury. "They have no business here, anyway; no right to come down here without my permission," then, according to Admiral Porter, he sat back down in the chair "looking like a man it would be dangerous for anyone to anger."[31] "Mr. Lincoln disliked Mr. Johnson very much," Porter wrote in his journal.[32]

Midshipmen were ordered to divert the unwelcome guests with champagne and cigars on a nearby dispatch boat, expressing regrets about the president's unalterable schedule. There was much grumbling amid the puffing and swilling. But once he cooled down, Lincoln dispatched yet another boat to take Johnson and King down to Richmond, which was fast becoming a fashionable tourist destination of the day.

As the first lady's party steamed down the James River, Elizabeth Keckley saw "fair fields, emblematic of peace—and here deserted camps and frowning forts, speaking of the stern vicissitudes of war." Keckley worried about what she would find. "I wondered what had become of those I once knew; had they fallen in battle, been scattered by the relentless tide of war, or were they still living as they lived when last I saw them?" She wondered, "If the people would come together in the bonds of peace."[33]

They were driven around Richmond in a coach and stopped at the Confederate capitol, with its "desolate appearance—desks broken, and papers scattered promiscuously in the hurried flight of the Confederate Congress." One of these papers was a personally ironic resolution forbidding "all free colored people from entering the State of Virginia."

In a moment of sublime triumph, Elizabeth Keckley sat in the chair of the Confederate senate chamber. When they toured the Confederate White House, Keckley noticed that her presence caused some of the Southern women staffing the joint to scowl "darkly upon our party as we passed through and inspected the different rooms."

It was, she declared, a "delightful visit."[34]

On the morning of Friday, April 7, Lincoln received a telegram from General Phil Sheridan after a decisive victory at Sailor's Creek, where more than 7,000 Confederates were casualties, comprising roughly one-third of General Lee's remaining army. The survivors were malnourished, eating dry corn meant for horses, and greatly outnumbered by the Union troops in hot pursuit. They had nowhere to run.

"If the thing is pressed," Sheridan telegraphed, "I think Lee will surrender to Grant."

Lincoln quickly responded: "Let *the thing* be pressed."[35]

History was accelerating. The fall of Richmond already seemed like old news. All eyes were on what was left of Lee's army as they gathered near Appomattox Court House, blocked by Union troops in every direction. Grant could see the endgame and wrote a note to Lee, saying he felt compelled "to shift from myself the responsibility of any further effusion of blood," and asked for the surrender of the Army of Northern Virginia. He sent it off behind enemy lines via courier and pressed on.

When Mary and her party returned midmorning, Lincoln suggested they tour Petersburg together. A private rail car was secured, and Lincoln climbed in along with several black waiters who served on the *River Queen* and wanted to see the captured city for themselves. "The President," wrote the Marquis de Chambrun with a hint of amazement, "is blinded by no prejudices against race or color."[36]

The fractured fronts of brick buildings framed the skyline while crowds of newly freed slaves clustered around the car as they arrived in town. When Lincoln met with the generals now in command of Petersburg, he was presented with the locals' demands that the Union army pay rent for the use of a building for their headquarters. Lincoln could not help pointing out that the surrounding destruction constituted rent enough.

But he took heart from the progress that had been made by pacifying the former rebel stronghold since his last visit, telling his traveling party that "animosity in the town is abating. The inhabitants now accept as accomplished facts, the final downfall of the Confederacy and the abolition of slavery. There remains much for us to do, but every day brings new reason for confidence in the future."[37]

As Lincoln took the party on a carriage ride across the city, he stopped at a massive tree he had admired on his trip three days before, describing it in great and odd detail, how the wide trunk and "vigorous and harmoniously proportioned branches" reminded him of the oak and beech trees from his youth. His comments seemed to the marquis as showing "no poetic desire to idealize nature; but . . . it denoted extraordinary observation, mastery of descriptive language and absolute precision of mind."[38]

On the slow train ride back to City Point, Lincoln and Tad noticed a large turtle basking in the sun and ordered the train to stop so the animal could be brought into their cabin. "The movements of the ungainly little animal seemed to delight him," Elizabeth Keckley recalled.[39] Father and son spent much of the rest of the ride laughing and playing with their newfound terrapin friend. The president seemed "in perfect health and exuberant spirits."[40]

Dixie and Macbeth

Saturday, April 8, dawned clear and warm, but still Lincoln could not sleep. This would be Lincoln's final day at City Point after two weeks. He had unfinished business: a visit to thousands of wounded troops at what was then the largest hospital in the nation.

The Depot Field Hospital, administered by the U.S. Sanitary Commission, stretched over 200 acres. Beneath tents were long rows of beds, beside each of which sat a washbasin and a Bible, with gravel-lined corridors to absorb the spring's muddy floods. But all the whitewash in the world could not remove the stench from the freshly amputated limbs poured out of wheelbarrows into piles outside.

The hospital administrators wanted to show off their state-of-the-art facilities to the president. He wasn't there for the show: "Gentlemen, you know better than I how to conduct these hospitals," Lincoln said, "but I came here to take by the hand the men who have achieved our glorious victories."[1]

Lincoln went from bed to bed, shaking hands with each one of the soldiers, stopping to ask a question or make a connection, telling them that the war would soon be over and they would all be going home.

"Not one of us did he pass by," a wounded soldier from Vermont recalled, "and to every one he had some word of good cheer tenderly spoken, while his homely face became absolutely beautiful as it beamed with love and sympathy." His spirit shone through his features as his tall frame bent over each of the beds. "We all felt impatient to get well as fast as possible that we might fight as never before for our President, the great heart who came to cheer and love us while we lay disabled from our wounds."[2]

Some of the meetings were heartening, others heartbreaking. Captain Charles Houghton was recovering from wounds received in the final fight over Fort Stedman at Petersburg, and Lincoln asked, against the doctors' advice, to see his recently amputated left leg.

Upon seeing the bloody stump, the president recoiled, and said, "Oh this awful, awful war!" Then with a few tears streaming down his face, Lincoln leaned down and said "Poor boy! You must live! You must!" Houghton summoned the strength to whisper, "I intend to, sir."[3] And he did, living another fifty years after being awarded the Medal of Honor for his valor at Petersburg.

When Lincoln began to head for a set of tents set apart from the others, a young doctor tried to intervene, saying that the president should not waste his time because they contained only "sick rebel prisoners."

"That is just where I *do* want to go,"[4] Lincoln responded firmly. He proceeded to make his way down the line of captured Confederates, talking with them just as he had with the Union soldiers. Years later, Colonel Henry L. Benbow recalled their conversation at his bed:

"Looking him in the face, as he stood with extended hand: Mr. President, I said, 'do you know to whom you offer your hand?' 'I do not,' he replied. Well, I said, you offer it to a Confederate colonel, who has fought you as hard as he could for four years. 'Well,' said he, 'I hope a Confederate colonel will not refuse me his hand.' No, sir, I replied, I will not, and I clasped his hand in both mine. I tell you, sir, he had the most magnificent face and eye that I have ever gazed into. He had me whipped from the time he first opened his mouth."[5]

Lincoln was leading by example, living up to his belief that you destroy your enemies when you make them your friends.

But Lincoln's more fatalistic instincts found expression when a nurse named Helen Gilson handed him a self-help booklet she'd found in the jacket of a soldier who'd died a few days earlier. It was titled "How to Make One's Way in the World."[6]

Trying to shake off the dark irony, Lincoln went outside and spied an ax laying beside a pile of wood. He'd once been regarded as a good wood chopper and after some urging agreed to take a few whacks. He then held the ax with his arm outstretched at a right angle in a surprising show of strength for a fifty-six-year-old man.

That night, as a military band played beneath glowing colored lanterns on the deck of the *River Queen*, the Lincolns said goodbye to City Point.

Lincoln's taste in music ran toward the melancholy, like his taste in poetry. He loved sentimental ballads like "Annie Laurie" and "Twenty Years Ago," as well as the popular tunes of Stephen Foster, who dominated sheet music sales of the day with songs like "Hard Times Come Again No More." Lincoln even enjoyed the occasional Mozart, attending a performance of *The Magic Flute* in Washington the week before he left for City Point.[7]

But at tonight's party for officers, he was in a more buoyant mood and requested the band play "La Marseillaise" for the benefit of the Marquis de Chambrun. It was a tune that had been banned in France by the second Emperor Napoleon because of its revolutionary overtones. "You have to come over here to hear it," Lincoln wryly observed.[8]

Then, perhaps thinking of songs that had fallen out of favor because of their political significance, he asked Chambrun if he'd ever heard the rebel song "Dixie," which had become a Confederate battle hymn and unofficial national anthem despite having been written on New York City's Lower East Side.

Chambrun replied he was not familiar with it, and Lincoln then scandalized the officers and musicians by requesting they play "Dixie," saying, "That tune is now Federal property and it is good to show the rebels that, with us in power, they will be free to hear it again."[9]

The floating party was in mid-swing when a steamer bearing Julia Grant, so memorably snubbed by Mary Lincoln, passed by the *River Queen*. At that moment, the military band on Mrs. Grant's boat asked her if she had any requests. "Yes," she replied. "Play 'Now You'll Remember Me'"[10]—a pointed diss that the first lady probably missed.

It was past ten on Saturday night when the band packed up and the officers disembarked with grateful thanks from the commander in chief, and the *River Queen* sped off toward Washington.

Lincoln stood on deck in silence for a long while, passing more than a hundred ships at anchor, as the lights of City Point receded in the darkness. "Mr. Lincoln remained absorbed in thought," Chambrun recalled, "and pursued his meditation long after the quickened speed removed the lugubrious scene forever from our sight."[11]

It had been a momentous sixteen days, a time of dreams achieved—or, at least, nightmares ending. Lincoln had gotten away from the grasping ambition and vengeance of Washington. He had seen Petersburg finally fall after nine months of siege and strode through the streets of Richmond with his son, witnessing the joy of liberated slaves, vindicating his belief that right makes might.

Around midnight, Ulysses S. Grant lay in a farmhouse bed near Appomattox, suffering from a crippling headache as his staff banged away on a piano the floor below him. Grant applied hot mustard plasters to his wrists and the back of his neck to alleviate the pain. His fitful sleep was broken by an apologetic aide bearing a note from General Lee.

The Southern commander rejected Grant's earlier suggestion that it was time for surrender—but opened the door to an in-person meeting to discuss peace. "To be frank, I do not think the emergency has arisen to call for the surrender of this army; but as the restoration of peace should be the sole object of all, I desired to know whether your proposals would lead to that end. I cannot, therefore, meet you with a view to surrender the Army of Northern Virginia; but as far as your proposal may affect the C. S. forces under my command, and tend to the restoration of peace, I should be pleased to meet you at 10 a.m. to-morrow, on the old stage road to Richmond, between the picket-lines of the two armies."[12]

Now Grant was wide awake. Lee's letter was a sign of progress, but Grant could not meet with Lee on these terms. He had been specifically ordered not to negotiate the political terms of peace by the president. He could only offer terms of surrender. But he knew Lee was not in a position to make demands.

Grant passed the dispatch to his chief of staff John Rawlins, who argued that Lee was bluffing to buy time and escape again. But Grant read between the lines and believed Lee was looking for an honorable way to surrender.

"He is only trying to be let down easy," Grant told Rawlins,[13] unintentionally echoing Lincoln's advice to Weitzel in Richmond.

Grant decided to sleep on it and, upon waking before sunrise, walked down to General Meade's tent for coffee. There he put pencil to paper and replied in a diplomatic manner designed to coax Lee into accepting the inevitable.

"I have not authority to treat on the subject of peace; the meeting today could lead to no good. I will state, however, General, that I am equally anxious for peace with yourself and the whole North entertains the same feeling. The terms upon which peace can be had are well understood." They had been articulated by Lincoln many times in public and private. "By the South laying down their arms they will hasten that most desirable event, save thousands of human lives, and hundreds of millions of property not yet destroyed. Seriously hoping that all our difficulties may be settled without the loss of another life."[14]

As the sun rose on Palm Sunday, April 9, Lincoln looked out over the shimmering waters of the Chesapeake Bay, 150 miles from Appomattox.

All was relaxed upon the *River Queen*. Unable to receive telegraphs between ports, Lincoln was able to focus on his family and friends. The information-obsessed president would be unreachable for most of the day.

As the conversation in the main cabin turned to literature, the president read aloud to his captive audience. Characteristically, he alternated from comedy to tragedy, from the slapstick wisdom of Artemus Ward to Shakespeare's *Macbeth*, his favorite play.

It does not take great feats of imagination to understand why Lincoln gravitated toward *Macbeth*. It is a cautionary tale set amid civil war—the story of a striver with a wife who simultaneously drives him upward toward power and downward toward despair. Guilt robs him of sleep. He is surrounded by many but feels alone, forced to wear a mask of genial command, concealing a mind on fire. No matter how high he climbs the ladder of success, he cannot outpace his fate.

That day on the *River Queen*, Lincoln read one soliloquy repeatedly, the anguished cry of a victorious king confronting the bloody cost of his ambition.

> We have scotch'd the snake, not kill'd it; She'll close, and be herself; whilst our poor malice Remains in danger of her former tooth. But let the frame of things disjoint, both the worlds suffer, Ere we will eat our meal in fear, and sleep In the affliction of these terrible dreams
>
> That shake us nightly: better be with the dead, Whom we, to gain our peace, have sent to peace, Than on the torture of the mind to lie, In restless ecstasy.
>
> Duncan is in his grave; After life's fitful fever he sleeps well; Treason has done his worst: nor steel, nor poison, Malice domestic, foreign levy, nothing, Can touch him further.[15]

"Either because he was struck by the weird beauty of these verses, or from a vague presentiment coming over him, Mr. Lincoln paused here while reading," Chambrun recalled, "and began to explain to us how true a description of the murderer that one was; when, the dark deed achieved, its tortured perpetrator came to envy the sleep of his victims and he read over again the same scene."[16]

At a moment of unknown triumph, Abraham Lincoln was meditating on murder. It was a desolate vision of victory. The South, like the snake, was bloodied but still dangerous. Peace was elusive to the living who bore a responsibility for war. But perhaps Lincoln's fate was not yet set—he could still redeem something from all the blood and loss, if he could reunite the nation and rededicate it to the proposition that all men are created equal.

Section IV

Appomattox and the Art of Peace

"This too shall pass away. Never fear. Victory will come."[1]

—*Abraham Lincoln*

L ee planned one last attack. At dawn, General John B. Gordon's remaining troops charged through the morning fog with a rebel yell and briefly overwhelmed the federal line at the top of the ridge, only to discover 30,000 Union infantrymen in blue marching toward them across the valley. Outnumbered two to one, with no food and no way out, Lee's men could no longer escape their fate.

The Confederate commander had prepared for the worst that Palm Sunday, dressing for surrender in a new gray uniform, polished black boots with gold spurs, and a ceremonial sword that hung from his leather belt with a red sash. "I have probably to be General Grant's prisoner," Lee explained, "and thought I must make my best appearance."[2]

Thirty-year-old General Edward Porter Alexander argued against the surrender, saying they could scatter their soldiers and live off the land, extending the fight with guerrilla war.

Lee shook his head. "We must consider its effect on the country as a whole," he said. "If I took your advice, the men would be without rations and under no control of officers. They would be compelled to rob and steal in order to live. They would become mere bands of marauders, and the enemy's cavalry would pursue them. . . . We would bring on a state of affairs it would take the country years to recover from." While younger officers might go underground, "the only dignified course for me would be to go to General Grant and surrender myself and take the consequences of my acts."[3]

Shamed into silence, Alexander later wrote, "He had answered my suggestion from a plane so far above it that I was ashamed of having made it."[4]

A Confederate courier waving a white towel was dispatched to the Union lines with a message from Lee. As the guns fell silent, soldiers on either side of the line stared at each other with the unaccustomed feeling of peace descending on men who had been conditioned to kill each other on sight. They would all live to see Easter.

Grant was riding with his officers across rough ground, his head still throbbing. They stopped at a clearing where logs were being burned and availed themselves of the bonfire to light cigars. As they puffed, they saw an officer riding toward them at full gallop, waving his hat over his head and shouting. It was Lieutenant Charles Pease from Meade's staff, spurring a black stallion. He carried the note from Lee.

Grant read it with quiet intensity, his jaw clenched. Then with a nod, he handed the note to Rawlins, and asked him to read it aloud:

General: I ask a suspension of hostilities pending the discussion of the Terms of surrender of this army in the interview which I requested in my former communication of Today. Very respectfully, Your obt servt.- R E Lee

At first, there was stunned silence. Then Colonel Duff, chief of artillery, jumped on a log, waved his hat, and offered three cheers.

"A feeble hurrah came from a few throats, when all broke down in tears," reported war correspondent Sylvanus Cadwallader, noting that "there was no more expression in Grant's countenance than in a last year's bird nest."[5]

"We are all Americans"

Lee was sitting under an apple tree when couriers presented him with Grant's acceptance of surrender. His trusted lieutenant, Charles Marshall, was dispatched to find a suitable place for the meeting in the nearby hamlet of Appomattox, between the two armies.

On the desolate dirt streets, Marshall spied Wilmer McLean, a grocer who moved from Manassas after the first battle of Bull Run after a cannonball came careening through his house. He wanted to get his young family far away from the fighting, but he could not escape history. Soon McLean would be able to proclaim, "The war began in my front yard and ended in my front parlor."[1]

He lived in a nearby red-brick home with white columns, a broad front porch, and a rickety wooden staircase.

Lee was waiting in the McLeans' parlor room by the fireplace when Grant arrived at 1:30 in the afternoon. In the distance, a Union military band played "Auld Lang Syne" as he strode up the steps.

They were a study in contrasts: the tall, dignified man in a gray dress uniform; Grant wearing mud-spattered boots and no sword, in a simple uniform adorned only with shoulder straps signifying the first lieutenant general in the U.S. army since George Washington.

They were fifteen years apart in age: Lee's beard a fading gray, Grant's beard a ruddy brown. Lee behaved with "great dignity and courtesy but no cordiality," remembered Grant's aide Adam Badeau.[2] The Union general tried to cut the tension with a friendly handshake and then led Lee around the room to meet his staff.

When Lee came upon Colonel Ely Parker, a full-blooded Seneca Indian on Grant's senior staff, he fixated upon Parker's dark features for a second and then said, "I am glad to see one real American here."

"We are all Americans," Parker replied.[3]

As they sat down, Grant mentioned that they had served together in the Mexican–American War, when Grant was a young supply officer and Lee already a renowned field commander. Lee replied he had often searched his mind to see if he could remember meeting Grant. "Our conversation grew so pleasant that I almost forgot the object of our meeting," Grant recalled,[4] until Lee called his attention to the business at hand and asked him to write out the terms of surrender.

Grant sat at a small round wooden table in the center of the room in a black leather-backed swivel chair. Lee sat at a marble table in a high-backed wicker chair. Charles Marshall stood to the side by the fireplace. "A gladiatorial contest of millions of swords," recalled Colonel Parker, "was about to be settled by a stroke of the pen."[5]

"When I put my pen to the paper, I did not know the first word that I should make use of in writing the terms," Grant wrote in his memoirs. "I only knew what was in my mind, and I wished to express it clearly, so that there could be no mistaking it."[6]

Lincoln's vision for winning the peace guided Grant's pen as smoke from his cigar swirled around his head. He hesitated a moment, focusing his mind.

Then he started writing. In one taut paragraph, Grant stated that Confederate soldiers would be given parole, rather than taken prisoner, provided they agreed "not to take up arms against the Government of the United States of America." Their weapons and artillery would be handed over to Union officers.

Perhaps remembering Lincoln's wish on the *River Queen* to see Confederates back at their homes with "their horses to plow with," Grant allowed the Confederate officers to keep their personal horses, side arms, and baggage, items "which were important to them, but of no value to us," wanting to avoid "unnecessary humiliation."

The end of slavery was unspoken; it was now understood to be inevitable and therefore literally unremarkable. The cause of the war was a casualty of the war.

Then in one final line, Grant essentially offered a conditional pardon to calm any impulse to continue the rebellion. "This done, each officer and man will be allowed to return to their homes, not to be disturbed by United States authority so long as they observe their paroles and the laws in force where they may reside." This was a commitment with far-reaching implications: all Confederate soldiers and officers would be free from prosecution for treason if they accepted the terms of surrender and followed the law going forward.

Handed the document, Lee read through the terms intently, peering at the paper through steel-rimmed spectacles. When he got to the line allowing officers to keep their side arms and horses, Lee looked up and asked whether this extended to all soldiers beyond the officer corps. Grant replied that it did not, but after some thought, relented on the point with an eye toward speedily returning men to their farms, as Lincoln requested.

Grant's secretary, a former journalist named Theodore Bowers, began to write a clean version of the final terms, but his hands began to shake as he tossed out one copy after another in a crumpled-up ball. He then asked Ely Parker to step in, with steady penmanship honed by legal training.

Colonel Parker finished the draft in clean strokes and passed the document to Grant to review. He then passed it on to Lee. After reading the final version, Lee wrote out a separate letter accepting the terms of surrender and handed it to Grant.

"What General Lee's feelings were I do not know," Grant recalled. "As he was a man of much dignity, with an impassible face, it was impossible to say whether he felt inwardly glad that the end had finally come, or felt sad over the result, and was too manly show it . . . but my own feelings, which had been quite jubilant on the receipt of his letter, were sad and depressed. I felt like anything rather than rejoicing at the downfall of a foe who had fought so long and valiantly, and had suffered so much for a cause, though that cause was, I believe, one of the worst for which a people ever fought, and one for which there was the least excuse."[7]

Before departing, Lee asked for food for his starving army. Grant asked him how many soldiers he had left, and Lee admitted he didn't know. "My losses in killed and wounded have been exceedingly heavy, and besides, there have been many stragglers and some deserters," Lee said. "Many companies are entirely without officers."[8]

Grant suggested sending 25,000 rations, asking if it would be sufficient. "I think it will be ample," Lee replied. "And it will be a great relief, I assure you."[9]

With a final handshake between the two generals, Lee was free to leave. Union soldiers saluted as Lee strode by, lost in thought, punching one fist in the palm of his hand out of muted frustration, before mounting his horse, Traveler. Grant stood on the porch and doffed his hat to Lee, who nodded and returned the gesture in a sign of mutual respect. Then the gray man on the gray horse rode in silence toward the remains of his army.

In the uneasy stillness of the afternoon, one Pennsylvania soldier wandered into the Confederate lines, searching the faces of his foes turned fellow countrymen and recounted the surreal experience: ". . . as soon as I got among these boys I felt and was treated as well as if I had been among our own boys, and a person would have thought we were of the same Army and had been fighting under the same Flag."[10]

As word of the surrender spread, Union troops began to celebrate, throwing their hats in the air, as a hundred-gun salute began to echo. Grant ordered it stopped. This was not a time for celebration, but reconciliation.

"The war is over," he said. "The rebels are our countrymen again."[11]

At 4:30 p.m., almost as an afterthought, Grant wrote out a simple notification on the side of the road to be telegraphed to the Department of War: "General Lee surrendered the Army of Northern Virginia this afternoon on terms proposed by myself."

At roughly the same time, Lincoln was steaming by George Washington's home at Mount Vernon, perched high on the banks of the Potomac River. He seemed lost in thought, taking in the scene. The Marquis de Chambrun broke the silence to compare the two men and their legacies. "Mount Vernon, with its memories of Washington, and

Springfield, with those of your own home—Revolutionary and Civil War—will be equally honored in America."[12]

"As though awakened from a trance," Lincoln said, "Springfield, how happy I shall be four years hence to return there in peace and tranquility!"[13]

Their conversation turned to war and peace. "It was impossible to discover in Lincoln any thought of revenge or feeling of bitterness toward the vanquished," Chambrun reflected. "His only preoccupation was to recall the Southern States into the Union as soon as possible. When he encountered opposition on this point, when many of those surrounding him insisted on the necessity of strong reprisals, he would exhibit signs of impatience, for though uninfluenced by such opinions, on hearing them he gave evident signs of a nervous fatigue which he partially controlled but was unable to dissimulate entirely. On one point his mind was irrevocably made up. The policy of pardon, in regard to those who had taken a principal part in the rebellion, appeared to him an absolute necessity. Never did clemency suggest itself more naturally to a victorious chief."[14]

One of those exchanges occurred back inside the saloon, when Mary said that she hoped Jefferson Davis would be hanged. Lincoln swiftly responded with the biblical phrase he'd used so often in recent days: "Let us judge not that we be not judged."

As the sun set, the *River Queen* docked at Washington. News of Lee's surrender had not yet reached the capital due to a transmission delay in the telegraph. Lincoln bade goodbye to the crew, tipped his hat to the dockworkers, and climbed into a waiting carriage with Mary.

As they rolled toward the city, the first lady pointed to the buildings in the distance and said, "that city is full of enemies." Lincoln waved it off, saying, "Enemies—never again must we repeat that word."[15] Peace was ahead of them.

After dropping Mary off at the White House, Lincoln went to Seward's townhouse where the gaslights were turned low as the secretary of state lay in bed, wrapped in bandages and a neck brace. The president sat by his friend's sickbed and whispered the week's events to him—from the visits to Petersburg and Richmond to the hundreds of handshakes at the military hospital. "I think we are near the end at last," he said.[16] Seward nodded, with a glimmer of gratitude in his eyes. It was the last time the two men would meet.

Shortly after 9 p.m., the Department of War telegraph crackled with the news of Lee's surrender to Grant. As Stanton read the announcement, "his iron mask was torn off," one witness recounted, and the secretary of war began "trotting about in exhilarated joy."[17]

Stanton delivered the news personally to his chief. At the White House, the two men embraced in an uncharacteristic hug, which Stanton remembered as "some of the happiest moments of my life."[18]

Bidding Stanton good night, Lincoln went upstairs to rouse Mary and tell her the good news. Lee's army was in their hands.

At daybreak, the nation's capital shook with the first blast of a five-hundred-cannon salute so loud that it shattered windowpanes in Lafayette Square across from the White House. People began to stream out of their houses into the streets as grown men and women danced alongside their children. "The nation seems delirious with joy," Gideon Welles recorded in his diary. "Guns are firing, bells ringing, flags flying, men laughing; all, all are jubilant."[19]

A crowd gathered outside the White House and serenaded Lincoln with "The Star-Spangled Banner" as he ate breakfast. Work was canceled for the day and an impromptu parade made its way from the Navy Yard to the White House, growing in size as they marched, disregarding a rainstorm in their revelry, announcing their presence with patriotic songs and occasional fire from one of the howitzers rolled through the streets like parade floats.

By the time the celebration reached the executive mansion, the crowd was thirsty for recognition, which they received from Tad, who waved a captured Confederate flag from a second-floor window to cheers before he was yanked back by White House staff.

Military bands played as the crowds clamored for a speech. When President Lincoln finally appeared at the window waving, they exploded with cheers and hats were thrown high into the air.

"From the windows of the White House, the surface of the crowd looked like an agitated sea of hats, faces and arms," Noah Brooks reported.[20] Lincoln tried to calm everyone down and then offered congratulations to the American people and three cheers for General Grant. He said he did not have a speech to give just yet, joking that if he spoke then he would have nothing to say at the following day's official victory celebration.

But reprising his request from the *River Queen* the night before, Lincoln asked that the military band play "Dixie."

"I have always thought 'Dixie' one of the best tunes I have ever heard. Our adversaries over the way attempted to appropriate it, but I insisted yesterday that we fairly captured it," Lincoln said to laughter and applause. "I presented the question to the Attorney General, and he gave it as his legal opinion that it is our lawful prize."[21]

Lincoln was sending a message about reconciliation in a way that folks could understand: Dixie was back in American hands.

At Appomattox the next day, all was quiet in the two army camps as Grant's and Lee's officers met again in McLean's house to determine the logistics of laying down arms. Confederate General James Longstreet was passing through the room when Grant looked up and recognized him with a grin.

The two men had been close friends at West Point, when Longstreet had been known as Pete and Grant went by the name Sam. Stationed together in Missouri before the Mexican–American War, Longstreet served as a groomsman at Grant's wedding. Despite the war, their friendship was still undimmed.

Grant strode up with easy humor and outstretched his hand, offering a cigar, which Longstreet gratefully accepted. "Pete, let us have another game of brag"—a form of poker popular in the army—"to recall the days that were so pleasant," Grant said. Longstreet thought to himself, "Why do men fight who were born to be brothers?"[22]

Reconciliation was personal. Reconstruction was political. Back at the White House, Lincoln summoned Francis Pierpont, the long-exiled Unionist governor of Virginia, to his office to discuss plans for restoring the state government.

Lincoln explained that he was still developing the particulars of his policy and he wanted more information about the feeling of the Southern people. "How will they receive you who have antagonized them from the beginning of the war," Lincoln asked Pierpont. "Will they refuse to have anything to do with the Federal government? Will they sulk and do nothing?"[23]

With the momentous changes, Pierpont said that there was very little fixed sentiment in the South at the moment. They were still reeling from loss and living with rumors. Until the railroad connections were restored, Pierpont believed that public opinion would be unsettled and therefore malleable. How they internalized "the new order of things," Pierpont said, "would depend upon the manner in which the people were treated by those in authority."[24]

This fit with Lincoln's liberal instincts and his concern that the radicals' vindictive approach to Reconstruction would harden opposition and sow the seeds of future conflict. He asked Pierpont to go on the road and report back on public opinion, consistent with his long-held belief that "public sentiment is everything: with it, nothing can fail; against it, nothing can succeed."[25]

Public sentiment certainly seemed to be moving in his favor, though there were already hints of the problems that lay ahead. In Concord, Massachusetts, the transcendentalist philosopher Ralph Waldo Emerson wrote, "Tis far the best that the rebels have been pounded instead of negotiated into a peace. They must remember it." But he was concerned about what was to come: "General Grant's terms certainly look a little too easy . . . and I fear that the high tragic historic justice which the nation with severest consideration should execute will be softened and dissipated and toasted away at dinner tables."[26]

Lincoln was steeling himself for the next challenge, one more suited to his practical and peaceable personality. His schedule was dotted with meetings to discuss necessary steps to bring the South back into the Union, though Jefferson Davis was still on the run and General Joseph Johnston's army had not yet surrendered to Sherman in North Carolina.

When asked what he would do with Jeff Davis when caught, Lincoln straightened up in his chair and crossed his legs, as he always did before he was going to tell a story.

"Gentlemen, that reminds me of an incident which occurred in a little town in Illinois where I once practiced law," Lincoln said. "One morning I was on my way to the office, when I saw a boy standing on the street corner crying. I felt sorry for the woebegone little fellow. So I stopped and questioned him as to the cause of his griefs. He looked into my face, the tears running down his cheeks, and said, 'Mister, do you see that coon?'—pointing to a very poor specimen of the coon family which glared at us from the end of the string. 'Well, sir, that coon has given me a heap of trouble. He has nearly gnawed the string in two—I just wish he would finish it. Then I could go home and say he had got away.'"[27]

Everyone laughed, perhaps none so hard as the president himself. But the point was clear: Lincoln hoped that Davis would escape to hasten the healing of the nation while depriving the South of a martyr.

Most of his day was spent working on his much-anticipated speech marking the end of the war. Lincoln decided to use the opportunity to not simply mark the successful end of the long struggle, but to pivot the American people's attention forward to the task ahead: Reconstruction. It was a problem that would, as Noah Brooks explained, "demand the highest statesmanship, the greatest wisdom, and the firmest generosity."[28]

Lincoln's Last Speech

It was the first formal address he'd given since the Second Inaugural, six long weeks before. It would also be his last.

Lincoln wrote speeches in longhand, sitting in a favorite armchair with his long legs crossed to serve as a sturdy border against which he would write the first draft in pencil on stiff sheets of white boxboard.[1] He wrote slowly, with a lawyer's logic and precision of language. He understood that as president every word carried great weight. Accordingly, he often wrote multiple drafts of major addresses and read them aloud to get a sense of how they sounded before pronouncing them ready for public consumption.

Expectations were high and time was tight. Lee's surrender had come more suddenly than Lincoln anticipated. And so Lincoln did something unusual: he combined portions of an older, undelivered speech with a lengthy new opening to mark the momentous occasion.

In the early evening, Elizabeth Keckley caught sight of Lincoln through an open door as he prepared for its delivery. He was at his desk, "looking over his notes and muttering to himself," Keckley recalled. "His face was thoughtful, his manner abstracted, and I knew, as I paused a moment to watch him, that he was rehearsing the part that he was to play in the great drama soon to commence."[2]

Washington was illuminated that night. The new dome of the Capitol building was lit in the evening mist, viewable from miles away. Across the river, Robert E. Lee's former home, Arlington House—which had been seized by the federal government for nonpayment of taxes and converted from a plantation to a Union cemetery—had colored lights on its broad lawn as hundreds of liberated slaves gathered there to sing "Year of Jubilee."

Thousands crowded the torchlit White House lawn waiting to hear the president translate their emotion into meaning. Inside, Noah Brooks saw Lincoln on a staircase with his rolled-up manuscript in one hand. As the president stepped out into public view from the balcony of a second-floor window, Elizabeth Keckley marveled at the sea of humanity that stood outside.

"The swaying motion of the crowd, in the dim uncertain light, was like the rising and falling of billows—like the ebb and flow of the tide upon the stranded shore of the ocean," Keckley recalled in her memoir. "Close to the house the faces were plainly discernible, but they faded into mere ghostly outlines on the outskirts of the assembly; and what added to the weird, spectral beauty of the scene, was the confused hum of voices that rose above the sea of forms, sounding like the subdued, sullen roar of an ocean storm, or the wind soughing through the dark lonely forest. It was a grand and imposing scene, and when the President, with pale face and his soul flashing through his eyes, advanced to speak, he looked more like a demigod than a man crowned with the fleeting days of mortality."[3]

There was a collective shout as the president appeared in the misty evening air.

The torchlight from below cast shadows onto the hollows of his face, leaving his manuscript in the dark. As he waited for the cheers to subside, he called for a candlestick to cast light on the text. Noah Brooks—transitioning from his role as journalist to his promised position as the president's new secretary—held it aloft from behind a curtain as Lincoln began:

"Fellow Citizens. We meet this evening not in sorrow, but in gladness of heart. The evacuation of Petersburg and Richmond, and the surrender of the principal insurgent army, give hope of a righteous and speedy peace, whose joyous expression cannot be restrained."

This was the iconic opening the crowd had been hoping for—after years of sorrow and loss, it was time for celebration and appreciation. But that was all the triumphalism Lincoln would indulge that night.

Despite the temptation to declare victory and damn the enemy,

Lincoln was determined to turn this into a teachable moment: there is no enemy in the aftermath of civil war, there is only us. And so the next step was a sublime de-escalation, offering praise to God and Grant.

"In the midst of this, however, He from whom blessings flow must not be forgotten. A call for a national thanksgiving is being prepared, and will be duly promulgated. Nor must those whose harder part gives us the cause of rejoicing be overlooked. Their honors must not be parceled out with others. I myself was near the front, and had the pleasure of transmitting much of the good news to you. But no part of the honor for plan or execution is mine. To General Grant, his skillful officers, and brave men, all belongs . . ."

A demagogue would have tried to claim credit for the victory, but Lincoln did the opposite in private as well as in public. When he'd received congratulations for the victory behind closed doors, he refused to accept praise. "I want you to stop those congratulations right there," he'd said to Governor Pierpont. "About every gentleman I've met this morning has congratulated me that way, and I want it distinctly understood that I claim no part nor lot in the honor of the military achievements in front of Richmond. All the honor belongs to the military."[4]

Now Lincoln turned the page, letting the first fall to the floor, where it was scooped up by Tad, delighted to be playing a role in the night's drama next to his "Papa-Day."

It was time to focus on the future with a sense of shared responsibility, "the re-inauguration of national authority—Reconstruction."

Lincoln's choice of the word *Reconstruction* was heavy with implications in contrast to the conservatives' preferred term *restoration*. Under Lincoln's leadership, there would be no restoring the plantation class to power, but rather a rebuilding of the South for a future forever free from slavery.

The practical challenge stemmed from the essential fact of civil war, Lincoln said: "Unlike a case of war between independent nations, there is no authorized organ for us to treat with," perhaps reflecting on his inconclusive conversations with Judge Campbell in Richmond. Instead, the peacemakers must "mold from disorganized and discordant elements." An additional degree of difficulty—which Lincoln termed an "embarrassment"—were enduring disagreements about the "mode, manner and means of reconstruction."

This is where Lincoln's newly written text stopped. The first two pages were labeled "A" and "B," but the next page began with the number "1"—as the historian Louis P. Masur notes.[5] Judging by its focus and Lincoln's travel schedule, it had apparently been written in late February—when debate was raging in Congress about Reconstruction policy in Louisiana and Lincoln was caught in the crossfire.

"As a general rule, I abstain from reading attacks upon myself," he told the crowd in a revealing segue, "wishing not to be provoked by that to which I can not properly offer an answer." But the fight in Congress over Louisiana's Reconstruction drove him to make an exception.

He argued that critics of the Louisiana plan based their objections against the standard of perfection rather than progress. The advances in the new state constitution were undeniable: a former slave-owning state had abolished slavery, voted to endorse the Thirteenth Amendment, integrated public schools, and extended a limited right to vote to African-Americans. These issues were all interconnected.

Lincoln's goal was to bring the rebellious states back into "proper practical relation" with the federal government. He repeated this phrase five times in the speech, giving it a talismanic quality. It was typical Lincoln—logical and lyrical—rather than inflexible and ideological. As historian Eric Foner explained, "he urged Republicans to think of reconstruction as a practical problem rather than a philosophical one."[6]

They would be guided by what worked. "So new and unprecedented is the whole case, that no exclusive, and inflexible plan can be safely prescribed," Lincoln said. He would be willing to admit he had been wrong if the results were wrong: "Bad promises are better broken than kept," he explained. He would change his course if it was revealed to be "adverse to the public interest."

Rigidity carried its own risks: "such exclusive, and inflexible plan, would surely become a new entanglement." Lincoln "would not stickle about forms, provided he could attain the desired result," Gideon Welles recalled. "He thought it was best to meet the rebels as men, fellow countrymen, who were reasonable and intelligent."[7]

But there seemed to be something nihilistic, not idealistic, in making the perfect the enemy of the good and refusing to seat Louisiana's duly elected congressional delegation. Lincoln asked the crowd to imagine the message that it would send. "We in effect say to the white men 'You are worthless, or worse—we will neither help you, nor be helped by you.' To the blacks we say 'This cup of liberty which these, your old masters, hold to your lips, we will dash from you, and leave you to the chances of gathering the spilled and scattered contents in some vague and undefined when, where, and how.'" Progress delayed could mean progress denied.

Grounding his argument, Lincoln offered up a homespun metaphor: "The government of Louisiana is only to what it should be as the egg is to the fowl, we shall sooner have the fowl by hatching the egg than by smashing it." This was the sole line in the speech that elicited laughter from the audience.

If they approved the Louisiana delegation, Congress would be giving crucial encouragement to the forces of reform: "To adhere to their work, and argue for it, and proselyte for it, and fight for it, and feed it, and grow it, and ripen it to a complete success." It was the language of a farmer who cultivates his crop, rather than a tyrant who would wipe cultures clean and attempt to remake them in his, rather than God's, image.

Then Honest Abe told a little white lie by publicly sidestepping the issue of whether the rebellious states had ever truly left the Union. Lincoln long believed that the alleged right to secession was the "essence of anarchy," definitively unconstitutional. But some radical Republicans were now arguing that the seceded states had given up their rights upon leaving the Union, giving victorious Northerners the power to entirely remake the Southern states at the point of a bayonet. Now Lincoln dismissed this debate as a "pernicious abstraction"—arguing that because the Southern states now found "themselves safely at home it would be immaterial if they had ever been abroad."

Because there was no established path to guide them, there must be bold experimentation by the states. But that did not mean that Lincoln was willing to let Reconstruction drift, unmoored from core principles. The opposite was true—as Lincoln said, "important principles may, and must, be inflexible." It was precisely because he was determined to achieve the overarching goals of the war that he was willing to change tactics.

The essential principle was the end of slavery. But that historic change did not settle the many questions of how liberated slaves would integrate into American life. There were questions about education and economic assistance as well as whether and when they would be given the vote. Some conservatives opposed giving the formerly enslaved the right to vote at all, others argued that participating in elections was a privilege that needed to be earned in order to be exercised responsibly. Democrats accused Republicans of wanting to give blacks the vote solely so they could ensure a permanent political majority.

Lincoln now carved out a more progressive position on black voting rights than he'd ever acknowledged in public: "I would myself prefer that it were now conferred on the very intelligent and on those who serve our cause as soldiers."

This may sound miserly to modern ears, but it was a radical statement: the first time that any president ever endorsed even a limited right to vote for African-Americans.

Lincoln was publicly echoing his private comments to Governor Michael Hahn of Louisiana the year before, suggesting "some of the colored people" ought to be given the vote: "for instance, the very intelligent, and especially those who have fought gallantly in our ranks. They would probably help, in some trying time to come, to keep the jewel of liberty within the family of freedom."[8]

There was a continuity in Lincoln's principles even as he evolved in public. Though black Americans had the right to vote in only six Northern states, some radical Republicans complained that Lincoln's position was insufficient.

At least one of the listeners in the crowd had the opposite reaction. "That means nigger citizenship," John Wilkes Booth said as he urged his drunk coconspirator Lewis Powell to shoot the president from the crowd. "That is the last speech he will make."[9]

Elizabeth Keckley had a similar thought flash through her mind as she watched from an adjoining window of the White House. "As the light from the lamp fell full upon him, making him stand out boldly in the darkness, a sudden thought struck me, and I whispered to the friend at my side: 'What an easy matter would it be to kill the President, as he stands there! He could be shot down from the crowd, and no one be able to tell who fired the shot.'"[10]

But the crowd was too jubilant to fixate on the remaining danger. After all, the war was over.

Lincoln believed that there would be plenty of time for a more formal presentation of peacetime policy. And so the speech ended abruptly, almost awkwardly, with a hint that a more detailed statement about Southern Reconstruction might soon come: "In the present *'situation'* as the phrase goes, it may be my duty to make some new announcement to the people of the South. I am considering, and shall not fail to act, when satisfied that action will be proper."

This left the president's intentions open to some interpretation, but as John Nicolay reflected, "Can anyone doubt that this new announcement which was taking shape in his mind would again have embraced and combined justice to the blacks and generosity to the whites of the South, with union and liberty for the whole country?"[11]

Lincoln laid down a marker, articulating the practical principles that he intended to guide Reconstruction. And as he departed the White House window with a wave, the band played "Battle Hymn of the Republic."

As the cheers faded, Mary Lincoln led the French envoy, Marquis de Chambrun, to visit the president in his office, unannounced. He found Lincoln lying down on a large horsehair sofa, exhausted from the oratorical effort. But Lincoln leaped up when he saw Chambrun and greeted him with the earnest handshake that comes from seeing a travel companion sooner than expected.

Chambrun praised the speech as being "extremely moderate" while Lincoln again "declared his firm resolution to stand for clemency against all opposition."[12] They soon joined more friends in the Red Room, where tea and cakes were served at ten. It was a jovial reception, with Mary in full plume, amid hearty congratulations and smiles of relief after the long struggle. Seeing Noah Brooks, Lincoln joked, "That was a pretty fair speech, I think—but you threw some light on it."[13]

When one overserved guest suggested that the rebels should be hanged, Tad channeled his father and impulsively interjected, "Oh no, we must hang *on* to them."

Upon hearing that, Lincoln perked up with paternal pride: "That's right Tad," he said with a grin. "We must hang on to them."[14]

As the crowd thinned, Lincoln called over his friend from Illinois days, the U.S. Marshal for the District of Columbia and sometime bodyguard, Ward Hill Lamon, and asked him to travel to Richmond. He wanted the latest intelligence and penned a note for safe passage. Lamon agreed but asked that the president stay close to home for safety and avoid his usual trips to the theater. With mock-solemnity, Lincoln promised he would do the best he could.

The newspaper reaction to Lincoln's speech reflected the divisions that he sought to bridge. *The Cincinnati Commercial* saw "real statesmanship in it—that is the application of common sense to public affairs."[15] *The Philadelphia Press* agreed, declaring, "Radicals and Conservatives, Republicans and Democrats and in some cases even original Secessionists are eulogizing it."[16] While the *National Intelligencer* proclaimed, "The speech is from a lofty stand-point; it soars away above party; it is paternal as well as fraternal."[17]

But, of course, there were critics ready to grumble and pounce. The reflexively hostile, pro-Democrat *New York World* called it "vague and vacillating . . . Mr. Lincoln gropes in his speech like a traveler in an unknown country without a map."[18] Even the usually friendly, pro-Republican *New York Times* admitted that "those who expected from the President a statement of settled reconstruction policy have been disappointed."[19] *The Baltimore Sun* predicted that "the signs are unmistakable of an impending disagreement between what are called extremists and the administration, relative to the reconstruction policy. The breach is said to be widening but the policy of the President seems most likely to win and be accepted by the people as the most practical one."[20]

By morning, the mist cleared and the promise of spring seemed to surround the executive mansion. Lincoln enjoyed breakfast with his family and began to relax.

He took renewed pleasure in horsing around with Tad and doting on the boy's pet goats, Nanny and Nanko, whom he proudly pronounced "the kindest and best goats in the world."[21] They responded to his voice and bounded up next to him. While watching his goats leap and prance on the White House lawn, he mused to Elizabeth Keckley that he would rather wear his goat's "horns and hairy coat through life, than demean myself to the level of the man who plunders the national treasury in the name of patriotism."[22]

The plunder of the national treasury was on his mind almost as much as Reconstruction policy. That day, he'd dealt with war profiteers who'd defrauded the government on military contracts. But those sums were paltry compared to the national debt, which exceeded $2.3 billion[23]—an astronomical sum at the time, almost twice the federal budget. It was a constant preoccupation for President Lincoln because, out of necessity, he increased the budget fifteenfold from its pre–Civil War size.[24] He knew Reconstruction would be expensive—but far better to invest in rebuilding the South than have it degenerate into chaos and sow the seeds of further conflict.

Lincoln was already thinking about ways to spur American industry. He was determined to invest in national expansion and education, from the transcontinental railroad to land-grant colleges. His initial skepticism about the outsized influence of Wall Street had been tempered by experience, telling a friend that "finances will rule the country for the next fifty years."[25]

Standing next to a window in his second-floor executive office overlooking the still unfinished Washington Monument, his old mahogany writing desk stuffed with papers, Lincoln immersed himself in the torrent of administrative life. Fortified by cups of coffee, Lincoln worked through the backlog, matching job seekers with open positions and addressing requests for pardons, while finding time to ask Stanton to secure some flags for Tad.

Although harried, Lincoln never lost the human touch. On a brief trip to the War Department, he passed a person William Crook described as "a ragged, dirty man in army clothing," sitting outside the White House. He'd been wounded, recently released from the hospital, and called out to the president. Lincoln walked over and sat down on the curbside next to the man, listened to his story, and reviewed his papers. Convinced of the merits of his appeal, Lincoln smiled and told him to come by the White House the next day. "You would never know, from his manner to the plainest or poorest or meanest, that there was the least difference between that man and himself," Crook recalled. "The President could meet every man square on the plane where he stood and speak to him, man to man.... He was the only man I ever knew the foundation of whose spirit was love."[26]

But Lincoln was far from infallible and he had made mistakes that needed to be cleaned up that day. Lincoln's spur-of-the-moment suggestion in Richmond to convene the Virginia legislature unleashed dissent in Lincoln's cabinet as well as unhinged reactions among radicals in Congress, with Senator Benjamin Wade declaring, "If he authorized the approval of that paper ... by God, the sooner he was assassinated the better."[27]

Wary of signs that Confederates might misinterpret his gesture, Lincoln was persuaded to backtrack by Gideon Welles's argument that "negotiating with large bodies of men" was more difficult than reasoning one on one, especially "when we were now in a condition to prescribe what should be done."[28] Lincoln sent word to General Weitzel to stand down on the request. The fact of Appomattox erased its intended purpose.

At Appomattox that morning, Confederate troops stood in line for miles to formally surrender their weapons and battle flags under the eye of Maine's general Joshua Chamberlain, a college professor turned veteran of twenty battles, including Gettysburg. As the Confederates solemnly deposited their weapons in a pile, Chamberlain instructed the Union troops to stand silently at attention in a position of respect with their rifles on their shoulders.

As the bugle blew, Chamberlain saw the "downhearted and dejected" Confederate general John B. Gordon respond to the "machine-like snap of arms" and "instantly assumed the finest attitude of a soldier. He wheeled his horse facing me, touching him gently with the spur, so that the animal slightly reared, and as he wheeled, horse and rider made one motion, the horse's head swung down with a graceful bow, and General Gordon dropped his swordpoint to his toe in salutation."[29]

There was evidence of mutual respect. Some Union troops, silent and steady in line, found their "battle-bronzed cheeks were not altogether dry." The ceremony took almost the entire day, with 27,000 rifles laid down, as the defeated men dispersed and headed home.

On the streets of Washington there was a noticeable change in feeling as well. Celebration overwhelmed any feelings of bitterness, evidence that a magnanimous peace might be possible.

"Just now, on all lips, the noble maxim, 'Forgive and forget' is to be heard," the Marquis de Chambrun recorded. He saw columns of Confederate prisoners marched through the streets of Washington without being jeered by the citizens, "not wanting to hurt the feelings of these misled creatures." Instead, the democracy's energy was shifting toward civic debate: "Almost every citizen boasts of possessing the right formula for re-edifying the Union," realizing "that virulent political discussions can lead to nothing constructive."[30]

That afternoon, Lincoln left the White House for a ride to the Soldiers' Home, a place he often used as a retreat from the summer heat. It was located on the highest point in the District of Columbia, and he'd had many productive days and nights in a cottage there, even working on the final draft of the Emancipation Proclamation. Now he seemed to be looking for solitude, riding without a companion, trailed by a cavalry guard. He kept a brisk trot on the trip, passing a carriage carrying Maunsell B. Field, the assistant secretary of the treasury. The two men stopped and exchanged pleasantries "upon indifferent subjects," as Field recollected in his delightfully titled memoir, *Memories of Many Men and of Some Women*. But what made the gravest impression was Lincoln's exhaustion. "He was on one of those moods when 'melancholy seemed to be dripping off him,'" Field recalled, "and his eye had that expression of profound weariness and sadness that I never saw in other human eye."[31]

But trips to the Soldiers' Home always seemed to revive

Lincoln's spirits and he returned to the White House to see Washington basked in a sunset, street corners lit up with incandescent displays of Lincoln's and Grant's faces that set off a sparkling, colorful glow. There was a lightness in the night air, punctuated by fireworks in the sky.

Good Friday, 1865

It began as a perfect spring day, warm with clear skies. The lilacs and Judas trees were blooming by the Potomac. For the first time in months, the entire Lincoln family sat down to breakfast at the White House. The president had his customary coffee and an egg, splurging that morning with a few pieces of crisp bacon.

Robert had arrived from the front with Grant and brought to the table a picture of Robert E. Lee to show his father. Lincoln studied it closely. "It is a good face," he said. "It is the face of a noble, brave man. I am glad the war is over at last."

Then he reached out a hand to Robert and gave thanks for his safe return. "The war is now closed, and we soon will live in peace with the brave men that have been fighting against us."[1]

Despite the clamor of a few drunks still celebrating at the White House gates, it promised to be a momentous day. Not only was the reality of peace beginning to sink in, but in a bit of symmetry, Lincoln knew that morning in Charleston Harbor, the American flag would be raised over Fort Sumter almost four years to the day after it came down.

The morning's editorial in the *New-York Tribune* echoed Lincoln's hopes. "The path of Peace opens pleasantly before us. There may be thorns in the way as we advance, obstacles to overcome, pitfalls and snares to avoid, but we look back to the dread road we have travelled for four long and weary and painful years, the road before us smiles with summer sunshine."[2]

Harper's Weekly reached for the hopes of Palm Sunday, juxtaposing illustrations of Jesus riding into Jerusalem with the surrender at Appomattox.

"So great an event our history has not known. For peace, under her joyous palms, brings justice and union," they wrote. "That God works in history is only a way of saying that the progress of human development will inevitably assert itself against all resistance. Four years ago, it was hard for us in this country to believe that we, too, must be forced through blood and sorrow to defend this truth. We thought we fully believed it. But in the fierce glare of war we can now see that even this sharp and bitter struggle was necessary to establish our own principles, not only before the world but in our own hearts. Let us thank God that we have not faltered. Let us rejoice that, through all the doubt and darkness, through the fires of opposing guns, and the sneers and taunts and skepticism of those who believed and wished those fires might prevail, the great heart of the American people has beat steadily on to victory . . . Let us fervently pray that God may strengthen us to secure the victory they have won, and perpetuate a peace which shall not shame their memory, and that Palm Sunday may henceforth be the symbol of a national repose founded upon the true brotherhood which the Prince of Peace proclaimed."[3]

While others celebrated the hard-won victory, the work of waging peace would not wait for Lincoln. But its urgency would have to be balanced against paperwork, personnel, and politics.

Heading to his office, Lincoln thumbed through the morning newspapers and readied himself for a full day of meetings, kicking off with a visit from his friend, Speaker of the House Schuyler Colfax of Indiana.

The forty-two-year-old Hoosier was planning a trip west during the nine-month congressional recess and wanted to see the president before he left. He brought along with him Congressman Cornelius Cole of California, a former gold prospector and Sacramento newspaper editor.

Colfax began with a recitation of his view of Reconstruction: hang 'em all—specifically, his former colleagues in Congress who'd turned coat to the Confederate side. He could "forgive those who'd been swept up into the vortex of rebellion by the force of public sen-timent in the South,"[4] but members of Congress should have known better. They were willful traitors and the punishment for treason was death. Personal feelings aside, the rules must be applied.

Lincoln tried to change the conversation. "You're going to California, I hear," he said. "How I would rejoice to make that trip! ... I can only envy you its pleasures." Lincoln launched into a message to the miners he wanted Colfax to deliver as he traveled west to the Rockies.

"I have very large ideas of the mineral wealth of our Nation," said Lincoln. "I believe it practically inexhaustible. It abounds all over our Western country from the Rocky Mountains to the Pacific, and its development has scarcely commenced. During the war, when we were adding a couple of millions of dollars every day to our national debt, I did not care ... We had the country to save first. But, now that the Rebellion is overthrown, and we know pretty nearly the amount of our debt, the more gold and silver we mine makes the payment of that debt so much easier."[5]

Slowing down to hammer home his main point, he said, "I am going to encourage that in every way possible. We shall have hundreds of thousands of disbanded soldiers, and many have feared that their return home in such great numbers might paralyze industry by furnishing suddenly a greater supply of labor than there will be a demand for." Lincoln understood their anxiety, but he had a solution. "I am going to try to attract them to this hidden wealth of our mountain ranges, where there is enough room for all. Immigration, which even the war has not stopped, will land upon our shores hundreds of thousands more per year from overcrowded Europe. I intend to point them to the gold and silver that waits for them in the West. Tell the miners for me that I shall promote their interests to the utmost of my ability; because their prosperity is the prosperity of the nation. And we shall prove in a very few years that we are indeed the Treasury of the world."[6]

The sweep of this prescription conveyed Lincoln's continental vision for reuniting our nation. It was ambitious but practical, seam-lessly pro-enterprise, pro-worker, and pro-immigrant. It paid down America's debts while aiming for global influence. And it would gain thunderous applause as Colfax recounted their conversation to audiences from mining camps to the Mormon Tabernacle Choir in the coming months.

But for now, there was only head nodding agreement punctuated by a gentle pushback from the president against Colfax's earlier, uncharitable remarks. Kindness had a practical benefit in Lincoln's political mind, and while he wanted to give the "skeer" to high-ranking traitors, his hope was to chase them out of the country to avoid making martyrs. Then, he said, "We can be magnanimous to the rest, and have peace and quiet in the whole land."[7]

Lincoln's absence of malice impressed Colfax, who recalled that Lincoln spoke with calm determination to secure "liberty and justice to all, with full protection to the humblest, and to re-establish on a sure foundation the unity of the Republic after the sacrifices made for its preservations."[8]

Next in line was the portly former New Hampshire senator John Parker Hale. He was an old friend from Lincoln's one term in Congress, with a long history in Republican politics, but he'd become an occasional critic of the administration for being too slow to move against slavery. He'd recently lost his seat and Lincoln, overlooking their disagreements, appointed him to the plum post of ambassador to Spain at a salary of $12,000 a year. Hale was eager to accept—his daughter Lucy was a prominent Washington socialite who'd fallen for an alcoholic Southern-sympathizing actor named John Wilkes Booth.[9] He hoped the travel overseas would cool their passion. He did not know that they were already engaged—or that Booth would be found carrying his daughter's picture when he was killed by Union soldiers one week later.

Lincoln's mercy was tested by another morning visitor, Senator John A. J. Creswell of Maryland. They greeted each other warmly—after all, Creswell had done more than any other politician to keep Maryland in the Union and Lincoln was in a buoyant mood, saying, "Everything is bright this morning. The war is over. It has been a tough time but we may have lived it out," adding with dark afterthought, "or some of us have."[10]

But Creswell came calling for an unexpected favor: a pardon for a Confederate soldier being held prisoner at Point Lookout, Maryland.

He was the cousin of a college classmate, the senator explained, a good kid who'd fallen in with a bad crowd. He'd been a fool, but Creswell promised to look after him.

This reminded Lincoln of a story. Back in Illinois, there'd been a group of teenagers who decided to go for a May Day outing on an island, which meant they had to cross a shallow stream in a flat boat. When they were done with their party, they found the boat had drifted off. "They were in sore trouble and thought over all manner of devices for getting over the water, without avail. After a time, one of the boys proposed that each fellow should pick up the girl he liked best and wade over with her," Lincoln said with a chuckle. "The masterly plan was carried out until all that were left upon the island was a short little chap and a great, long gothic built lady. Now, Creswell, you are trying to leave me in the same predicament. You fellows are all getting your friends out of the scrape and you will succeed in carrying off one after another until nobody but me and Jeff Davis will be left on the island."[11]

Even as he expressed a genial dissatisfaction with favoritism, Lincoln reveled in his reputation as a presidential pardon factory.

That day he saved at least one more young soldier's life with a stroke of his pen, remarking: "I think this boy can do more good above ground than under-ground."[12]

Heading downstairs, Lincoln bumped into Mrs. Hess, wife of the owner of the local Grover's Theatre. He apologized that he wouldn't be attending their presentation of *Aladdin and His Magic Lamp* that night. Tad would be there, but Mary had made plans to see a comedy over at Ford's Theatre.

Without missing a beat, Mrs. Hess explained that she'd brought her sister-in-law to visit the White House conservatory. Lincoln asked if they'd seen his favorite lemon tree and—throwing his favorite dark shawl, with red and yellow stripes, over his shoulders—he escorted the two to see it in bloom. They asked Lincoln if he was feeling happy over the "glorious news" and he replied, "For the first time since this cruel war began I can see my way clearly."[13] He picked a lemon for each of the ladies, asked his Scottish gardener to gather a few flowers for them, and departed.

Over at the Department of War, Ulysses S. Grant was hunched

over paperwork, puffing on a cigar with his military jacket unbuttoned. He'd been tasked by Secretary Stanton with suggesting budget cuts to something resembling peacetime troop levels while slashing nonessential munitions contracts to help reduce the debt. He'd been at the job for hours, departing his confines only to check in at the telegraph office to see if there was any news from Sherman as he pressed Confederate general Johnston for a final surrender in North Carolina.

Realizing that it was nearing 11 o'clock, Grant hustled over to the White House, where he'd been asked to attend the cabinet meeting. As he entered the dark green room on the second floor, Lincoln rose to greet him and the assembled secretaries broke into applause for the general who won the war.

With the exception of the two heavyweights—Seward was still recovering in bed and represented by his son Frederick, the assistant secretary of state, and Stanton, who was typically late—the cabinet was assembled around a massive walnut table, cleared of its customary military maps and stacks of books to begin the work of securing the peace.

The president sat down in his oak armchair by the south window. In an expansive mood, Lincoln told his cabinet of a recurring dream that reappeared the night before. It involved the water—"your element," he said, gesturing to Secretary of the Navy Welles. He was on "some singular, indescribable vessel," Lincoln explained, "moving with great rapidity towards an indefinite shore."[14]

He'd had the dream before "nearly every great and important event of the War": Sumter, Bull Run, Antietam, Gettysburg, Stones River, Vicksburg, and Wilmington. Grant interjected that Stones River had not been a victory, but Lincoln waved off the point, saying, "We shall, judging from the past, have great news very soon. I think it must be from Sherman. My thoughts are in that direction, as are most of yours."[15]

Grant expressed confidence that his old friend would defeat the remaining rebel army and secure the peace along the terms Lincoln recommended back on the *River Queen*.

As Grant described the surrender at Appomattox in his gravelly voice, Lincoln asked what terms had been provided to the common soldiers. "I told them to go back to their homes and families and they would not be molested, if they did nothing more," Grant said.

The president beamed at hearing his words from the *River Queen* repeated back to him, as Grant described the feeling on the ground: "Kindly feeling toward the vanquished, and hearty desire to restore peace and safety of the South, with as little harm as possible to the feelings or property of the inhabitants, pervaded the discussion."[16]

Then Stanton burst into the room, carrying an immense roll of paper under his arm that contained his plans for Reconstruction. He'd been up all night and came to the meeting prepared to bigfoot any competing policies by dropping a mammoth proposal that would rip secession out by the roots and remake the South by taking control of some state governments indefinitely. Lincoln was consistent with his resistance: "We can't undertake to run State Governments in all these Southern States. Their people must do that, though I reckon that, at first, they may do it badly."[17]

Stanton and Seward, War and State, often dueled for maximum influence. Frederick Seward came loaded with directives from his father, which he said had been whispered from his sickbed. It was, Lincoln noted, a rather lengthy list from a man who could barely speak.

Stanton countered that his plan for Reconstruction would temporarily erase some Southern state borders entirely, combining Virginia and North Carolina under one federal military governor while the state governments reconstituted. Lincoln approved Stanton's request that his full proposal be circulated among the cabinet for future discussion and debate. But with regard to Virginia, Lincoln stated that the long-suffering government-in-exile, led by Governor Pierpont, would be given the power to follow through on their mandate: "We must reanimate the states."[18]

Even with the sweep of history in front of them, Lincoln and his cabinet had to make small, practical calls. They decided to open Southern ports to trade, to speed a return to normal life through the complementary self-interest of commerce.

Stanton wanted Confederate forts destroyed to remove any temptation of further use or turning them into relics. Lincoln deferred to the experts at the table, explaining they had spent more time thinking of the particulars. He would set the direction, but the agencies would address the execution. Lincoln always made the final decision and owned it, good or ill. "President Lincoln never shunned any responsibility," Welles recalled, "and often declared that he, not the cabinet was in fault for any errors imputed to them, when I sometimes thought otherwise."[19]

At noon, Lincoln's cabinet could hear church bells across Washington begin to ring, marking the moment when darkness fell across the land during Jesus Christ's crucifixion.

In Charleston Harbor, a resurrection ceremony was taking place. The same American flag that had been taken down four years before under cannon fire was being slowly raised over the battered ruins of Fort Sumter by the war-weakened hands of Major General Robert Anderson, the commander who'd lowered the flag at the start of the war. "Thank God that I have lived to see this day,"[20] he tearfully declared.

Federal artillery celebrated the occasion with salutes that rattled the windows of stately homes on the Battery. As slate blue smoke hovered over the water, a prayer of Thanksgiving was offered up by the celebrated Reverend Henry Ward Beecher of Brooklyn—the younger brother of the author of *Uncle Tom's Cabin*—to more than a thousand assembled local leaders, freed slaves, and Union soldiers—including members of the battle-scarred African-American Massachusetts Fifty-Fourth infantry regiment—as the abolitionist leader William Lloyd Garrison looked on with satisfaction.

Beecher's sermon echoed within what he called "this pulpit of broken stone." He gave thanks to God for sustaining the life of Lincoln, and for the president's "disinterested wisdom . . . under the unparalleled burdens and sufferings of four bloody years, and permitted him to behold this auspicious confirmation of that national unity for which he has waited with so much patience and fortitude."[21] Then Beecher launched into a vision of Reconstruction that could have been dictated by Lincoln, a vision of mercy guided by justice.

One nation under one government, without slavery, has been ordained and shall stand. There can be peace on no other basis. On this basis, reconstruction is easy, it needs neither architect nor engineer . . . We do not want your cities nor your fields, we do not envy you your prolific soil, nor heavens full of perpetual summer. Let agriculture revel here, let manufacturers make every stream musical; build fleets in every port; surprise the arts of peace with genius second only to that of Athens; and we shall be glad in your gladness and rich in your wealth. All that we ask is unswerving loyalty and universal liberty and in that name of this high sovereignty of the United States of America, we demand, and that, with the blessing of almighty God, we will have.

We raise our father's banner, that it may bring back better blessings than those of old, that it may oust out of the devil of discord; that it may restore lawful government and a prosperity purer and more enduring than that which it protected before; that it may win parted friends from their alienation . . . that it may heal all jealousies, unite all policies, inspire a new national life, compact our strength, purify our principals, ennoble our national ambitions, and make this people great and strong; not for aggression and quarrelsomeness, but for the peace of the world, giving to us the glorious prerogative of leading all nations to more just laws, to more humane policies, to sincere friendship, to rational instituted civil liberty, and to universal Christian brotherhood.[22]

Even some Southerners seemed moved by this prospect of peace without rancor, as select attendees departed for a rare interracial dinner hosted downtown on Church Street by the African-American chef Nat Fuller. Glasses were raised and toasts were given to freedom and Lincoln, whose "brave heart beats for human freedom everywhere."[23]

Back at the cabinet meeting, Lincoln savored the opportunity to establish a successful framework for Reconstruction throughout the next eight months, without congressional interference. As long as the administration was "wise and discreet," they could "accomplish more without than with them," Lincoln said. "There are men in Congress, who, if their motives are good, are nevertheless impracticable and who possess feelings of hate and vindictiveness in which I have no sympathy and could not participate."[24]

"I hope there will be no persecution, no bloody work, after the war is over. No one need expect me to take part in hanging or killing those men, even the worse of them. Frighten them out of the country, open the gates, let down the bars, scare them off,"[25] Lincoln said, waving his hands across the table as if shooing sheep.

"Enough lives have been sacrificed," he explained. "There has been too much of a desire on the part of some of our very good friends to be masters, to interfere with and dictate to those states, to treat the people not as fellow citizens; there is too little respect for their rights. I do not sympathize in these feelings."[26]

There remained disagreements within the cabinet, but Lincoln felt confident he could bridge them all. The radicals detected a shift to their position now that victory had been achieved, while the moderates trusted that Lincoln's more liberal vision would prevail.

All agreed that they had never seen Lincoln looking finer. "Didn't our chief look grand today," Stanton said.[27] Senator James Harlan of Iowa found him "transfigured" with his "indescribable sadness . . . suddenly changed for an equally indescribable expression of serene joy."[28]

As the cabinet meeting ended a little after 1 o'clock, Lincoln called Grant over and asked if he would accompany them to the theater that night. The general gave his regrets, explaining that Mrs. Grant already made plans to reunite with their children in Burlington, New Jersey, near Philadelphia, where they were safely in school during the war. Left unspoken was Julia's desire to spend as little time with Mary as possible.

Lincoln took no offense but turned to Stanton and asked for a guard to be detailed to him that night as Ward Hill Lamon was on assignment in Richmond. He asked specifically for Major Thomas J. Eckert, a Stanton aide whom the president had seen break five metal fire pokers across his arm in a show of strength that probably doubled as evidence of bad procurement policy.

But the Department of War was short staffed because of the Easter holiday and, hoping to dissuade Lincoln from attending the theater, Stanton said he needed Eckert to work that night. So Lincoln reluctantly agreed to have a local police officer named John Parker fulfill guard duties while Mary went about finding companions for the presidential box at Ford's Theater, which had already begun publicizing their attendance at that night's benefit performance of the British comedy *Our American Cousin*, starring the celebrated Miss Laura Keene. Lincoln didn't feel like going to the theater, but he didn't want to let anyone down.

John Wilkes Booth heard about the president's plans while he was picking up his mail at Ford's Theater midday. He had eight hours to update his plot, fortifying his will with whiskey shots at a local saloon.

Chomping on his favorite snack of an apple, Lincoln returned to his work. Typically, this is when Lincoln would throw open the doors of his office for what he called his "Beggar's Opera"—a time when anyone could come and petition the president. But today, there was too much unfinished business. Lincoln rang the bell on his desk to send in Vice President Andrew Johnson, who'd been waiting outside during the cabinet meeting.

The president had been avoiding the vice president since his disastrous drunken display on Inauguration Day. It was time to clear the air, and Lincoln greeted Johnson warmly, calling him "Andy." It had never been customary to include vice presidents in cabinet meetings, but Lincoln wanted Johnson to understand the intended direction for Reconstruction. They met for a half hour, but Johnson never recounted their conversation and Lincoln would not have the opportunity to do so.

The remainder of the midafternoon was spent paging through various pardon requests and official correspondence. One letter caught his eye—from Brigadier General James H. Van Alen, of Kinderhook, New York—asking that the president take special precautions to guard against the threat of assassination. The trip to Richmond had been seen by some as reckless. In response, Lincoln dashed off a note thanking Van Alen for his concern, assuring him that he intended "to adopt the advice of my friends and use due precaution." Then Lincoln pivoted to the politics of Reconstruction, thanking Van Alen for being in support of his plan to restore "a Union of hearts and hands, as well as states."[29] It was the last letter he would ever write.

As Lincoln readied himself for a long-promised afternoon carriage ride with Mary, he found the assistant secretary of war, Charles Dana, at this door. It seemed that the head of the Confederate secret service, Jacob Thompson of Mississippi, was in Portland, Maine, trying to board a steamer bound for England. Did Lincoln want him arrested? "No, I rather think not," Lincoln said. "When you have got an elephant by the hind leg, and he's trying to run away, it's best to let him run."[30] He wanted unrepentant Confederates to flee the country, and many did just that, including more than 10,000 Southerners who headed to Brazil, where slavery remained legal until 1888.

Around 3 p.m., as Lincoln was making his way down the staircase to join Mary, he overheard a one-armed soldier say he'd give his other arm if he could meet Abraham Lincoln.

"You shall do that and it shall cost you nothing, my boy!" Lincoln said as he grasped the surprised soldier's hand and gave it a hearty shake.[31]

The weather was a comfortable 68 degrees as the presidential carriage rolled out of town, with the first couple cuddled up close. Lincoln wanted to travel alone with his wife and he was in high spirits. "He was so gay," Mary recalled, "that I said to him, laughingly, 'Dear Husband, you startle me by your great cheerfulness. I have not seen you so happy since before Willie's death.'"

"I consider *this* day, the war, has come to a close," Lincoln replied. "We must both be more cheerful in the future—between the war and the loss of our darling Willie—we have both been very miserable."[32]

They talked about the future and life together after the White House. Lincoln expressed a desire to visit the Holy Land and even spoke of settling in San Francisco where their sons might find more opportunity than within the confines of Springfield. Lincoln would need to work; they did not have enough money saved up to retire in comfort and there was no presidential pension. Before leaving Springfield, he'd asked his law partner Herndon to keep their old wooden law office sign, Lincoln & Herndon, swinging on its shingle. "If I live," Lincoln told Herndon, "I'm coming back sometime and then we'll go on practicing law as if nothing had happened."[33]

Abraham and Mary rolled up toward the Soldiers' Home and then turned back toward the Navy Yard, as Lincoln reminisced about their early days as young parents on the prairie. When they arrived, Lincoln waved to the working men and asked which ship had seen the most action. He was directed to the ironclad USS *Montauk* and shook the hand of everyone aboard. The ship had been stationed in South Carolina, fired on Fort Sumter, and in a few days would be used to imprison the men who plotted to assassinate the president. The ship's medical officer, Dr. Todd, wrote his brother that the president and first lady "seemed very happy, and so expressed themselves, glad that this war was over, or near its end."[34] Todd would also attend Ford's Theater that night.

At the White House gates, Lincoln spied two old friends from Illinois—Governor Richard J. Oglesby and General Isham N. Haynie. He called them into the White House, where they sat by the fireside in the reception room and swapped old stories. The president whipped out a recent selection of humor columns from the *Toledo Blade* written by David Ross Locke, in the voice of a character named Petroleum V. Nasby: a hypocritical, illiterate country preacher of Confederate prejudices. Lincoln read several dispatches aloud to his guests, including this selection on Lincoln's recent visit to Richmond:

> Lee surrenderd! Why, this ends the biznis. Down goes the curtain. The South is conkered. CONKERED! Linkin rides into Richmond! A Illinois rale-splitter, a buffoon, a ape, a gorrriler, a smutty joker, sets hisself down in President' Davis' cheer, and rites dispatches! ...The Dimokrasy has likewise given up the ghost. It may survive this, but I can't see how ...Linkin will serve his term out—the tax on whiskey won't be repealed—or leeders will die of chagrin and delirium tremens and inability to live so long out uv offis and the sheep will be scattered. Farewell vane world. I'll embrace the Catholic faith and be a nun and in a cloister find that rest that pollytix can never give.[35]

Lincoln laughed at each absurd line. He took comfort in the company of old friends and did not want them to leave his side.

"How long we remained there I do not know," Oglesby recalled.

"They kept sending for him to come to dinner. He promised each time to go but would continue reading the book. Finally, he got a sort of peremptory order that he must come to dinner at once." White House doorman Tom Pendel had been dispatched to break up the party, explaining the need to dine promptly before the theater. But Lincoln was reluctant to depart, saying, "I'd much rather swap stories than eat."[36]

He finally sat down with Mary and their children for a simple meal and then tried to coax Robert to join them at the theater. His son declined, citing exhaustion from the front and a still-burning cigar he wanted to finish. They would make do with Major Henry Rathbone and his stepsister-cum-fiancée Clara Harris—the daughter of New York senator Ira Harris.

Before the Lincolns departed, the president excused himself and ducked out to the War Department to check on the latest cables. Accompanied by William Crook, Lincoln's mood drifted back toward melancholy. He did not want to go to the theater that night and his usually brisk steps slowed.

He mused about assassination in the evening fog as the gas lamps began to glow. "Do you know I believe there are men who want to take my life? And I have no doubt they will do it." Crook said he hoped the president was mistaken. "Other men have been assassinated," Lincoln said with a matter-of-fact fatalism. "I have perfect confidence in those who are around me—in every one of you men. I know no one could do it and escape alive. But if it is to be done, it is impossible to prevent."[37]

At the end of their visit to the War Department, with Mary in the carriage waiting, Lincoln encouraged Crook to go home and rest. Instead of saying his customary "Good Night," Crook heard him say "Good-Bye."[38]

And then, with a wave, Lincoln climbed into the waiting black carriage and left for the theater.

Reconstruction

A Tragedy in
Three Acts

"It is more dangerous to make peace than to make war."[1]

—*Rev. Henry Ward Beecher*

A t Ford's Theater, the shot rang out after a laugh line in the third act. Lincoln slumped forward, Mary screamed, and John Wilkes Booth jumped out of the president's box yelling, "Sic Semper Tyrannis." He caught his spur on the frame of an unsmiling portrait of Washington, breaking his ankle while landing onstage. After a beat, shouts filled the theater and spilled out into the misty gaslit streets.

Blood oozing from the back of his head, with a .41 caliber bullet lodged in his brain behind his right eye, Lincoln's body was carried to a boardinghouse across the street. His soul lingered for nine hours; long legs folded and wrapped in a bloody sheet; laid diagonally across a sleigh bed, the walls a murky kaleidoscope of Victorian browns and purples with hazy faces weeping and whispering. As he drew a final breath at 7:22 a.m., Stanton said, "Now he belongs to the ages."

The promise of rebirth seemed distant that Easter weekend. Red, white, and blue bunting was changed to black crepe. Church bells tolled at 3 o'clock on Saturday afternoon, summoning citizens across the country to pray for their fallen leader while synagogues commemorating Passover—the end of Hebrew slavery—offered Kaddish for a gentile for the first time.[2] In Connecticut, the Reverend C. B. Crane spoke for many when he declared, "On that last Good Friday, peace was secured between the contending regions of our distracted country . . . Jesus Christ died for the world and Abraham Lincoln died for his country."[3] America witnessed the crucifixion of Abraham Lincoln, a martyr to the cause of liberty and union.

As the telegraph sped the news across the nation, joy over the war's end turned to shock and anger. "There unfolded a transition so vast," recalled Frederick Douglass, "from victory to the very dust and ashes of sorrow and mourning—that few among us could believe the dreadful news to be true."[4]

The *Washington Chronicle* declared that "the indignation and horror created by this foul murder will serve, more than anything else could possibly do, to destroy the feeling of commiseration and brotherly love for the misguided people of the South, and the policy of magnanimity toward the leaders of the rebellion, which had taken root in the North."[5] The *Unconditional Union* in Little Rock editorialized, "Rebels have slain the greatest and best friend they had in the Republic."[6]

Not everyone felt that way. Alabama's *Demopolis Herald* blared "Glorious News: Lincoln and Seward Assassinated," followed by the fact-free headline "Lee Defeats Grant."[7] In South Carolina, diarist Emma LeConte described excitement in Columbia amid shouts of "Isn't it splendid!" and let her enthusiasm for Lincoln's death spill out onto the page: "Hurrah! Old Abe Lincoln has been assassinated! It may be abstractly wrong to be so jubilant, but I just can't help it . . . We have suffered till we feel savage. There seems no reason to exult for this will make no change in our position and will only infuriate them against us. Never mind, our hated enemy has met the just reward of his life."[8]

But many Confederate leaders realized that Lincoln's death would unleash more devastation upon their battered lands. As General Joe Johnston met with General Sherman to discuss surrender in the woods of North Carolina, he dropped his head upon hearing of the assassination. "Mr. Lincoln was the best friend we had," he said. "His death is the worst thing that could happen for the South."[9]

Former critics overseas now honored the fallen president. In London, *The Economist* editor Walter Bagehot eulogized Lincoln as a great leader: "Power and responsibility visibly widened his mind and elevated his character. Difficulties, instead of irritating him as they do most men, only increased his reliance on patience; opposition, instead of ulcerating, only made him more tolerant and determined."[10]

Tributes transformed grief into myth. In New York, Walt Whitman was briefly stunned into silence, passing newspapers across the kitchen table with his mother, before penning four poems honoring Lincoln, including "O Captain! My Captain!" The novelist Herman Melville was moved to poetry the day of Lincoln's death, writing: "They killed him in his kindness/In their madness and their blindness . . . They have killed him, the Forgiver—the Avenger takes his place."[11]

As the "Avenger" assumed the presidency, there was unexpected optimism inside radical Republican circles. Senator Benjamin Wade heartily shook Andrew Johnson's hand and declared: "I thank God you are here. Mr. Lincoln had too much of human kindness in him to deal with these infamous traitors, and I am glad that it had fallen into your hands to deal out justice to them."[12]

Now that Lincoln was dead, radicals and reactionaries would try to kill his legacy. The tragedy of Reconstruction would teach Americans the terrible cost of failing to win the peace.

As waves of despair rolled out from Washington, Abraham Lincoln's body was brought back to the White House where Mary, Robert, and Tad were holed up in the residence, shaking with grief. "Who has killed Papa-Day?" Tad cried, while Robert tried to put on a brave face; their mother, inconsolable, called for Elizabeth Keckley.

Abraham Lincoln's body was prepared for burial in the same black Brooks Brothers suit he'd worn at his inaugural six weeks before. His bloodied overcoat with the embroidered lining that read "One Nation, One Destiny" was given to a favorite White House doorman as a keepsake. The contents of the president's pockets were emptied. They included gold-rimmed spectacles with a broken hinge tied together by string, an ivory pocketknife, a monogramed Irish linen handkerchief, and a large brown leather wallet lined with purple silk containing the $5 Confederate bill he had picked up on his visit to Richmond eleven days before.

Within a spacious compartment of the wallet labeled "notes" were eight newspaper articles, neatly folded and kept close at hand for reference. They offered insight into Lincoln's mind during the last weeks of his life, showing the tender areas in need of praise, personal interests, and flashes of humor. Together, they provided evidence to the lonely president that his instincts had been vindicated despite violent opposition.

The packet included a condensed copy of the 1864 political platforms of Lincoln and McClellan, a copy of Sherman's orders for his March to the Sea, and an article commemorating Missouri's vote to end slavery.

Two letters written by rebel soldiers, reprinted in Union newspapers, detailed their disenchantment with the Confederacy. One admitted that "the negro emancipation policy, at which we so long hooted, is the most potent lever of our overthrow."[13] The other was a bawdy bit of defiance titled "A Conscript's Epistle to Jeff. Davis," which denounced him as a "bastard President of a political abortion" before announcing the soldier's intention to defect to the Union.[14]

Lincoln's favorite British statesman, Liberal leader John Bright—whose portrait hung in Lincoln's office at the White House—penned a letter in the *New York Tribune* endorsing Lincoln's reelection, praising his "grand simplicity of purpose and a patriotism that knows no change and which does not falter . . . a brightness of personal honor on which no adversary has yet been able to fix a stain."[15]

A second dispatch from England came from the *Liverpool Post*, which reprinted—without permission—a letter Lincoln wrote the Shakespearian actor James Henry Hackett, praising his performance as Falstaff. The *Post* noted that Lincoln's favorite plays—including *Macbeth, Hamlet,* and *Richard III*—constituted a great library for leaders of men, before going on to compliment the president by saying, "He has never given up on a good servant or a sound principle. He has never shut his eyes to facts or remained in ignorance of them."[16]

Finally, there was an article recounting a speech by Reverend Henry Ward Beecher endorsing his reelection to wild applause at a speech in Philadelphia. It concluded by saying, "after a term of war he is entitled to a term of peace."[17]

While Lincoln pretended to be unaffected by public criticism, these clippings showed how vindication in the eyes of his fellow citizens soothed Lincoln's soul.

But these articles seemed like sad, small details in the face of the staggering loss that was being assimilated into American life. The relics were kept by Robert Lincoln and then sealed up, forgotten, in the Library of Congress for a half century.

Lincoln's open casket was displayed in the East Room of the White House, fulfilling the nightmare he had aboard the *River Queen*. Americans lined up for miles to pay their respects, a river of life honoring the dead. Preachers from four denominations spoke at his services. A funeral train then reversed the route that he traveled to Washington for his inauguration four years before, carrying his corpse 1,700 miles through some 400 cities and towns, with Lincoln's casket accompanied by the smaller coffin of his son Willie, who would be buried alongside his father in Springfield.

The Anti-Lincoln

In six weeks, Andrew Johnson traveled from a disastrous drunken performance on Inauguration Day, to the purgatory of the vice presidency, to the sudden assumption of the presidency itself.

He was the opposite of Lincoln in all things except humble beginnings. Where Lincoln had been steady and selfless, Johnson was erratic and egotistical. Where Lincoln was tolerant of criticism, Johnson was consumed by feuds and perceived slights. While Lincoln was a reconciler, Johnson was alternately radical and reactionary.

These qualities were not well hidden. *The Atlantic* called Johnson "egotistic to the point of mental disease, insincere as well as stubborn, cunning as well as unreasonable, vain as well as ill-tempered."[1] Union general Carl Schurz saw no "sunlight" in Johnson, but instead "something sullen, something betokening a strong will inspired by bitter feelings."[2]

Radical Republicans believed Johnson was a fellow traveler who hated slavery, but they soon found out his populist resentments were really focused on the wealthy southern planter class. He was a class warrior rather than a race warrior.

But in the wake of the assassination, Johnson briefly basked in the glow of Lincoln's halo. Always a strong opponent of secession, he tried to base his actions on what he understood to be Lincoln's plan—a focus on bringing the Southern states back into the Union as quickly as possible, provided they passed new constitutions ending slavery and swore allegiance to the Union. It was when he began making decisions of his own that the trouble began.

At the end of the five-week mourning period, Johnson produced an almost ludicrously lenient bill of amnesty upon the South that required little and invested nothing. The vast majority of white Southerners would regain their rights and property if they took a loyalty oath. High Confederate officials and plantation owners with more than $20,000 in property were excluded. But they could request a pardon directly from the president, effectively disregarding Lincoln's prohibition on full amnesty for Confederate leaders.

Drunk on power if not on whiskey, Johnson seemed to enjoy approving these personal appeals from his one-time social superiors in the South. Always susceptible to flattery and displays of personal fealty, he granted more than 7,000 of these individual petitions,[3] empowering former Confederates to reclaim as much of their privilege and property as possible, while vehemently opposing black voting rights. Responding to Southern complaints, Johnson ordered all black troops to be removed from the region by the end of the year.[4]

Reporting from Richmond, Thomas Morris Chester raged against the spectacle of former Confederate officers "strutting about in their red sashes, swords and pistols," with looks of barely suppressed jubilation over Lincoln's death. In his dispatches, Chester argued that they should "be stripped of the villainous gray in which they delighted to murder soldiers of the Union, and the color stamped with infamy."[5] With disbelief, he chronicled the reappointment of the Confederate-era Richmond mayor, Joe Mayo, and his police force's new abuses of power against freed blacks. This federal backsliding amounted to betrayal.

As former Confederates consolidated power, it bred contempt. As General Carl Schurz reported back to the White House after a fact-finding tour of the South in the summer of 1865, "the generosity and toleration shown by the government to the people lately in rebellion have not met with a corresponding generosity."[6]

There had not been enough accountability to ensure unity. Schurz noted that the former rebels did not recognize the criminality of secession—treason had not, in fact, been made odious—and there was an "utter absence of national feeling." Southerners reluctantly accepted the end of slavery and secession as a matter of necessity, but not equal rights under the law.

As the new Mississippi governor, Benjamin Grubb Humphreys—a Confederate Brigadier General—declared in his first message to the legislature: "The negro is free, whether we like it or not; we must realize that fact now and forever. To be free, however, does not make him a citizen, or entitle him to political or social equality with the white man."[7]

By the fall of 1865, legislatures in the deep South began to implement "Black Codes," designed to enforce white supremacy in the absence of slavery. There were restrictions on equal pay, carrying guns, and purchasing land. Vagrancy laws criminalized unemployment. Children could be separated from parents and work requirements led to indentured servitude. Imprisonment escalated while blacks were prohibited from testifying against whites in court—all creating a legal minefield for freedmen under the cloak of law and order. It was slavery without the chains.

Andrew Johnson accepted these "Black Codes," citing states' rights; they suited his vision of the South. The states checked the box with the minimum standards for readmittance to the Union—and Congress was still adjourned, giving the president unchecked power to determine Reconstruction. In October, Johnson paroled five members of the Confederate cabinet including Vice President Alexander Stephens. This was not the magnanimous peace Lincoln had envisioned. The reversal caused whiplash within the administration. Ulysses S. Grant recalled that "Mr. Johnson, after a complete revolution of sentiment, seemed to regard the South not only as an oppressed people, but as the people best entitled to consideration of any of our citizens," making congressional Republicans more radical in their views while spurring some Southerners to feel that "they would be able to control the nation at once . . . and many of them acted as if they were entitled to do so."[8]

When Congress convened in December, a group of former secessionists arrived in Washington, ready to take their place as newly elected congressmen. Furious, Republicans refused to seat them, contesting their legitimacy and asserting their power over the president to direct Reconstruction.

Despite this skirmish, within three years of Appomattox, there would be seven former Confederate soldiers in the U.S. Congress.[9] Within a decade, they would be joined by four ex-Confederate generals, fifty-eight members of the military and Confederate congress, and six former Confederate cabinet secretaries, including Alexander Stephens.[10]

Some said Johnson's change of heart toward the men he once denounced as traitors came from partisan considerations—he was a Democrat, after all, and intended to run for reelection in his own right. But there was also a more fundamental resentment at work.

"This country is for white men," Johnson told the governor of Missouri, "and by God, as long as I am President, it shall be governed by white men."[11] After Frederick Douglass met with him in the White House to appeal for giving African-Americans the vote in Washington, D.C., Johnson launched into a tirade in front of his secretary: "I know that damned Douglass; he's just like any nigger, and he would sooner cut a white man's throat than not."[12]

Much of the country was starting to look away from problems of race, ready to turn the page toward prosperity. In October 1865, the lead article in *Harper's* magazine was a fifteen-page report on the booming new business of mercury mines in California,[13] validating Lincoln's vision of former soldiers moving west to work. But he had not imagined that shift of focus would be accompanied by the abandonment of freedmen in the South.

President Johnson and the Republican-controlled Congress were on a collision course. In December, Johnson issued an executive order demanding that all confiscated land that had been given to freedmen be returned to the planter class. This was another reversal, as W. E. B. Du Bois perceptively noted: Johnson "dropped his demand for dividing up plantations when he largely realized that Negroes would be beneficiaries."[14]

This was a betrayal of promises made by the Freedmen's Bureau under the leadership of thirty-five-year-old General O. O. Howard, who'd lost his right arm in battle and now was determined to help lift the former slaves to self-sufficiency.

With a total budget the equivalent of only one week's fighting the Civil War, the Freedmen's Bureau helped avoid starvation in the

South, issuing nearly 30,000 rations a day to black and white refugees alike.[15] Confronting the legacy of anti-literacy laws for slaves, they built schools in major cities like Richmond and taught reading, writing, and arithmetic as well as Bible study. With more than 850,000 acres of land at their disposal—some seized from enemy combatants, others for failure to pay federal taxes—they devised a plan to allow freed slaves to lease the land for up to three years, giving them the opportunity to buy the land outright. When word of Johnson's executive order restoring the rebel land was received, some generals refused to recognize it as legitimate. They were fired. This was more than a power struggle—it would have far-reaching effects on freed blacks' ability to accumulate wealth.

But Johnson's assault on the freedmen was just beginning. Two months later, he shocked Washington by vetoing a Republican bill to extend the Freedmen's Bureau—a direct repudiation of Lincoln's legacy.

Johnson's veto statement said he objected to the Freedmen's Bureau as a massive expense and an unconstitutional expansion of federal power that would not only overwhelm states' rights but create a special class of rights for blacks in the South.

The government "has never founded schools for any class of our own people," Johnson complained, nor "authorized to expend the public money for the rent or purchase of homes for the thousands, not to say millions, of the white race who are honestly toiling from day to day for their subsistence. A system for the support of indigent persons in the United States was never contemplated by the authors of the Constitution. Nor can any good reason be advanced why, as a permanent establishment, it should be founded for one class or color of our people more than for another."[16]

Of course, this ignored the crucial context—there had never been an enslaved class suddenly made free and therefore in need of support to guarantee their equal rights. Johnson's strained colorblind argument—while railing against supposed special rights for blacks—neatly summarized arguments from states' rights conservatives that would echo through the ages.

The day after this veto, Andrew Johnson gave one of the strangest presidential speeches in American history. In a keynote speech at a fundraiser to complete the Washington Monument, Johnson was in full martyr mode, asking, "Who has suffered more for the Union than I have?" in view of wounded veterans and the parents of slain sons.

Wielding a wounded ego, Johnson referred to himself in the first person more than 200 times, compared Republican leaders to Confederate rebels, and accused a nineteenth-century version of the deep state of plotting his assassination: "Are those who want to destroy our institutions, and to change the character of the government . . . not satisfied with one martyr in this place?"[17]

The president seemed unhinged while the Union was still being glued together. This was not good. It would get worse.

In March, the Civil Rights Act came to the president's desk after passing Congress with almost unanimous Republican support. Johnson again wielded the veto pen, pushing back on the bill's promise of equality under the law and rejecting citizenship for freed slaves. It was a "stride towards centralization," Johnson declared, strengthening the national government at the expense of states' rights, while he again raised the specter of special rights for the former slaves: "The distinction of race and color is by the bill made to operate in favor of the colored and against the white race."[18]

Johnson and Republicans were now at war. In June, Congress passed the Fourteenth Amendment, codifying birthright citizenship and equality under the law—but not yet voting rights—in the Constitution, bypassing the president and sending it to the states for ratification.

Johnson was now obsessed with blocking black citizenship and voting rights at the ballot box and embarked on a "swing around the circle" speaking tour through the Midwest and South, where his demagogic instincts were unleashed in front of audiences. Even the nonpolitical General Grant considered the president's rhetoric a "national disgrace."[19] Deadly race riots broke out Memphis and New Orleans, convincing many Northerners that enforcement needed to be imposed on the South to fulfill Lincoln's vision and avoid a new rebellion.

Republicans triumphed in the 1866 midterm elections, returning to Washington with a veto-proof majority. They quickly passed sweeping Reconstruction laws over Johnson's now impotent objections, dividing the South into five federally controlled military districts and requiring the former Confederate states to register black voters, pass new constitutions, and ratify the Fourteenth Amendment as a condition of their full return to the Union.

Ohio congressman James Garfield—a Civil War veteran and future president—declared that because Southerners "would not cooperate with us in building what they had destroyed . . . we must lay the heavy hand of military authority upon these Rebel communities . . . and plant liberty on the ruins of slavery."[20]

Just as the Confederates' violent response to Lincoln's election ultimately created the condition that they were afraid of—the end of slavery—Johnson's efforts to block the bills of radical Republicans ended up creating the more militant imposition of Reconstruction he tried to resist. It was a lesson in the unintended consequences of overreach and backlash.

Politically weakened, the president continued to fight. In February 1868, Johnson tried to fire the secretary of war. Stanton refused to leave, literally barricading himself in his office. The fallout from this bizarre power struggle led to Johnson becoming the first president impeached by the House of Representatives. Johnson's obstruction of congressional Reconstruction was the core complaint, but the articles of impeachment also cited his "intemperate, inflammatory and scandalous harangues." After nine weeks and forty-one witnesses, Johnson survived Senate conviction by a single vote.

Johnson's defenders always insisted that he tried to remain faithful to Lincoln's vision of Reconstruction. None other than Gideon Welles, who spanned Lincoln and Johnson's eight years in office, argued that Johnson's opposition to giving African-Americans the vote was consistent with Lincoln's position in 1862.

But this willfully ignored Lincoln's evolution. He'd been trying to lead the country toward equality while Johnson wanted to stop this progress. Lincoln pressed for black voting rights in private letters to governors and in his last public speech, making his purpose plain to his secretary, William Stoddard, saying that the ballot "will be about the only protection they have after the war is over."[21] Johnson fought black voting rights, decrying the "Africanizing of the southern part of our territory" in a veto message to Congress, while declaring that "to force the right of suffrage out of the hands of white people into the hands of the Negros is an arbitrary violation" of states' rights.[22]

This contrast was clear to Frederick Douglass, who told an audience at the Brooklyn Academy of Music in 1866: "Mr. Lincoln would have been in favor of the enfranchisement of the colored race. I tell you, he was a progressive man; he never took any step backwards." But Andrew Johnson, he said, promised to be a Moses to the colored race and ended up playing Pharaoh, "a man who wants to enfranchise our enemies and disfranchise our friends."[23]

Johnson ultimately managed to alienate majorities on both sides of the Mason-Dixon Line. His obsessive focus on restoring states' rights to Southern whites—at the expense of anything resembling equal rights for freed slaves—empowered Confederate resistance. In response, Congressional Republicans sent more federal troops to the South, spurring local white resentment. In his final months in office, Johnson erased accountability by offering all ex-Confederates a full pardon and amnesty.[24]

When the nation needed steady, principled leadership to secure the war's gains for liberty and union, Andrew Johnson was the wrong man at the wrong time. Political reform had been resisted at a malleable moment, economic expansion in the South was stalled, and cultural integration was stillborn. Out of the chaos, white vigilante violence spread throughout the South. Defeating the KKK would be the defining challenge of the next stage of the fight for peace.

USA vs. KKK

The Ku Klux Klan grew from a secret society formed by six ex-Confederates in Pulaski, Tennessee, on Christmas Eve 1865, into a savage force for white terror.

In April 1867, the Klan named former Confederate general Nathan Bedford Forrest—who presided over the infamous slaughter of black Union troops at Fort Pillow—as "Grand Wizard" during its first national convention at the Maxwell House Hotel in Nashville.

From the Maxwell House's white tablecloths to midnight rides in white hoods, the KKK were homegrown terrorists, an organized force for hate and violence, trying to intimidate freed blacks back into subservience while accelerating a scourge of lynching that would stain the South for almost a century. But in an 1868 interview, Forrest described the KKK as a "protective political military organization"[1] that claimed as many as a half-million members throughout the South, though he lied and denied being a member himself.

The Klan offered its members the illusion of dignity and morals in their oath, which stated, "We are on the side of justice, humanity, and constitutional liberty as bequeathed to us as purity by our forefathers." They said they merely objected to "the principles of the radical party," by which they meant the party of Lincoln. They pledged mutual aid to each other, but also warned that any members who broke ranks and spoke out "shall meet the fearful penalty and traitor's doom, which is Death! Death! Death!"[2]

It was the vigilante wing of a new resistance to Reconstruction that tried to rewrite history. The mythology of the Lost Cause—popularized by a book of the same name by the former wartime editor of the *Richmond Examiner*, Edward A. Pollard—recast the Civil War as a conflict over states' rights and constitutional liberty, not slavery, while Confederate soldiers were seen as honorable patriots and defenders of the traditional Southern way of life. They denied the legitimacy of their defeat, blaming it on overwhelming numbers from invading Northern hordes. Some hoped for another war. All idolized Robert E. Lee. But U. S. Grant was on the rise.

In 1868, Grant was the unanimous pick to carry the Republican banner into the presidential election under the slogan "Let Us Have Peace," while Andrew Johnson could not even muster the support of his Democratic Party. Grant had internalized Lincoln's wisdom on winning the peace. Now Lincoln loomed even larger in death.

Observing the customs of the day, Grant spent the election in his adopted hometown of Galena, Illinois. He did not campaign or even give speeches from his front porch. While promising peace and reconciliation, the Republicans were not offering a "peace at all costs" platform. After a sensational but failed push by *The New York Herald* to have Robert E. Lee serve as Grant's vice president to "unite the North and South in a solid bond of practical union,"[3] Lincoln's friend and Speaker of the House Schuyler Colfax was tapped to be vice president, as Republicans strengthened their commitment to black voting rights.

In contrast, Democrats tacked harder to the right, running Lincoln critic and former New York governor Horatio Seymour at the top of the ticket, joined by Missouri's Francis P. Blair—a scion of Washington's influential Blair family who had become obsessed with the dangers of equal rights. He declared that the western territories should be reserved for "free white men" while railing against the "semi-barbarous race of blacks" who, he said, would "subject white women to their unbridled lust."[4] It was a fear-based campaign that ran under the slogan "The White Man's Banner."[5]

On election day, the results were surprisingly close: Grant won by only 300,000 votes, despite a nearly three-to-one victory in the electoral college. Bigotry still had a powerful constituency.

At forty-six, Grant was the youngest man elected to the presidency. On Inauguration Day, the typically bitter Andrew Johnson refused to attend the ceremony after issuing a final flurry of pardons, including three imprisoned members of the conspiracy to kill Lincoln, while granting John Wilkes Booth's family permission to claim his body.

Under a cold blue sky, surrounded by American flags, Grant took the oath of office from Chief Justice Chase and then walked to the podium at the center of the inaugural stage. "Self-possessed, as though he were at his own fireside,"[6] as *The New York Times* described, Grant took out of his pocket a speech that extended Lincoln's principles of peace to the new challenges of Reconstruction, calling for the country to confront its work "calmly, without prejudice, hate, or sectional pride, remembering that the greatest good to the greatest number is the object to be attained."[7]

His utilitarian declaration did not mean a retreat in minority rights: "The question of suffrage is one which is likely to agitate the public so long as a portion of the citizens of the nation are excluded from its privileges in any State," Grant said in his cigar-ripened voice. "The question should be settled now."

Grant declared that he would push for the ratification of the Fifteenth Amendment: "The right of citizens of the United States to vote shall not be denied or abridged by the United States or by any State on account of race, color, or previous condition of servitude." The principle was clear. The problem would lie in realizing the amendment's seemingly self-evident second clause: "The Congress shall have the power to enforce this article by appropriate legislation." Enforcement was just what Southern states were resisting with increasing violence.

The governor of North Carolina, William W. Holden, wrote Grant of the horror his state was enduring at the hands of the Klan: "An organized conspiracy is in existence in every County in the State, and its aim is to control the government," Holden wrote. "Bands of these armed men ride at night through various neighborhoods, whipping and mal-treating peaceable citizens, hanging some, burning churches and break-ing up schools which have been established for the colored people."[8]

Violence, intimidation, and fraud were the ways in which the Klan and other ex-Confederates tried to suppress the vote now that democracy was no longer rigged entirely in their favor. Between 1865 and 1870, more than 2,000 black Americans were lynched.[9]

Violence escalated in the run-up to the 1870 midterm elections, as black candidates—especially Union veterans—ran as Republicans. In South Carolina, where blacks had long outnumbered whites but for the first time could vote, Governor Robert K. Scott told Grant about scenes that "chilled my blood with horror . . . Colored men and women have been dragged from their homes at the dead hour of night and most cruelly and brutally scourged for the sole reason that they dared to exercise their own opinions upon political subjects."[10]

This was a twisted new manifestation of the prewar Southern tactic of "aggressive defensiveness," with white mob violence frequently framed as self-defense, but now bolstered by killing skills they had learned in war. A favorite tactic was to provoke a riot at Republican political rallies by starting a fistfight or firing a shot and then blaming it on blacks as an excuse for bloody escalation that could last for days.[11] There were always initial reports of "heavily armed negroes attacking a handful of harmless whites," noted foreign correspondent and future French prime minister Georges Clemenceau, but when it came time to actually tally the casualties, "a few negroes are always down, but of white men, not a trace."[12]

Despite all the murder and mayhem, they did not initially succeed in suppressing the black vote. In 1870, Joseph Rainey of Charleston, South Carolina, became the first African-American popularly elected to the House of Representatives. He joined Senator Hiram Revels, who had been appointed to Jefferson Davis's old senate seat by the Mississippi State Legislature. Their ranks were soon filled by black congressmen from Georgia, Florida, and Alabama, who would serve throughout the 1870s.

The presence of ex-slaves in the Senate and running Republican state legislatures in the deep South enraged ex-Confederates. This was not democracy but black domination, they said, and vigilante violence escalated. Seven African-American state legislators were murdered by the Klan for simply trying to serve in office. Their killers walked free.

Grant recoiled at the reports of racial violence. Lincoln's fears that disbanded armies would turn into robber bands and guerrillas[13] seemed to be coming true.

Grant swung into action, demanding enforcement legislation that gave federal judges power to oversee the resolution of contested elections by reviewing paper ballots and insisting that Congress address the violence in the South before going on their nine-month recess. Grant marched up to Capitol Hill to lobby for an anti-Klan bill, personally writing out a request for legislative action, stating that the law was necessary to "secure life, liberty, and property, and the enforcement of law, in all parts of the United States."[14] He said this was his sole priority. Congress got the message.

Congress passed the Enforcement Acts, giving the president the power to use military force and impose heavy penalties to combat domestic terrorist groups like the Klan. In a presidential proclamation, Grant explained it was his hope that "citizens of every race and color" could live in "peaceful enjoyment of the rights guaranteed to them by the Constitution."[15] Now his hope had the legal and military force behind it to make it a reality.

Grant had another tool at his disposal: the newly created Department of Justice. Previously, the attorney general was little more than a glorified White House counsel. Now there would be an independent department. While his cabinet was generally dominated by friends and congressional cronies with an eye toward personal chemistry, Grant made an inspired choice for the first independent attorney general: the forty-nine-year-old U.S. attorney from Georgia, Amos T. Akerman.

Akerman was the only former Confederate to serve in a Reconstruction cabinet—which made him a perfect choice to lead the crackdown on the KKK.

He was New Hampshire born, but a Southerner by choice—graduating from Dartmouth College, then moving to North Carolina and then Georgia to soothe his asthmatic lungs. After serving as a tutor to the children of Andrew Jackson's former attorney general, Akerman became a Southern Whig. He was opposed to secession, but joined the Confederate Army in 1864, fighting William Tecumseh Sherman's troops in their March to the Sea.

But at the war's end, Akerman became a prominent local Republican arguing for acceptance of Reconstruction in an 1868 letter republished in *The New York Times*, condemning local Democrats for being motivated by "revenge for military defeat, revenge for political disappointment and revenge for the loss of slaves."[16]

Akerman praised the "forbearance by the conquerors unprecedented in the world's history" that had spared the lives of Confederate leaders, "the common fate of leaders in an unsuccessful rebellion." Denouncing the "ignorance" that underlay the KKK, Akerman argued in favor of black voting rights, stating that "the abolition of all political distinctions founded on color, will remove effectually and forever, a conflict of the races. There is no necessary antagonism between white men and black men. It is only when one race claims what the other refuses, that the conflict exists."[17]

As attorney general, Akerman set up the new Department of Justice offices and began his legal push to eradicate the Klan, aided by an increased military presence in the South. The basic conditions of Lincoln's liberal vision of Reconstruction had to be backed up with both the force of law and firepower.

Akerman won over his new colleagues in Washington with evident intelligence and honesty—a reputation heightened by the appointment of the U.S. attorney from Kentucky, Benjamin Bristow, to serve as solicitor general. Together, they could empathize with the Southern perspective without making excuses for inexcusable actions. In turn, Southerners could not easily accuse them of Yankee discrimination.

Empathy did not mean leniency. Akerman dismissed critics who said the federal government was being too harsh, responding that Southern "malcontents" "take all kindness on the part of the Government as evidence of timidity." And he was unsparing in his moral clarity when it came to the Klan, calling it the "most atrocious organization that the civilized part of the world has ever known."[18]

The attorney general deployed the full force of his new department to crush the KKK. Integrated federal grand juries delivered more than 3,000 indictments in the first year of deployment.[19] Akerman went relatively easy on rank-and-file Klan members who confessed and repented as long as they turned in their hooded superiors. His policies resulted in more than 1,000 convictions; sixty-five Klan leaders served hard time at a federal prison in Albany, New York.[20]

It worked. In less than one year, the Klan was in retreat across the South. Mississippi Senator Adelbert Ames wrote: "As it is, the K.K.'s, cowards as they are, have for a time at least suspended their operations in all but the eastern parts of the state. Recent convictions in North Carolina and the President's action in putting a part of South Carolina under martial law has had a very subduing effect all over the South. It is perceptible here."[21]

In 1871, Congress held hearings into the Klan, with testimony from formerly enslaved men and women. "The United States never had a Truth and Reconciliation commission after slavery ended. The Klan hearings were as close as we came," reflected the scholar Henry Louis Gates. "Congress was actually listening to black people testifying about the atrocities committed against them."[22]

But progress was fleeting. Even Attorney General Akerman admitted that confronting the Klan caused him to fear for the future. "I feel greatly saddened by this business," he wrote. "It has revealed a perversion of moral sentiment among the Southern whites which bodes ill to that part of the country for this generation."[23]

Grant understood the power of having former Confederates enforce Reconstruction. His old friend James Longstreet became a Grant-backing Republican in New Orleans, serving as head of an integrated state militia, whose ranks included Thomas Morris Chester, and clashed with white vigilante groups as they tried to storm City Hall after a contested election. The legendary Confederate cavalry raider, John Mosby, ran Grant's reelection campaign in Virginia.

These loyalists were denounced by former colleagues as traitors to the Lost Cause, but they embodied Lincoln's vision of reconciliation. Deploying former Confederates to enforce national laws helped depolarize enforcement and avoided the hated carpetbagger label. But it would not be enough to cool the simmering resentments forever.

The Star-Spangled Betrayal

In 1876, as America celebrated its one hundredth birthday, voters prepared to elect a new president.

The postwar economic expansion had been gutted by a global depression sparked by an 1873 stock market collapse. Mass unemployment drained support for the Grant administration, which came under criticism for cronyism and corruption.

Exhausted by the Civil War and strained by the personal struggle to keep financially afloat, many citizens turned inward and abandoned the country's ambitious plans to protect the freedmen. "People are becoming tired of . . . abstract questions, in which the overwhelming majority of them have no direct interest," a Republican newspaper admitted. "The Negro question, with all its complications, and the reconstruction of the Southern States, with all its interminable embroilments, have lost much of the power they once wielded."[1]

As Republicans backed off Reconstruction and relented on general amnesty, they were routed in the 1874 midterm elections, with Democrats rocketing from eighty-eight to one hundred and sixty-nine seats in the House of Representatives. Fifty-nine former Confederates were now members of the U.S. Congress, comprising 77 percent of Democrats from the South.[2]

In the North, support for Reconstruction that strengthened emancipation was replaced by a focus on reconciliation with whites below the Mason-Dixon Line. In the South, Reconstruction was replaced by Redemption—a Christian-sounding name for the decidedly un-holy goal of restoring the white caste system. It was the revenge of the planter class. The Redeemers won governorships throughout the South on a platform of white supremacy and tax cuts. They slashed social spending to the bone, despite the need for rebuilding after the war, determined to defund public institutions—from schools to hospitals—where African-Americans could enjoy equal access. This was politics as war by other means.

In the election of 1876, they were able to strike a corrupt bargain with Republicans to regain power throughout the South.

Democrats had been out of power for fifteen years. Now, they nominated New York governor Samuel Tilden, continuing the Cop-perhead affinity for the South that had long existed in the Empire State. Tilden was a protégé of former president Martin Van Buren and helped establish the antislavery Free Soil Party before returning to the Democratic fold, warning that Lincoln's election would spur a civil war. Holding court in his majestic mansion overlooking Gramercy Park (now home to the National Arts Club), the life-long bachelor rose through the party ranks. When he took the courageous step of condemning the corrupt Tammany Hall political machine that con-trolled New York City, his independence was rewarded with the gov-ernorship. After one term in Albany, Tilden aimed for the presidency, running on an anti-corruption platform.

Republicans nominated three-term Ohio governor Rutherford B. Hayes, a mild-mannered abolitionist who'd been wounded in the Civil War. He was a successful Cincinnati attorney and the father of eight children with a college-educated wife. Hayes's pledge to serve a single term made him a compromise candidate at the convention.

Southern votes mattered more than ever before. In one of the great ironies in American political history, the Fifteenth Amendment dramatically increased the political power of the South through full representation in Congress and the electoral college. But this ended up disproportionately benefiting Southern whites as Black Codes and vicious intimidation tactics were deployed to deny voting rights to African-Americans.

On election day, Lincoln's tomb was raided by grave robbers

who wanted to hold the president's body for ransom. They lifted the heavy stone lid of the sarcophagus, on which was carved "With Malice Toward None," but they fled before they could steal the coffin and get it past the gates of the Oak Ridge Cemetery in Springfield.

The deeper insult to Lincoln's memory came with the election results. Tilden swept the South as well as New York and border states from Maryland to Missouri. It was almost enough to make him president.

Instead, Samuel Tilden became the first presidential candidate in American history to win the popular vote outright—by some 250,000 votes—but lose the electoral college. It threw the country into chaos. Recounts dragged on for months in Florida, South Carolina, and Louisiana amid Democratic accusations that Republicans were stealing the election. There was talk of armed partisans marching on Washington and fears of reignited violence between the states. In January 1877, Congress appointed a fifteen-member Electoral Commission comprised of five Republicans and five Democrats from Congress and five members of the Supreme Court.

The corrupt bargain that ended Reconstruction was finalized at Wormley's Hotel in Washington, a block from the White House. It was owned and operated by an African-American businessman named James Wormley, who raised funds to build a school to educate local black children named for his friend Charles Sumner, who had died in 1874. His efforts at achieving equality would be undone through the compromise brokered at his hotel.

Behind closed doors, Democrats agreed to give the presidency to Hayes in exchange for Republicans' commitment to remove the remaining troops from the South, appoint a Southern Democrat to the Hayes cabinet, and support legislation to fund industrial development in the South. In return, Democrats promised that they would not suppress civil rights or permit attacks on political enemies. But without troops to enforce this promise, it proved meaningless.

On March 2, Congress certified Hayes as the nineteenth president of the United States with a one-vote electoral college margin. Two days later, he took the oath of office in a closed-door ceremony in the

White House Red Room to reduce the chance of violent clashes at a public inauguration.

Republicans traded their principles for another presidential term. As historian C.Vann Woodward noted, "The compromise laid the political foundation for reunion. It established a new sectional truce that proved more enduring than any previous one," but "it preserved one part of the fruits of the 'Second American Revolution'—the pragmatic and economic part—at the expense of the other part—the idealistic and humanitarian part."[3]

President Hayes—forever known as "Ruther-Fraud"—felt oddly powerless to stop the rollback of black rights in the South, despite his longtime commitment to abolition. "The House was against me and I had no army," he explained, "and public sentiment demanded a change of policy."[4] Nonetheless, he tried to argue that the withdrawal of federal troops from the South represented a "fulfilment of [Lincoln's] aspirations" while conveniently forgetting his commitment to constitutional equality and black voting rights.

In the end, Reconstruction's revolutionary experiment in interracial democracy lasted a decade. As federal troops withdrew, segregation replaced slavery as the law of the South and lynching proliferated, as white hoods were replaced by White Leagues. The great migration to the North was as much a matter of seeking relative safety as economic opportunity.

Partisan politics in the South divided along racial lines as white Democrats took control of local, state, and federal offices. Through a combination of violence and legislative mechanisms like literacy tests and the poll tax, African-American men were systematically denied the right to vote throughout the South and removed from voter rolls.

The Lost Cause became part of the curriculum in Southern schools, as groups like the Daughters of the Confederacy began whitewashing the Civil War by ensuring textbooks presented a sanitized Southern version of American history.[5] Without truth, there could be no real reconciliation. An increasingly conservative Supreme Court overturned the convictions of white militia members who'd been convicted under the Enforcement Act of the slaughter of freedmen in Louisiana and declared the 1875 Civil Rights Act unconstitutional less than a decade after its passage. Eventually three ex-Confederates would sit on the Supreme Court—including Chief Justice Edward Douglass White—approving the twisted logic of "separate but equal" that gave segregation a black-robed cloak of respectability.

It happened slowly and then all at once. In Louisiana, the number of black registered voters fell from 130,000 to 5,000.[6] In 1901, there were 181,315 black men eligible to vote in Alabama. Two years later, there were less than 3,000.[7] The number of black elected officials plummeted as well—from some 1,500 at the height of Reconstruction to just a handful in the 1880s.[8] By 1902, there was not a single African-American left in Congress.

In the spring of 1884, a New Orleans lawyer and sometime journalist named William Taylor paid a visit to the home of an ex-president in permanent exile.

Imprisoned for treason but never tried in court, Jefferson Davis had lived off the largess of wealthy supporters in the North and South and now, past his sixty-fifth birthday, lived in a benefactor's mansion near Beauvoir, Mississippi, in view of the Gulf of Mexico.

He encouraged his visitor to spend the night and regaled him with assessments of the Civil War and its principal actors. When he got to Lincoln, now dead almost twenty years, Davis sighed.

"Mr. Lincoln was a vulgar joker," Davis said, "but withal he was a great man. He was wise and he was honest. He could have been of great good to the South if he had lived, and his untimely death was a great loss to us."

He fell silent for a while by the fire and then picked up his thought: "Yes, it was a great loss, for he was succeeded by a low, mean demagogue—Johnson—and a demagogue is the worst of men. Johnson was unschooled, but a man of great native ability. He had no convictions and tried to please all. Lincoln was a man of great vigor of mind, although he was plain and rough. If Mr. Lincoln had lived, the South would have had a President that understood her condition, and he would have been of more benefit to her than any other man could possibly have been. He was an honest man. His death was a great misfortune to the South."[9]

In the twilight of his life, even the traitorous Jefferson Davis was speaking truth that would have been considered heresy by many of his one-time followers.

Davis died on a visit to New Orleans in December 1889. He received a funeral procession through the French Quarter, celebrated in the South and denounced in the North, as he had been in life. By 1916, ten Southern states recognized Davis's birthday as a holiday—a practice that continues in Alabama.[10]

Robert E. Lee died two decades earlier and was even more venerated than Davis. His birthday was celebrated as a holiday in all the states of the former Confederacy, while roads and schools were named after Lee across the country, even though his own stately home, Arlington, remains a military cemetery.

Grant died in 1885, hailed as a national hero but tarred as a presidential failure after scandals in his second term. In truth, he had done more than any other president to keep Lincoln's legacy alive by ensuring the passage of the Fifteenth Amendment and crushing the KKK. At the end of his life, faced with financial ruin after a stock market crash, he finished his Civil War memoirs while dying of throat cancer at a cabin in the Adirondacks, leaving his family secure when his book became a national best seller.

Frederick Douglass outlived the other giants of his time. He died in 1895, spending his last day with Susan B. Anthony at the annual meeting of the National Women's Rights Convention. In his later lectures, he continued to rail against white supremacy and the failures of Reconstruction, preaching the strength of a diverse and inclusive "composite nation"—founded on "the principle of perfect civil equality to the people of all races and of all creeds."[11] Douglass hung a portrait of Lincoln over his fireplace at home in Washington.

Lincoln's literary acolytes continued to spread his political gospel. Noah Brooks wrote four books on Lincoln. Lincoln's private secretaries John Hay and John Nicolay worked on a ten-volume biography of their president, between stints in journalism and the diplomatic corps. Hay would go on to serve as Secretary of State to Republican Presidents William McKinley and Theodore Roosevelt, where he declared the basis of American foreign policy to be "the Monroe Doctrine and the Golden Rule."[12] Thomas Morris Chester moved from journalism to the law, traveled to Britain, and became the first African-American admitted to the English bar. He visited Russia as a guest of U.S. ambassador Cassius M. Clay and dined with the tsar. In 1873, he returned to the United States and became the first black man admitted to the Louisiana bar, warning that civilizations fall because of their failure to "be governed by public virtue and impartial justice."[13]

Walt Whitman became the grand old man of American poetry, but supported himself on the lecture circuit, giving an annual address on "The Death of Lincoln," presenting the fallen president as a hero of a historic drama that could stand one day alongside the works of Homer and Shakespeare. "The final use of a heroic-eminent life—especially a heroic-eminent death—is its indirect filtering into the nation and the race . . . then there is a cement to the whole people," Whitman said. "Strange (is it not) that battles, martyrs, agonies, blood—even assassination, should so condense—perhaps only really, lasting condense—a Nationality."[14]

By the turn of the century, almost all of those who knew Lincoln best were gone.

Mary died after decades of internal exile, unable to find a welcoming home, first trying Chicago then fleeing overseas to France and Germany. Institutionalized for a time, she seemed to many an apparition, dressed always in black, her face swollen, eyes ghostly, looking back to the past for comfort and looking forward to death.

Tad preceded her to the grave. The jolly boy who was his father's greatest joy never got to grow into full adulthood, returning from education in Europe with a faint German accent, felled by tuberculosis in Chicago at the age of eighteen.

Robert outlasted them all. As the last direct connection to the flesh and blood of Abraham Lincoln, he rose reluctantly through the ranks of the Republican Party and American business. He was a lawyer, like his father, but he possessed none of the old man's charm as he went about the grim business of legacy protection. He was enthusiastic about astronomy but became chairman of the hugely profitable Pullman Car Company and served in cabinet positions as Republican administrations strained to gain a credible connection with Lincoln.

In a twist of fate, Robert bore the bizarre historical scar of having been in close proximity to the murder of three presidents—not only in his father's dying hours, but with President James Garfield and William McKinley,[15] the last veteran of the Civil War to serve as president. On Memorial Day, 1922, seventy-eight-year-old Robert joined President Warren G. Harding at the dedication of the Lincoln Memorial.[16] He declined to speak.

The surviving Lincoln loyalists spent much of their lives evangelizing about the character of the man they'd known. Over time the stories grew bigger, shorn of the interesting deficiencies that make a man fully human. But they were witnesses: Lincoln had given them a glimpse of how goodness could be combined with greatness. Amid the pressures of war and peace, Lincoln's simple kindness transformed their idea of leadership.

The power of his example carried forward, inspiring a new generation of leaders with a similar spirit to follow his path and extend it to the world stage.

Section VI

The Fight for Peace

"The most impressive lesson to be drawn from the life and sayings of Abraham Lincoln is that battles that are won in hate provoke later conflicts, whilst those that are won by love leave no sting and are therefore permanent victories."[1]

—*Herbert Hoover*

The children of the Civil War would lead the nation in the first decades of the American century. The scars of the war and the lessons of Lincoln's leadership—now amplified into legend—would play a surprising role in America's rise, as the fight for a just and lasting peace was pursued on the global stage.

In the wake of two world wars, two paths to peace emerged. The Lincoln path focused on unconditional surrender followed by a magnanimous peace—reconciliation and rebuilding. The other path combined premature peace negotiations with a policy of retribution. Those who followed the Lincoln path succeeded in securing peace; those who didn't saw war return with a vengeance.

It's a curious fact that the two American presidents entrusted with making peace after world war—Woodrow Wilson and Harry Truman—were respectively the son and grandson of Confederate sympathizers. Their families had suffered through Reconstruction with feelings of resentment that festered even decades later. They took very different lessons from this difficult period on the domestic front, with Wilson resegregating the federal government and Truman finally desegregating the armed forces. But both men sought to apply Lincoln's wisdom in the international arena.

After America's entry into the First World War, the Treaty of Versailles would be negotiated with Allied leaders who exhaustively lauded Lincoln but failed to apply his principles to winning the peace. With a punitive policy of reparations on a Germany that never really accepted defeat, the Second World War ignited on the ashes of the First.

Determined to learn the lessons of this failure, a new generation of Americans took pains to plan for winning the peace even as the Second World War raged. Juggling competing proposals in his cabinet, President Franklin Delano Roosevelt was consistent in his insistence on unconditional surrender. After FDR's sudden death in April 1945, Harry Truman picked up the mantle and presided over the two most successful occupations in modern history, carried out by two talented but very different generals—Lucius Clay and Douglas MacArthur—who descended from opposite sides of the Mason-Dixon line.

After the war, America did not retreat from the world but expanded its engagement with the Marshall Plan, feeding and rebuilding Europe into a network of liberal democracies while containing communism in the ultimate expression of what Truman called "The Golden Rule for World Peace."

Woodrow Wilson's
Lost Cause

W oodrow Wilson was the only American president who grew up
in a state that lost a war.

"A boy never gets over his boyhood,"[1] Wilson said. His first memory was hearing someone outside the family gate say that Lincoln
had been elected and a civil war would soon start.[2] His father, Joseph,
was a pro-Confederate Presbyterian minister in Augusta, Georgia,
who gained notoriety for a widely published sermon titled "Mutual
Relations of Master and Slave as Taught in the Bible."[3] Woodrow
remembered seeing Robert E. Lee ride by his house and watched
Confederates turn the churchyard outside his bedroom into a military
hospital. In the wake of the war, he watched Union troops march Jefferson Davis through town in shackles as his mother struggled to feed
the family with soup made from whatever she could forage.

People who lose wars have long memories. To the extent that a
person's political instincts are psychology projected onto the world, Wilson's biographer August Heckscher believed that "a sense of the war's
encroaching chaos remained with him later in life, less in the form of
conscious memories than of the impulses to create unity and stability in
the world around him."[4]

This impulse to impose order on chaos was reflected in Wilson's
personal evolution. He'd grown up in the shadow of the "Lost Cause"
and entered Princeton University in 1875, alienated from his Northern

classmates. But over the course of his education, he became a political science professor who championed Lincoln's national perspective over arguments in favor of states' rights. "Because I love the South," Wilson would say, "I rejoice in the failure of the Confederacy."[5]

His early books like *Division and Reunion* and a 1901 essay in *The Atlantic* dealt with the lessons of Reconstruction: "Had Mr. Lincoln lived, perhaps the whole of the delicate business might have been carried through with dignity, good temper, and simplicity of method," Wilson wrote.[6] He also developed a keen appreciation for Lincoln's management style. "It was of the nature of Mr. Lincoln's mind to reduce complex situations to their simples, to guide men without irritating them, to go forward and be practical without being radical—to serve as a genial force which supplied heat enough to keep action warm, and yet minimized the friction . . . to put them back, defeated, but not conquered or degraded, into the old-time hierarchy of the Union."[7]

Wilson's wild ride to the presidency in 1912 was almost as abrupt as Lincoln's ascension in 1860. After just two years as a reform governor of New Jersey, taking on corrupt bosses with a progressive agenda aimed at the middle class, he reached the presidency thanks to a divided opposition, just as Lincoln had, defeating a GOP torn between incumbent William Howard Taft and former President Theodore Roosevelt's third-party challenge under the Progressive Party's "Bull Moose" banner, which Roosevelt believed advanced Lincoln's "tempered radicalism."

Wilson was a cerebral leader, compassionate yet cool: a moralist who was comfortable wielding authority. "If I cannot retain my moral influence over a man except by occasionally knocking him down," Wilson said, "if that is the only basis upon which he will respect me, then for the sake of his soul I have got occasionally to knock him down."[8]

As the only president with a doctorate in political science, Wilson focused on systemic reforms. He carried forward Lincoln's belief in internal improvements: he built rural roads and enacted corporate reforms to establish the eight-hour workday while warring against monopolies to ensure equal competition and boosting wages. He reduced tariffs and imposed the first permanent income tax, which Lincoln first introduced as a war-time measure.

But when Wilson presided over ceremonies marking fifty years since the end of the Civil War, he celebrated North–South reconciliation while ignoring the legacy of emancipation. Reflecting his own native prejudice, Wilson empowered Southern Democrats in Congress and presided over the final rollback of Reconstruction by resegregating federal government agencies. It was an immoral trade-off that tarred Wilson's legacy as a progressive while fundamentally contradicting Lincoln's vision of a more fair and free nation.

Wilson wanted to focus on domestic reforms. "It would be the irony of fate," he said days before his inauguration, "if my administration had to deal chiefly with foreign affairs."[9]

Fate had other plans. Across the Atlantic, Europe was burning, with a quarter century of peace crushed under the uncontrollable escalation of a war that would ultimately claim 40 million casualties.

Wilson's childhood experience made him recoil from war, and American tradition forbade involvement in foreign conflicts. But the world was smaller now, and when a German U-Boat sank the passenger ship *Lusitania*, public outrage compelled Wilson to join the continental conflict. He would consent to American intervention only if it was a war to end all wars, a war that would "make the world safe for democracy."

Wilson proposed a novel "peace without victory, a peace among equals" to the Senate in 1917. "Victory would mean peace forced upon a loser, a victor's terms imposed upon the vanquished," Wilson argued. "It would be accepted in humiliation, under duress, at an intolerable sacrifice, and would leave a sting, a resentment, a bitter memory upon which term of peace would rest, not permanently, but only as upon quicksand."[10]

In those lines, it is not hard to hear the personal lessons Wilson took from living on the losing side of the Civil War and Reconstruction. He was proposing a peace that would skip over victory and its humiliation and move straight to reconciliation.

A half-century after his death, Lincoln was idolized on both sides of the Atlantic. British Liberal Party prime minister David Lloyd

George grew up with a framed picture of Lincoln over the family's modest mantelpiece in Wales, and he spoke of how he was "often struck by the growth of both tenderness and stern determination in the face of Lincoln."[11]

Lloyd George tried to coax America into the war by invoking the lessons of Lincoln, calling the war a fight of freedom against "a new form of slavery, a militarist slavery" and declaring "we are fighting for a just and a lasting peace."[12]

Two months before America entered the war in 1917, Lloyd George published an essay in American newspapers to mark Lincoln's birthday, writing, "The American people under Lincoln fought not a war of conquest, but a war of liberation. We today are fighting not a war of conquest, but a war of liberation, a liberation not of ourselves alone, but of all the world . . . Lincoln held steadfastly to the belief that it was the freedom of the people to govern themselves, which was the fundamental issue at stake. So do we hold today."[13]

Lincoln proved such a powerful transatlantic symbol that French general Joseph Joffre, chairman of the Allied War Council, left Europe for two weeks during the war to lead a pilgrimage to Lincoln's tomb in Springfield shortly after the United States finally entered the war on the Allies' side.

Lincoln's image was used to rally the nation. A patriotic song called "Abraham Lincoln What Would You Do?" issued a call to arms and did brisk sales in sheet music.[14] "With Malice Toward None; With Charity For All," was used to promote American efforts to combat wartime famine in Europe, organized by an Iowa-born international mining engineer named Herbert Hoover. A classic recruiting poster that proclaimed the black 369th infantry regiment—known as the Harlem Hellfighters—"the first Americans who planted our flag on the front lines" showed Lincoln looking down approvingly from the heavens over the surrendering Huns. The Hellfighters saw more combat than any other U.S. regiment.

In September 1918, as the war raged, Czech president Tomas Masaryk visited Gettysburg and was inspired to write to Wilson, explaining, "Lincoln formulated these principles, which were to rule the internal policies of the United States. At a historical moment of worldwide significance, you, Mr. President, shaped these principles for the foreign policies of this great republic as well as those of the other nations: that the whole mankind may be liberated—that between nations, great and small, actual equality exists—that all just power of governments is derived from the consent of the governed."[15]

The parallels seemed clear to contemporaries even if strained by the fundamental difference between civil and world wars. But all this was grafted onto the conflict in an attempt to give patriotic continuity to what was then called the "Great War" in a country that had never intervened in a European war before. It appealed to Wilson's sense of destiny, and he shared Lincoln's determination to win the peace after winning the war.

But unlike Lincoln, Wilson agreed to an armistice without unconditional surrender. It was followed by six months of painful negotiations over specific treaty terms.

He could claim a moral victory: the Germans had surrendered without a single Allied troop on their soil. They did not feel defeated but felt compelled to negotiate because of the looming presence of the American army as well as the promise of a liberal peace put forward by Wilson's Fourteen Points, which recognized that "unless justice be done to others it will not be done to us." They hoped to benefit from Wilson's benign vision as opposed to the harsh retribution they expected to receive at the hands of the British and French.

But the commander of American forces, General John Pershing, warned that armistice before unconditional surrender would be a disaster: "Germany's desire is only to regain time to restore order among her forces," he wrote in a blistering memo to the Allied command. "There can be no conclusion to this war until Germany is brought to her knees."[16] Pershing was overruled, but in time the world would find that peace negotiations with a country that did not fully accept it had lost would lay the seeds for future conflict—just as Lincoln anticipated.

Nonetheless, when Wilson arrived in Paris in December 1918, two million Frenchmen lined the streets. As he passed, Wilson doffed his black top-hat with a broad, thin-lipped smile. He was hailed as a prince of peace, leading a new world power.

Inside the palatial negotiations, Wilson's idealism collided with the other Allied nations, who had suffered far greater loss of life and property than the United States. To them, the United States' mediation smacked of arrogance and ignored their real material and political needs. They wanted revenge and reparations.

Prime Minister Clemenceau of France was a onetime journalist who, as a young man, covered Reconstruction in the United States and admired the radical Republicans. He encouraged Wilson to visit the apocalyptic front lines in France only a few hours outside of Paris. The president refused, unleashing a torrent of criticism from French newspapers.

"I don't want to see the devastated regions," Wilson explained. "As a boy, I saw the country through which Sherman marched to the sea. The pathway lay right through my people's properties. I know what happened, and I know the bitterness and hatreds which were engendered. I don't want to get mad over here, because I think there ought to be one person at that peace table who isn't mad."[17]

A magnanimous peace required self-discipline. But Wilson's missionary zeal grated on the other Allied leaders who felt constrained by their constituents' demands for revenge after so much devastation.

In closed door meetings of the Big Four, Wilson would offer up "a few simple and elementary truths about right being more important than might, and justice being more eternal than force," Lloyd George wrote, briskly nodding to Wilson's invocation of Lincoln. "No doubt Europe needed the lesson, but the president forgot that the Allies had fought for nearly five years for international right and fair play . . . They were therefore impatient at having little sermonettes delivered to them."[18]

Wilson, ever the minister's son, also ventured into religious territory, explaining that Jesus Christ had articulated his vision clearly but without detailing the practical means to achieve them: "That is the reason why I am proposing a practical scheme to carry out His aims."[19]

This exasperated the irreligious Clemenceau, who threw up his perpetually gloved hands (a device to hide his eczema), saying, "How can I talk to a fellow who thinks himself the first man in two thousand years to know anything about peace on earth?"[20]

Wilson's vast vision was not tempered by Lincoln's modesty or gradualism. He wanted nothing less than to remake the world. The mechanism he envisioned was a League of Nations that would sub-sume unchecked self-interest in a broad international network of in-terdependence, committing its members to the security of all.

But Wilson's increasingly partisan impulses made winning the peace more difficult. In a display of hubris, he refused to invite Re-publicans to join his delegation at the Paris Peace Talks, undercutting essential bipartisan support for the League of Nations in the Sen-ate. Wilson's refusal to compromise with Senate Republicans on key provisions would ultimately doom the treaty when it came time for ratification at home in the United States.

Weakened by what was believed to be a secret bout with the Spanish influenza pandemic in Paris, Wilson became brittle and er-ratic, so doggedly focused on the League's creation that he gave up key elements of the Fourteen Points—including dropping opposition to crippling reparations from Germany, totaling more than $400 billion in today's dollars.[21]

This was a painful trade-off, but a popular position at the time. A young artillery captain from Independence, Missouri, named Harry Truman wrote back to his best girl, Bess, "When Austria begs our grand President for the privilege of peace it really looks like some-thing. I'm for peace but that gang should be given a bayonet peace and be made to pay for what they've done to France."[22] On the last day of the war, Truman still struggled with bloodlust, writing: "It's a shame we can't go in and devastate Germany . . . and scalp a few of their old men, but I guess it will be better to make them work for France and Belgium for fifty years."[23] Revenge was in the air, but rep-arations would have to do.

The other Allied powers argued that Germany was wealthy and suffered no battles on its own soil. While the Hun would lose land through partitions—including valuable coal producing regions—they were still an industrialized nation and it was believed they could afford to pay almost open-ended reparations.

Critics like British economist John Maynard Keynes condemned this idea as a cruel "Carthaginian Peace"[24] and predicted that inflation would spike and reparations would not be delivered while resentment would fester. "If Germany is to be 'milked,' she must not first of all be ruined," he argued. In addition, Keynes warned that the decision to allow Germany to maintain even a small standing army of 100,000 troops could provide a push-off point for future conflict, while the means for enforcing the terms of the treaty were too weak, opening the door to further discord.

Wilson insisted that it was the best deal that could be achieved, but aides who read the final draft felt a deep foreboding. "Hate and revenge" was what Herbert Hoover—now coordinating European food relief for the Wilson administration—saw coursing through the treaty. "If there was to be lasting peace, the people had to be influenced into paths of peace; they had to be given an alternative more advantageous than war, and, at the same time, they had to have a definite reminder not to do it again," Hoover reflected in his book *The Problems of Lasting Peace*. "It required a delicate balance of tolerance and grim justice. But hate, fear and revenge overweighed the scale. By device after device, they appeared in the Treaty of Versailles."[25]

Unable to sleep, Hoover went for a predawn walk through the streets of Paris and bumped into Keynes and South Africa's Jan Smuts, who were also on a troubled walkabout. "We agreed that the consequences of many parts of the proposed Treaty would ultimately bring destruction," Hoover wrote. "We also agreed that we would do what we could among our own nationals to point out the dangers."[26]

But after six months of negotiations and more than a thousand days of a war that killed some 20 million soldiers and civilians, there was a desperate need for peace. The Treaty was signed at Versailles in the Hall of Mirrors. The celebrations belied a deeper despair.

"This is not a peace" declared Marshal Ferdinand Foch, the Supreme Allied Commander. "It is an armistice for twenty years."[27] He proved to be almost precisely right.

Deploying the
Lincoln Legend

As the Civil War generation faded, the Lincoln legend grew. Occupying the misty ground between folk hero and secular saint, the myth of Lincoln was deployed to reunite the nation, overcome the Great Depression, and defeat tyranny overseas.

America's first transcontinental road was called the Lincoln Highway. Proclaimed as "a most fitting and useful monument to the memory of Lincoln,"[1] more than 2,000 concrete markers topped with a bronze medallion featuring Abe's face were placed along the road, providing a paved path from Times Square to the Golden Gate Bridge, connecting the country via small towns, coast to coast.

For generations struggling to rise up from poverty, Lincoln was lionized as an exemplar of the ability of any honest and hardworking American to climb the ladder of success, despite setbacks. Lincoln's name was attached to a historically black college in Philadelphia and another in a poor white Appalachian community. Memorization of the Gettysburg Address's 272 words became standard in public schools. Lincoln's image was emblazoned on stained glass windows in churches from Washington, D.C., to Detroit,[2] as an example of Christian ethics in action, a leader who met hate with love.

Lincoln even made an early leap into celluloid, featured in more than seventy silent films,[3] though his character was simplified to represent national reconciliation at the expense of emancipation. The storyteller had become part of the story.

On the seventy-fifth anniversary of Gettysburg in 1938, President Franklin Delano Roosevelt rolled onto the Pennsylvania battlefield to dedicate a peace memorial in the national park where 50,000 men had fallen.

It would be the final reunion of the living veterans of the Civil War, with 1,845 on hand—including twenty-five veterans of the battle itself. With an average age of ninety-four, the old men—blue and gray, black and white—dressed in their old uniforms with medals pinned to their chests and shook hands over the stone wall, the scene of some of the bloodiest fighting at what was "the high tide of the Confederacy."

Hobbling on canes, they grinned and shouted "hello" for the cameras, reenacting rebel yells, and greeting one another like long-lost college classmates rather than former combatants who'd been trained to kill each other.

After a military parade and concert, FDR spoke as the cameras whirred and the aged veterans strained to hear. "Men who wore the Blue, and men who wore the Grey are here together, a fragment spared by time. They are brought here by the memories of old divided loyalties, but they meet here in united loyalty to a united cause which the unfolding years have made it easier to see," Roosevelt said. "All of them we honor, not asking under which flag they fought then— thankful that they stand together under one flag now."[4]

Then the president pivoted to the question of preserving peace with an intensity usually reserved for war. "Lincoln was a commander in chief in this old battle; he wanted above all things to be commander in chief of the new peace. He understood that battle there must be; that when a challenge to constituted government is thrown down, the people must in self-defense take it up; that the fight must be fought through to a decision so clear that it is accepted as being beyond recall. But Lincoln also understood that after such decision, democracy should seek peace through a new unity. For democracy can only keep alive if the settlement of old difficulties clears the ground and transfers energies to face new responsibilities . . . That is why Lincoln—commander of a people as well as of an army—asked that his battle end 'with malice towards none with charity for all.'"[5]

After the speech, one veteran from each army lit the eternal flame of the monument together using the beams of the setting sun re-fracted through a looking glass.

Even then, Roosevelt knew that a new world war was coming. He also knew the American people were not ready to accept it. Wilson's hard-won League of Nations had been rejected by the Senate, and by 1937, a stunning 70 percent of Americans believed that U.S. involvement in the First World War had been a mistake.[6] With America still caught in the grip of the Great Depression, many argued this was a time to stay focused on our domestic needs and to put "America First," which became the name of a powerful isolationist group. The U.S. military had been allowed to atrophy after the First World War in an attempt to enjoy peace at the expense of self-defense. But this hunt for a peace dividend proved costly.

Awash in nostalgia for lost power, Germans nurtured the myth of their own lost cause. They elevated notions of racial superiority, based on blood and soil. In their search for someone to blame for their loss, they focused on Jewish-Germans, longtime neighbors now blamed for an international finance system that crippled their country via reparations and war debt. In addition to the ancient virus of anti-Semitism, the threat of communism provided an urgency behind the rise of the populist and nationalist Nazi Party. A corporal from the First World War named Adolf Hitler rose because of fiery speeches and a narcissism that was mistaken for fearlessness. At first, Hitler was dismissed as an anti-Semitic crank, a fool with a Charlie Chaplin mustache, who duped his fellow veterans into believing he would deliver them from disgrace. But in the chaos of the Weimar Republic, awash in inflation and licentiousness, more men rallied around his message and the trappings of militarism that gave them the illusion of dignity and morals.

Hitler was seen by some elites as a useful idiot who could rally workers to stop the spread of communism. Accordingly, he was catapulted into a coalition government. In the summer of 1934, Hitler seized complete control, requiring a personal oath of obedience by the military and adopting the title of Fuhrer. A crackdown on civil liberties began, but it was ignored by people enjoying renewed prosperity from massive public works projects. He rebuilt the German military in contravention of the Treaty of Versailles, and his troops marched into the demilitarized zone of the Rhineland, to the cheers of Germans and the impotent gaze of Western powers who had no appetite for another war.

Stern diplomatic statements of disapproval did nothing to deter Hitler's aggression. Harsh terms, weakly enforced, were the worst of both worlds when it came to enforcing peace.

In September 1938, Germany invaded Czechoslovakia. The next month, as British prime minister Neville Chamberlain tried to negotiate with Hitler in Munich, Robert Sherwood's *Abe Lincoln in Illinois* opened on Broadway. The play would go on to win the Pulitzer Prize; it presented the tale of a pre-presidential Lincoln and recast some of Lincoln's own lines along with made-up dialogue, meant to resonate with a nation still climbing out of the Great Depression at home while preparing for conflict with totalitarians abroad.

In a climactic scene set at the Lincoln–Douglas debates, Sherwood framed the argument over slavery with an echo of the New Deal as "the old issue between human rights and property rights" and he took on Stephen Douglas's cynical argument for popular sovereignty over slavery in words that addressed the isolationist impulse in America.

"'Let each state mind its own business . . . why stir up trouble?'" Sherwood's Lincoln asked. "This is the complacent policy of indifference to evil—and that policy I cannot but hate. I hate it because of the monstrous injustice of slavery itself. I hate it because it deprives our republic of its just influence in the world, enables the enemies of free institutions everywhere to taunt us as hypocrites and causes the real friends of freedom to doubt our sincerity, and especially because it forces so many good men among ourselves into an open war with the very fundamentals of civil liberty, denying the good faith of the Declaration of Independence and insisting that there is no right principle of action except self-interest. There can be no distinction in the definition of liberty as between one section and another, one class and another, one race and another. A House divided against itself cannot stand!"[7]

As Raymond Massey, the gargantuan actor who played Lincoln in the stage and film versions, explained, "If you substitute the word dictatorship for the word slavery throughout Sherwood's script, it becomes electric with meaning for our time."[8] After winning his Pulitzer Prize, Sherwood went on to serve as a speechwriter for FDR, where he remained for the duration of the war.

In the period between world wars, Lincoln's presence grew on film, from early silent epics like D. W. Griffith's *Abraham Lincoln* to John Ford's *Young Mr. Lincoln* starring Henry Fonda, and he served as a patron saint of civic religion in Frank Capra's *Mr. Smith Goes to Washington,* starring Jimmy Stewart. He was an avatar of decency and homespun dignity.

But Lincoln was still controversial in a segregated America. The military had taken on a decidedly Southern flavor with the construction of military bases throughout the South, in many cases named after Confederate generals like Fort Bragg, Fort Benning, and Fort Hood. Mentioning Lincoln in military communities was considered disrespectful to Southern compatriots. When the director Frank Capra was recruited to film wartime movies to rally the troops, he was asked by military brass to avoid references to "Lincoln, emancipation, or any race leaders or friends of the Negro."[9]

Those generals might have been fighting the last war: a 1945 poll found that Lincoln was named as one of the "two or three greatest men in American history" by 44 percent of Southern whites, compared to 61 percent of their Northern counterparts.[10] Only a third of Americans had been alive in the late 1800s. The scars of war were still visible, but they were less personal and more an inherited prejudice.

After Pearl Harbor, Lincoln was drafted into the war effort by newspaper editorial boards to invest historic meaning into the conflict that was not necessarily evident to those fighting and dying at the time. In wartime cartoons, Lincoln was shown looking down on a little Hitler, comparing Nazi demands for more territory with demands for the extension of slavery, sympathizing with FDR in the Oval Office ("You have a greater task than I had. Slavery must be removed from the whole earth.") and overseeing the smashing of a Nazi swastika with an ax ("Let Us Strive to Finish the Work We Are In"). His image was used on government posters that hung in train stations and post offices across the country, urging everything from recruitment to the sale of war bonds. In London, a statue of Lincoln stood outside Parliament, the king quoted Lincoln in his 1942 Christmas Day broadcast,[11] and Lincoln's birthday was celebrated with a special service at Westminster Abbey in 1944.[12] In the Congressional Record, Lincoln was mentioned 131 times during the war years while *The New York Times* printed 215 articles about Lincoln between 1940 and 1944.[13] The memory of Lincoln gave courage and comfort in times of crisis.

Exhaustively lauded in poetry, theater, and film, Lincoln made his major classical musical debut in 1942, with the first performance of Aaron Copland's *Lincoln Portrait,* which broke down barriers between the spoken word and the symphony, as well as popular culture and classical music.

It was commissioned shortly after Pearl Harbor by the Russian-born American conductor Andre Kostelanetz "to mirror the magnificent spirit of our country." This was Copland's signature move. The Brooklyn-born son of Russian immigrants was Jewish and gay, possessing a populist patriotism that infused compositions from *Fanfare for the Common Man* to *Appalachian Spring.* He believed that "music no less than machine guns had a part to play and can be a weapon in the battle for a free world."[14]

Copland decided to let Lincoln's words speak for themselves against the backdrop of a full orchestra, infused with melodies from folk songs. "I wanted to suggest something of the mysterious sense of fatality that surrounds Lincoln's personality," Copland wrote, "something of his gentleness and simplicity of spirit."[15]

"Fellow citizens, we cannot escape history," is the first line from Lincoln in the composition. Copland chose texts that resonated with the international struggle of the time: "It is the eternal struggle between two principles—right and wrong—throughout the world . . . As I would not be a slave, so I would not be a master. This expresses my idea of democracy. Whatever differs from this, to the extent of the difference, is no democracy."

As American dead began to pile up in the early months of their entry into war, Copland's closing lines from the Gettysburg Address offered durable inspiration: "That from these honored dead we take

increased devotion to that cause for which they gave the last full measure of devotion. That we here highly resolve that these dead shall not
have died in vain. That this nation under God shall have a new birth
of freedom and that government of the people, by the people, and for
the people shall not perish from the earth."

Lincoln Portrait debuted in Cincinnati, Ohio, in May 1942, as Japanese and American forces clashed in the Coral Sea, Rommel's Afrika
Korps stormed through North Africa, and German U-boats struck
freighters in the St. Lawrence River in North America. With a world
at war, no place seemed safe.

It was greeted as an instant American classic. During the composition's national radio debut, the poet and Lincoln biographer Carl
Sandburg introduced the piece in his gravel road baritone, asking the
audience to note "how closely Lincoln's words sometimes fit into our
own needs today," making it clear that "the ideas of Lincoln fight the
ideas of Hitler."[16]

A Plan to Win
the Peace

I n the philosophy of war there is no principle more sound than this:
that the permanence of peace depends, in a large degree, upon the
magnanimity of the victor."

This was Lincoln's wisdom, but it was written by Colonel Irwin
Hunt in the official report on postwar military governance after the
First World War.[1] In 1942, the idea was finally being put into action
as the U.S. government tasked a group of men from the Department
of War, the Department of State, and the Department of the Treasury
to begin postwar planning behind closed doors, drawing on Hunt's
report.

They would attempt to apply the lessons of the First World War in
the middle of the Second World War to stop a Third.

The Department of State group was led by Under Secretary
Sumner Welles, a descendant of Lincoln's contemporaries: Senator
Charles Sumner and Gideon Welles. But unlike his namesake during
the Civil War, Sumner Welles favored a liberal peace with Germany,
believing that the harsh terms at Versailles created the conditions that
led to the rise of Hitler.

Learning from this experience—and drawing on outside advisers
from New York's Council on Foreign Relations—the postwar plan-
ners supported occupation, complete disarmament, reeducation, and
the prosecution of war criminals. But they opposed deep reparations

in the belief born of experience that they spurred instability, inflation, and resentment.

Secretary of the Treasury Henry Morgenthau thought they were making a historic mistake. An FDR confidant and wealthy Hudson River Valley neighbor, Morgenthau favored a far more punitive plan. He believed in German collective guilt, arguing that the entire society—not just high-level Nazis—should be made to feel the permanent pain that came from starting two world wars within three decades. Roosevelt seemed sympathetic in private conversation. Morgenthau believed that the failure of Versailles had been too few reparations that were unevenly enforced, while the Allies' lack of will in stopping Hitler's rearmament for fear of escalation only encouraged his aggression.

With more than a trace of anti-Semitism, his cabinet critics claimed that Morgenthau's Jewish heritage clouded his judgment. But Morgenthau's Treasury team was not deterred. They put forward a forceful counterproposal, recommending the destruction of all German industry that could be used to rearm, executing war criminals without trial, and generally returning Germany to an agrarian past, while dismissing concerns this could lead to mass starvation. They titled their recommendations report with all the subtlety of a sledgehammer: *The Program to Prevent Germany from Starting a World War III.*[2]

Roosevelt encouraged competition in his cabinet to the point of confusion. Aides with opposing views would leave the Oval Office convinced that the president agreed with them. In some meetings on postwar Reconstruction, he would fixate on the Prussian militarism he blamed for the world wars. "When Hitler and the Nazis go out," he said in 1943, "the Prussian military clique must go with them. The war-breeding gang of militarists must be rooted out of Germany—and out of Japan—if we are to have any real assurance of future peace."[3] In other conversations, the president would pump the brakes, telling Secretary of State Cordell Hull, "I dislike making detailed plans for a country we do not yet occupy."[4]

But FDR was steadfast in his insistence on unconditional surrender from Germany and Japan. It was official Allied policy, outlined in an unconditional surrender declaration issued by Roosevelt and Churchill at a 1943 summit in Casablanca. They would not repeat the mistakes of the First World War's armistice, which they had experienced as young men serving in the Lloyd George and Wilson administrations.

In a July press conference, flanked by his press secretary Stephen Early—a direct descendant of Confederate general Jubal Early—FDR made it clear he was drawing upon Lincoln's legacy in the Civil War by breezily retelling the story of Appomattox.

"There has been a good deal of complaint among some of the nice, high-minded people about unconditional surrender," Roosevelt said. "They complain that it is too tough and too rough. I will explain it a little this way: Back in 1865, Lee was driven into a corner back of Richmond, at Appomattox Court House . . ." The president then launched into a story of how Grant insisted on unconditional surrender and Lee initially resisted, saying he needed provisions for his troops and assurance that they would be able to hold on to their horses.

After some back and forth in this version, Lee relented, saying: "'All right. I surrender,' and tendered his sword to Grant. Grant said, 'Bob, put it back. Now, do you unconditionally surrender?' Lee said, 'Yes.' Then Grant said, 'You are my prisoners now. Do you need food for your men?' Lee said, 'Yes. I haven't got more than enough for one meal more.' Then Grant said, 'Now, about those horses that belong to the Confederate officers. Why do you want them?' Lee said, 'We need them for the spring plowing.' Grant said, 'Tell your officers to take the animals home and do the spring plowing.'

"There you have unconditional surrender," FDR gamely explained. "I have given you no new term."

This strategy was essential because "practically all Germans deny the fact they surrendered in the last war, but this time they are going to know it." After their surrender, FDR said, "we will help them get back on their feet physically. We don't believe in wholesale starvation. But it doesn't mean that we will send the first spare food that we have into Germany. We will take care of our own and our allies first."[5]

Roosevelt's vision for winning the peace was a work in progress, animated by the idea of extending the New Deal to postwar Europe. He called for a version of the Tennessee Valley Authority to be built on the continent to aid electrification and reduce dependence on coal producing regions that had often been a source of continental conflict. But Roosevelt's juggling act resulted in some dropped balls, including his belief that he could deal with Stalin's expansionist ambitions through the power of his personality when the war ended.

While FDR's cabinet squabbled and the president delayed making decisions beyond the horizon of winning the war, the military took the initiative to train a new generation to win the peace. In his post–World War I report, Colonel Irwin Hunt wrote that "in none of the service schools devoted to the higher training of officers has a single course on the nature or scope of military government been established."[6] This would now be remedied.

In the spring of 1942, the School of Military Government opened at the University of Virginia. It offered a curriculum in nation building across political, economic, and social spheres: not just government administration but legal affairs, banking, public health, public safety, transportation, and education. In addition to military men, the school admitted lawyers, doctors, and engineers. With a specific eye toward the occupation of Germany, Italy, and Japan, they anticipated everything from rebuilding infrastructure to the protection of art and archives, producing reference manuals to establish best practices.[7]

Their classes drew on U.S. experience in Reconstruction from the post–Civil War South to unhappy imperialist experiments in Cuba and the Philippines. Beyond steps to secure peace by suppressing guerilla forces, there was a focus on political and economic stabilization. One lecture drew on the difficulties of General Godfrey Weitzel in securing Richmond. Other lessons drew on Lincoln's suspension of habeas corpus, the use of military courts during the Civil War, and the need for applying Lincoln's Lieber Code to postwar tribunals.

In four years, more than one thousand students graduated from the program. It was expanded to satellite programs offered at campuses including Yale, Harvard, Stanford, Princeton, and the University of Michigan.[8] It produced dozens of manuals that would guide successful postwar occupations.

Soon two defeated Axis powers half a world apart would provide a real-world test for the students of the School of Military Government, while two U.S. commanders—General Lucius Clay in Germany and General Douglas MacArthur in Japan—would take very different approaches to winning the peace, but both inspired by Lincoln's vision of unconditional surrender followed by a magnanimous peace.

Denazification and Democratization

Harry S. Truman had been vice president for just eighty-two days when FDR suddenly died of a cerebral hemorrhage in Warm Springs, Georgia, in April 1945—eighty years after Lincoln's assassination. The former Missouri senator had been kept in the dark about military plans—including the development of the nuclear bomb. But with his battlefield promotion in the final stretch of the war, Truman set a brisk and decisive executive tone that contrasted with FDR.

In July 1945, Truman toured the wreckage of Berlin in advance of the Potsdam Conference. Wearing a Stetson in the back of a convertible, he saw the streets lined with German refugees—old men, women and children—carrying their belongings, trying to escape capture by Soviet troops. Millions of Germans were now homeless. It reminded him of the stories he'd heard from his Confederate-sympathizing family about the aftermath of the Civil War in the South, when they'd been "forced off the farm by Yankee laws," and wandered "along the hot Missouri roads until they found a safe place to stay."[1] He hated the Nazis, but he identified with the displaced.

"Having seen how the Treaty of Versailles bred political and economic conditions that brought Hitler to power, Truman favored a lenient peace that might lead to a self-supporting, non-militaristic, democratic Germany," wrote Robert J. Donovan, who covered the

Truman White House for the *Los Angeles Times*. "Otherwise, the administration feared that postwar impoverishment might either drive the Germans into the hands of the Soviets or make German survival a burden on American taxpayers."[2]

Fascism and communism were often seen as ideological opposites, but Harry Truman understood they were two sides of the same totalitarian coin. As a Democrat from the "Show Me" state, Truman would trust but verify. After meeting Joseph Stalin—and noting the dictator's disconcerting habit of doodling wolf's heads during negotiations—he realized that the Soviet leader was a man who could not be trusted.

During the reconstruction of Germany and Japan, most of Truman's attention was focused on stopping the surge of communism in Eastern Europe and Asia. But he also understood that stability, economic growth, and liberal democracy proved the most durable argument against the Soviets. It was a global application of the lesson Lincoln learned in the domestic politics of war and peace: overreach courts a backlash and can defeat the broader cause of progress.

"You can't be vindictive after a war," Truman reflected years later. "I know what it means to lose. My own family had been on the losing side in the Civil War. I remember my grandmother telling me stories about the Yankee redlegs who raided her farm and shot her chickens and butchered her pigs and set fire to the hay and the barns ... My mother hated the Yankees till she died, and I didn't want hate to be this war's gift to the future."[3] Truman's view was shared by General Lucius Clay, who was now in charge of day-to-day operations in postwar Germany.

Clay was a descendant of Lincoln's hero, Henry Clay, and the son of a three-term Georgia senator who had succeeded Confederate general John B. Gordon. The Clay family were not slave owners, but their first-born son was named after the Confederate vice president, Alexander Stephens. Their youngest son, Lucius, was born thirty-three years after the end of the Civil War at a time when its memory still loomed large in Clay's native Marietta. "I don't know whether it affected me," he said, "but the Civil War was always with us when I was growing up."[4]

Trained as a member of the Army Corps of Engineers, Clay missed service in the First World War but supervised the construction of public works programs during the New Deal. "He was the kind of man who could run General Motors or General Eisenhower's armies," said Secretary of State James Byrnes.[5] Clay's organizational skills kept him behind the front lines, to his great dismay, but when the war was over, Ike put the engineer in charge of the military government that would oversee the occupation and rebuilding, after telling the German people "we come as conquerors, but not as oppressors."[6]

"We are not here as Carpetbaggers," Clay announced at one of his first regular press conferences. While the comment sent Germans scrambling for translation, it meant more to Clay than just the postwar profiteers who descended onto the South. Clay was determined to apply the lessons of history to the rebuilding of Germany, even at the risk of contradicting cabinet officials like Secretary Morgenthau.

When Clay arrived in Berlin, any triumphalism was quickly drummed out of him. "It was like a city of the dead," wrote Clay. "I decided then and there never to forget that we were responsible for the government of human beings."[7]

"Technically, our instructions prevented us from doing anything to help the Germans financially or economically," he recalled. "I began to think about this thing in terms of reconstruction, in a period when even to talk about reconstructing Germany would have been enough to get you hung on the ellipse in Washington."[8]

Clay found inspiration for Reconstruction in Lincoln's vision: "I tried to think of the kind of occupation the South would have had if Abraham Lincoln had lived," he said.[9]

Clay's first priority was practical. Cities had been reduced to rubble, roads lined with burned cars and tanks. There were thirty-five bridges down across the Rhine, crippling commerce, and Clay set about clearing the waterway so trade could begin to flow again.

With Germany essentially divided between Soviet and Anglo-American control, Clay argued that a strong and prosperous Germany would help stop the spread of communism in those early days of the Cold War. For freedom to succeed, people needed to see how liberal democracy could improve their lives. "A self-supporting and self-responsible Germany is essential to the restoration of stability," Clay said, "and without a stable Europe lasting peace is impossible."[10]

But the orders from the joint chiefs of staff stood in contrast:

"The principal Allied objective is to prevent Germany from ever again becoming a threat to the peace of the world. Essential steps in the accomplishment of this objective are the elimination of Nazism and militarism in all their forms, the immediate apprehension of war criminals for punishment, the industrial disarmament and demilitarization of Germany, with continuing control over Germany's capacity to make war, and the preparation for an eventual reconstruction of German political life on a democratic basis."[11]

This was a neat summation of what became known as the four Ds: demilitarization, denazification, deindustrialization, and democratization.

Demilitarization was straightforward. The German war machine would be dismantled—from the arms-making industrialists to the underlying Prussian military culture. The terms of surrender required that "all German land, air and naval forces"—including support structures such as military schools and veterans' organizations—would be "completely and finally abolished."

This reflected a lesson learned from the failures of Versailles. German security would be established by the occupying allied forces.

Denazification required ripping the Third Reich up from the roots. The war crimes trials at Nuremberg captured the world's attention by bringing the Nazi leadership to justice for "crimes against peace" and "crimes against humanity," refusing to spare Hitler's top henchmen from accountability for their actions, including execution. With the prosecution led by U.S. Supreme Court Justice Robert Jackson, the proceedings drew on Lincoln's Lieber Code to define war crimes. The evidence presented at the trial—and America's insistence that German journalists cover the proceedings—was designed to ensure that future generations could not dismiss the horrors of the Holocaust as Allied propaganda.

But it was more difficult to ensure that the next layer of Nazi officials—millions of officers, bureaucrats, and business enablers—would not be allowed to retain or regain positions of power. This created a practical challenge: how could Nazi civilians be identified?

The process required sifting through Nazi files to establish guilt. It was painstaking work that the Americans pursued far more aggressively than the English or French in neighboring sectors. Special divisions were created to investigate and remove Nazis from positions of influence, deploying questionnaires and tribunals. Their efforts were aided by the discovery of Nazi Party records rescued from a dump before they were turned into pulp.

Former Nazis were forbidden from running for office or receiving employment beyond the level of a manual laborer. Eventually, the vetting process was passed to the German people to complete. "I had become convinced that this real task could not be accomplished by occupation officials without at some time making martyrs out of those we sought to condemn in the eyes of their countrymen," Clay explained. "The long-range job was one for the Germans to undertake."[12]

This was not without controversy, even in the American ranks. General George Patton blew up his legendary career when he questioned the wisdom of denazification: "More than half the German people were Nazis and we would be in a hell of a fix if we removed all Nazi party members from office," Patton said in his first on-the-record press conference as military governor of Bavaria. "The way I see it, this Nazi thing is very much like a Democratic and Republican election fight. The thing was that these damn Nazis got the other people by the scruff of the neck and the other Germans just didn't have the guts to go back."[13]

The statement's equivalence was politically untenable and morally indefensible. Patton—the California-born grandson and namesake of a Confederate colonel—was transferred by his old friend Eisenhower to a desk job, compiling the official record of the war. He would die in a Jeep crash three months later.

But the essential functions of government could not be abandoned without compounding postwar chaos. German soldiers could not be wisely sent home without any promise of future employment. The expertise required to maintain power stations and public sanitation could not be abandoned while looking for the perfect "Good German" to be trained up to do the job. Clay recruited college professors with relevant expertise who'd been relatively insulated from the Nazi regime; he also retained lower-level civil servants whose records demonstrated they had not been active party members. For all the practical challenges, Clay believed that "we came out better by getting an entirely new and different group of people into the political life of Germany."[14]

Deindustrialization looked simple from Washington, D.C. But despite Secretary of the Treasury Morgenthau's wishes, Germany could not be taken back to the seventeenth century. While the steel, coal, and munitions industries were largely dismantled, and equipment exported to neighboring nations, German workers needed jobs or it would invite further instability and create an opening for communists. "There is no choice between becoming a Communist on 1500 calories and a believer in democracy on 1000 calories," Clay remarked. "You cannot build real democracy in an atmosphere of distress and hunger."[15]

The economic constraints ordered by Washington were dismissed by Clay's special adviser for finance, Lewis Douglas, as being the work of "economic idiots."[16]

Clay and his advisers simply sidestepped the less sensible economic directives, taking advantage of the generous leeway provided to generals on the ground. American cigarettes were being used as currency in postwar Germany. The black market thrived. The specter of inflation reared its head, bringing back unwelcome memories of the Weimar Republic as well as Clay's family's stories about the suffering after Confederate currency became useless. In response, Clay replaced worthless Reichsmarks with Deutsche Marks at a ratio of 10 to 1, capped at 60 Deutsche Marks per citizen,[17] stabilizing the value of the currency, while cutting taxes on middle class Germans and spurring investment. This was well outside the U.S. Army's core competency, but it worked.

Democratization was the goal. Experts warned that this would take time. After all, the German people had been brainwashed by Hitler and burned by the democratic process he used to achieve complete power. But Lucius Clay did not believe in moving slowly.

Judicial reform was toward the top of Clay's agenda. Reestablishing the integrity of the courts—with a commitment to impartial justice—was essential to ensuring that other reforms would be built on a stable foundation.

President Abraham Lincoln in 1864. "Of all the men I ever met," said General William Tecumseh Sherman, "he seemed to possess more of the elements of greatness, combined with goodness, than any other."

Lincoln taking the oath of
office from his Republican rival,
Supreme Court Chief Justice
Salmon P. Chase, at the Second
Inauguration, in a front-page
illustration from *Harper's Weekly*.

Lincoln stands at the center of the stage,
reading his Second Inaugural Address,
proclaiming "with malice toward none,
with charity for all"—while the man
who would assassinate him in forty-one
days, John Wilkes Booth, overlooks the
ceremony to the right.

The last known photo of Lincoln, taken on
the White House portico, two days after his
Second Inauguration. Note the clean-shaven
cheeks, which turned Lincoln's famous beard
into a broad goatee.

THE REPUBLICAN PARTY GOING TO THE RIGHT HOUSE.

In the 1860 campaign, Republicans were depicted as a party of radical special interests carrying Lincoln into an insane asylum.

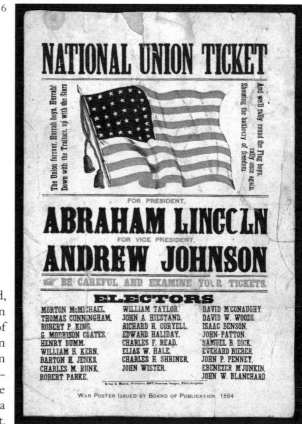

As the Civil War raged, Lincoln ran for reelection under the banner of the National Union Party, a centrist–fusion ticket balanced by vice-presidential nominee Andrew Johnson, a Tennessee Democrat.

Lincoln and his son Tad. "I believe he was the best companion Mr. Lincoln ever had," said bodyguard William Crook, "one who always understood him and whom he always understood."

Elizabeth Keckley was the first family's seamstress and friend. A biracial business owner, she purchased her freedom from slavery a decade earlier and lost her only son in the war.

By 1865, Frederick Douglass was the most famous orator in America. "Viewed from the genuine abolition ground, Mr. Lincoln seemed tardy, cold, dull, and indifferent," Douglass later reflected. "But measuring him by the sentiment of his country, a sentiment he was bound as a statesman to consult, he was swift, zealous, radical, and determined."

The poet Walt Whitman was a wartime nurse and great admirer of Lincoln. Looking back on the president's murder, Whitman wrote: "Strange (is it not) that battles, martyrs, agonies, blood, even assassination, should so condense—perhaps only really, lasting condense—a Nationality."

11

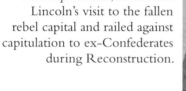

Thomas Morris Chester, a pioneering black war correspondent for *The Philadelphia Press*, chronicled Lincoln's visit to the fallen rebel capital and railed against capitulation to ex-Confederates during Reconstruction.

12

A contemporary sketch of Lincoln greeting Union soldiers at City Point, Virginia, drawn by Civil War soldier Charles Wellington Reed.

13

During the Civil War, 180,000 Black soldiers served in the Union Army. Twenty-five won the Medal of Honor. This is the 4th U.S. Colored Infantry, which participated in the siege of Petersburg. Lincoln came to believe that the "sight of fifty thousand armed and drilled black soldiers upon the banks of the Mississippi would end the rebellion at once."

The *River Queen* was a speedy side-wheeled steamship that functioned as an aquatic Air Force One during the final months of the war.

The Peacemakers by G. P. A. Healy shows Lincoln conferring with Sherman, Grant, and Porter aboard the *River Queen* at City Point. The title comes from the Sermon on the Mount: "Blessed are the peacemakers: for they shall be called the children of God." It hangs in the White House today.

Lincoln greeting Grant at his headquarters in Petersburg, Virginia, at the end of a nine-month siege. They discussed terms for Lee's surrender and magnanimous plans for Reconstruction on the front porch.

Lincoln walking into Richmond, holding Tad's hand on the boy's twelfth birthday— April 4, 1865.

Lincoln stopped on the front steps of the Confederate White House and spoke to the jubilant crowd of freedmen and women: "Although you have been deprived of your God-given rights by your so-called masters, you are now as free as I am . . . for God created all men free, giving to each the same rights of life, liberty and the pursuit of happiness."

Lincoln toured war-torn Richmond to riotous cheers. Before departing, Lincoln told the Union commander, "If I were in your place, I'd let 'em up easy."

Ulysses S. Grant's famously generous terms of surrender to Robert E. Lee at Appomattox Court House on April 9, 1865, were a direct expression of Lincoln's vision. Afterward, Grant quieted Union troop celebrations, saying, "The rebels are our countrymen again."

Commemorating Lee's surrender on Palm Sunday, *Harper's Weekly* reached for Biblical parallels, proclaiming: "Peace, under her joyous palms, brings justice and union."

Hopes were high for a
new birth of freedom
after emancipation.

Reconstruction offered a glimpse of multi-racial democracy, with Americans of
African descent serving in Congress and state legislatures, including Senators
Hiram Revels and Blanche Bruce—honored here alongside Frederick Douglass.

Ex-Confederates used terror as a
tool to reassert white supremacy
in the absence of slavery, captured
in this cartoon by Thomas Nast.
President Ulysses S. Grant used the
Enforcement Act to combat the
KKK with his Southern attorney
general, Amos T. Akerman.

Lincoln loomed large in the First World War, honored on both sides of the Atlantic. Here, Lincoln's spirit is seen inspiring President Woodrow Wilson, a child of the Confederacy.

In World War I, Lincoln's image was used to recruit troops while honoring the heroism of the "Harlem Hellfighters," who saw more combat than any other U.S. regiment.

LINCOLN said

"With malice toward none; with charity for all;······ let us strive on to finish the work we are in;····to bind up the nation's wounds;···· to do all which may achieve and cherish a just and lasting peace."

Save food
for world relief

UNITED STATES FOOD ADMINISTRATION

Lincoln's Second Inaugural was invoked to promote American charitable efforts to combat wartime food shortages overseas— "to do all which may achieve and cherish a just and a lasting peace."

THE STAIRWAY OF LIFE BEGINS AT THE DOOR OF OUR HOME

LOVE
SYMPATHY
IDEALISM
LOYALTY
PERSEVERANCE
HONESTY
HARD WORK

Lincoln in Pittsburgh
1861.

During the Great Depression, Lincoln was lionized as an exemplar of American virtues that could help any honest and hard-working individual climb the ladder of success in life.

Lincoln's ascension to secular saint in America's civic religion was symbolized with stained glass windows placed in churches across the United States.

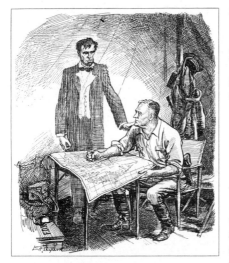

As America entered the Second World War, Lincoln was depicted guiding FDR toward the goal of eradicating slavery from the earth.

Lincoln looks down on a tiny Hitler swinging a sword, recalling Southern slave owners' demand for more land.

THAT WE HERE
HIGHLY RESOLVE
THAT THESE DEAD
SHALL NOT HAVE
DIED IN VAIN

BUY WAR BONDS

Amid the rising death toll during World War II, Lincoln's words from the Gettysburg Address were placed on posters to remind Americans of the need for resolve.

THIS WORLD CANNOT EXIST HALF SLAVE AND HALF FREE

BUY WAR BONDS

A War Bonds drive extended Lincoln's "House Divided" speech to inspire a global fight against tyranny.

The rail-splitter reimagined: overseeing the smashing of a Nazi swastika.

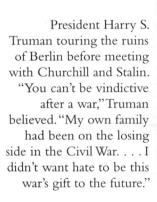

President Harry S. Truman touring the ruins of Berlin before meeting with Churchill and Stalin. "You can't be vindictive after a war," Truman believed. "My own family had been on the losing side in the Civil War. . . . I didn't want hate to be this war's gift to the future."

General Lucius Clay, who oversaw the occupation of postwar Germany, receiving a medal from President Truman. When asked what guided his decisions, Clay said: "I tried to think of the kind of occupation the South would have had if Abraham Lincoln had lived."

"History teaches . . . that almost every military occupation breeds new wars of the future," wrote General MacArthur. To break this cycle and stabilize Japan in defeat, MacArthur kept Emperor Hirohito in power instead of trying him for war crimes. But he widely disseminated this photo to convince the Japanese people that their emperor was a man rather than a god.

38

In 1946, a Japanese-language version of John Drinkwater's play *Abraham Lincoln* was performed by an acclaimed theater group known as the Kabuki Players, dramatizing the lessons of Lincoln's presidency for Tokyo audiences.

39

Secretary of State George Marshall at the 1947 Harvard graduation, where he announced the massive postwar economic plan that would bear his name. It was the opposite of reparations. It was an investment in peace.

"The Struggle Goes On" between freedom and tyranny as Lincoln glares at Soviet oppression during the Cold War.

Lincoln and King: "Two Martyrs" in the pages of *Ebony* magazine.

Nelson Mandela was eulogized by his biographer as "Africa's Lincoln." After his death, tributes piled outside his home in Johannesburg, including this painting depicting Mandela alongside other reconciling leaders: Martin Luther King Jr., Gandhi, JFK, Churchill, Obama—and Lincoln.

Education reform came next. The Hitler-heiling textbooks of the Third Reich taught grade school students to add and subtract using examples of guns and bullets. These were replaced by pre-1933 textbooks, as battered schools were rebuilt across the country. As many as 60 percent of German teachers had been members of the Nazi Party and were dismissed.[18] But through herculean effort—designed to remove roving bands of German youth from the rubble-strewn streets—schools were opened to nearly two million students by October 1945, six months after Hitler's death.[19]

Decentralization was a core to democratization. Germany was divided into five regional states emphasizing local community bonds over German national identity, which had been perverted with Prussian militarism through generations. The first local elections were held in January 1946, limited to small villages with fewer than 20,000 residents. On election day, U.S. troops remained out of sight and an astounding 86 percent of eligible Germans cast ballots to reclaim their democracy[20]—roughly twice the typical turnout in the United States at the time. Larger towns and cities followed in the spring and summer as a diverse array of new parliamentary parties proliferated—most notably the center-right Christian Democratic Party and the center-left Social Democratic Party, which traded power for more than half a century.

The rise of local elected officials free of the stink of Nazism created the conditions for the passage of a new German constitution, drafted in consultation with the military governors.

Modeled on the American Constitution but explicitly designed to block the rise of another Hitler, it guaranteed human dignity, democracy, and individual liberties—placing those values beyond the reach of any future amendment process—and limited the power of the executive through checks and balances, including an independent judiciary and legislature. It was passed to the German parliament for ratification and remains in effect.

By 1949, Lucius Clay had transferred many day-to-day administrative powers back to the German civil service, and he turned over his position as civilian high commissioner of Germany to the Under Secretary of State John J. McCloy. Military government was over in Germany, but the reconstruction continued. McCloy told the new

German chancellor, Konrad Adenauer, that his ambitions for rebuilding Germany reminded him of Lincoln's vision for Reconstruction after the Civil War.[21]

German fascination with Lincoln proliferated in the decade after the Second World War—between 1947 and 1958, no less than thirty-seven books about Lincoln were published in West Germany,[22] emphasizing him as a democratic ideal, a symbol of national reunion, and the rights of free labor. Streets and schools were named after Lincoln.

West Berlin mayor Willy Brandt—a future German chancellor and Nobel Peace Prize winner, who had been prosecuted by the Nazis and fled the country as a young man—idolized Lincoln and quoted him frequently in speeches. The construction of the Berlin Wall would add new relevance to his favorite Lincoln quote: "A house divided against itself cannot stand."

In October 1950, half a million Berliners turned out to dedicate the Freedom Bell, an homage to America's Liberty Bell. On the rim of the bell was an inscription that echoed the Gettysburg Address: "That This World under God shall have a new Birth of Freedom."[23]

MacArthur and
the Emperor

O n the morning of September 2, 1945, General Douglas MacArthur presided over the surrender of Japan on the deck of the USS *Missouri*. In front of whirring cameras and radio microphones, he spoke about his vision of the task that lay ahead.

"We must go forward to preserve in peace what we won in war. A new era is upon us," MacArthur said, referring to the nuclear bombs released over Hiroshima and Nagasaki. "Men since the beginning of time have sought peace ... Military alliances, balances of power, leagues of nations, all in turn failed, leaving the only path to be by way of the crucible of war. We have had our last chance. If we do not now devise some greater and more equitable system, Armageddon will be at our door." The foundation for the future, he said, would be built on "freedom, tolerance and justice."[1]

The Supreme Commander for the Allied Powers was the son of a teenage Union officer who won the Medal of Honor for heroism at the battle of Missionary Ridge. MacArthur grew up surrounded by stories of Civil War heroics and the challenges of Reconstruction. His father later served as military governor of the Philippines, giving his son insight into the difficulty of foreign occupations wrestling with insurgencies.

In his memoirs, MacArthur reflected: "History clearly showed that no modern military occupation of a conquered nation had been a success.

At first hand, I had seen what I thought were basic and fundamental weaknesses in prior forms of military occupations: the substitution of civil by military authority; the loss of self-respect and self-confidence by the people; the constantly growing ascendancy of centralized dictatorial power instead of a localized and representative system; the lowering of the spiritual and moral tone of a population controlled by foreign bayonets; the inevitable deterioration in the occupying forces themselves as the disease of power infiltrated their ranks and bred a sort of race superiority. If any occupation lasts too long, or is not carefully watched from the start, one party becomes slaves and the other masters. History teaches, too, that almost every military occupation breeds new wars of the future."[2]

MacArthur was determined to learn from the past to create a lasting peace. While MacArthur's official orders were essentially the same as those given to Lucius Clay, he did not pursue the Japanese equivalent of denazification. Instead of deposing the Japanese emperor Hirohito and trying him for war crimes, MacArthur kept him in place as a way of stabilizing the country in defeat.

For a thousand years, the Japanese had believed that their imperial family was descended from the Sun God, and they would be blinded if they looked at him directly.

MacArthur forced the Japanese emperor to reveal his humanity to his own people. The vehicles he used were sound and vision: one radio address from the emperor admitting he was not a God; one photograph to prove it.

With a click and a flash of the camera, the evidence was available for all Japanese to see.

There, in the American Embassy, stood MacArthur, hips cocked to one side, hands in his pockets, wearing military issue khakis, shirt open with no hat, tie, or jacket, casually towering over the diminutive emperor whose arms hung stiffly at his side. He was revealed to be a gentle man with a wispy mustache, wearing a western waistcoat. MacArthur ensured that the photo received wide distribution.

Hirohito was not of the warrior caste. He was a whiskey- and jazz-loving introvert who wrote books about marine biology. He spoke an ancient dialect that most of his subjects could not understand. But he took his responsibilities seriously and had come to resent the generals who steered his nation into a world war they could not win.

Given the alternative—death by hanging or firing squad—Hirohito grew to appreciate MacArthur's qualified support while the Japanese people grew to respect MacArthur.

The task at hand required few of the military skills MacArthur had perfected over decades. Instead, he explained, this new assignment required that he "had to be an economist, a political scientist, an engineer, a manufacturing executive, a teacher, even a theologian of sorts."[3]

Keeping the emperor in power but stripped of divine authority was essential to MacArthur's plan to win the peace. When faced with backlash in Washington, he explained that removing the emperor would require the deployment of an additional one million troops to put down counterinsurgencies. Instead, he proved able to rebuild the island nation of seventy million people with just 200,000 troops.[4]

MacArthur moved quickly, living by the maxim that "every mistake in war is excusable except inactivity and refusal to take risks."[5] Now he applied that wisdom to waging peace, writing down a brisk list of the occupation's goals and ticking them off one by one.

First, destroy the military power. Punish war criminals. Build the structure of representative government. Modernize the constitution. Hold free elections. Enfranchise women. Release the political prisoners. Liberate the farmers. Establish a free labor movement. Encourage a free economy. Abolish police oppression. Develop a free and responsible press. Liberalize education. Decentralize political power. Separate church and state.[6]

Within two years—working with deliberate speed and leveraging the cooperation of the emperor—he achieved them all.

The work was smoothed by MacArthur's strategy of consciously keeping an aura of mystery about him—echoing the Japanese emperors of old. He became known as the "blue-eyed Shogun." He did not tour the country—cultivating distance—traveling primarily between his residence at the U.S. Embassy and his general headquarters at the Dai-Ichi Insurance building, which lorded over the Imperial Palace grounds nearby.

In his spartan office, MacArthur kept a framed quote from Lincoln prominently displayed:[7] "I do the very best I know how ... If the end brings me out all right what is said against me won't amount to anything. If the end brings me out wrong, ten angels swearing I was right would make no difference."

Always mindful of the power of good press at home, he was fond of telling reporters, "My major advisers now have boiled down to almost two men—George Washington and Abraham Lincoln. One founded the United States, the other saved it. If you go back in their lives, you can find almost all the answers."[8]

But he understood that the lessons of American history needed to be refracted through the lens of Japanese culture to stick. While Japan was a feudal island nation that had been isolated for much of its history—until Admiral Perry of America opened it to foreign trade in 1854—its expansionist past half-century created toeholds for American influence. Among these was the popularity of the life of Lincoln.

The first Japanese language biography of Lincoln was published in 1890 and reprinted in thirteen editions. The author, Matsumura Kaiseki, presented the story as a hero's journey of moral development, describing Lincoln as a "good teacher for the impoverished," and a "model for our nation's politicians."[9]

By 1903, the life of Lincoln was included in a national curriculum that offered students twenty-eight lessons on values to live by. Lincoln was featured in five of these, including the virtues of honesty, empathy, and freedom. By comparison, the sitting Japanese emperor received only three sections devoted to the lessons of his life. The Japanese diplomat and scholar Nitobe—whose face graced the 5,000 Yen note—was a Lincoln enthusiast who contributed to several chapters in a popular Lincoln biography, *Tales of Lincoln*, which described him as "the kindest man among the great men, and the greatest man among the kind men."[10]

Enthusiasm for Lincoln was widespread in the region. The first president of the Republic of China, Sun Yat-Sen, based his political philosophy—"the three principles of the people"—on Lincoln, saying in 1912 that "we wish to see established in our country the system of government which the great Lincoln, in a memorable phrase, described as 'government of the people, by the people, for the people.'"[11]

This friendly fascination continued until a few years before the attack on Pearl Harbor. In 1936, a Japanese Christian evangelist named

Toyohiko Kagawa toured the United States in a pilgrimage to the sites of Lincoln's life, culminating at a sold-out speech in Springfield. "An Emperor of Japan once said that the greatest personality in the world's history is Abraham Lincoln. Even the great Emperor of Japan considered himself inferior to Abraham Lincoln," Kagawa said. "Abraham Lincoln does not belong to this country alone. He belongs to the world. He belongs to Japan also. Millions and millions of souls in Japan are inspired by his life."[12]

For all the vast differences between Japan and America, MacArthur could draw on the legacy of Lincoln to establish his legitimacy. His claim was bolstered by the fact that Emperor Hirohito prominently kept a bust of Lincoln in his office, before and after the war.[13]

MacArthur updated the conservative 1898 Meiji Constitution, which had officially elevated the emperor to the status of a living god. At first, he passed on his requests to a delegation from the Japanese legislature, known as the Diet. But when they came back with only cosmetic changes, MacArthur directed his staff to revise the document entirely according to his specifications, giving them just two weeks to complete the draft.

The result was nothing less than a revolution. While personally conservative, MacArthur enshrined equal rights for women and overturned prohibitions against labor unions by securing the right to collectively bargain. These were far beyond anything in the U.S. Constitution.

The most radical proposal was Article 9, which stated, "The Japanese people forever renounce war as a sovereign right of the nation and the threat or use of force as means of settling international disputes." No land, sea, or air forces would be maintained. The professional soldier was in effect outlawing war in Japan forever.

This man of war found his true genius in peace. He leveraged the emperor and had him endorse the new constitution in front of the Japanese parliament. Local and national elections would soon follow with massive turnout and the election of thirty-nine women to parliament.

Their new constitution made the Japanese people citizens rather than subjects. But MacArthur's own imperiousness was not covered in newspapers. His attempt to control dissenting information was functionally nothing less than censorship as the U.S. Military oversaw the one major national radio station that existed between 1946 and 1951 in Japan. While freedom of the press and freedom of expression were more widespread than they'd been under the old constitution, they were far short of what we would recognize as liberal democratic principles today.

The heavy hand was balanced with a lighter touch, as Americans opened public libraries and public hospitals. MacArthur encouraged the cultivation of Christianity and baseball, believing that these habits would help sow the seeds for democracy.

MacArthur drilled into his soldiers the importance of setting a good personal example. He told them that "by their conduct our own country would be judged in world opinion, that success or failure of the occupation could well rest upon their poise and self-restraint."[14] He encouraged the small kindnesses of GIs who became known for handing out candy and gum to local kids in a friendly breach of Japanese decorum. He also rejected the army's call for "non-fraternization"— dating Japanese women—in the belief that it would bond the two cultures in a personal way beyond policy.

But MacArthur did not compromise on demilitarization, destroying some 11,000 aircraft and 1.2 million guns. He broke up big companies and pursued a policy of decentralization to break the fever of nationalism. While he insisted that Hirohito not be tried for war crimes, he approved the trial of 5,700 Japanese for war crimes—920 were found guilty—and some 200,000 ultranationalists were purged from their positions, including schools.[15] In a calculated use of power and mercy, MacArthur commuted most death sentences before the end of the occupation and issued amnesties on Christmas Day.

He succeeded in changing the culture to the extent that the Japanese ministry of education became one of the "most zealous proponents of democracy"[16]—whereas three years before, the schools had lionized the imperial family and the honor of death in combat.

The lessons of Abraham Lincoln's life—which had been excised from Japanese textbooks during the war—were reintroduced. The full text of the Gettysburg Address was reprinted in standard school-books and a new round of Japanese-language Lincoln biographies appeared with titles like *Lincoln: The Embodiment of Democracy*. In 1946, a Japanese-language version of John Drinkwater's play *Abraham Lincoln* was performed by an acclaimed theater group known as the Kabuki Players, dramatizing the lessons of Lincoln's presidency for Tokyo audiences. They were rewarded with a spread in *Life* magazine.[17] By 1958, high school students in Tokyo ranked Lincoln "the most respected of all world figures."[18] There remains a center devoted to the study of Abraham Lincoln at Meisei University in Tokyo, and Lincoln even received the pop-culture benediction of having a Japanese comic book dedicated to the story of his life.[19]

The scholar Usao Tsujita explained the appeal of Lincoln in postwar Japan: "Lincoln as a figure needs to be accepted once more by our Japanese society for getting to know America and what a democracy means . . . Unless our country is able to turn out many persons like Lincoln, it can never be a civilized nation."[20]

Japanese enthusiasm for democracy was a success. MacArthur transferred more operational responsibility to the Japanese before the occupation officially ended in 1952. The Japanese economy grew at a rapid clip freed from the need to spend on national defense, while Americans viewed the transformed Japan as a check against communism.

Under MacArthur's implementation of a magnanimous peace, democratization and reindustrialization transformed Japan in record time, turning an enemy into one of America's most durable allies. MacArthur understood the strength of forgiveness. As Lincoln allegedly said, "Do not I destroy my enemies when I make them my friends?"

"The Golden Rule for World Peace"

Together, they have become known as "the good occupations." Never before had two defeated enemies half a world away been rebuilt to rejoin the world of nations.

Generals Clay and MacArthur followed a path imagined by Abraham Lincoln: unconditional surrender followed by a magnanimous peace, secured by political reform, economic growth, and cultural integration. It made the promise of a just and lasting peace a reality.

The grandchildren of the Civil War generation applied insights from the failure of the Treaty of Versailles to secure peace, prosperity, and liberal democracy in Western Europe. Studying history had been the basis of Harry S. Truman's self-education, and it helped him overcome inherited prejudices from his Confederate-sympathizing family. "My family didn't think much of Lincoln," Truman recalled. "I began to feel just the opposite after I'd studied the history of the country and what he did to save the Union."[1]

Truman became the first president to speak to the NAACP (from the steps of the Lincoln Memorial), created the Civil Rights Division of the Justice Department, backed a federal anti-lynching law, and desegregated the Armed Forces—which scandalized southern Democrats, causing them to run a segregationist Dixiecrat candidate against his reelection. In foreign affairs, Truman continued to idolize the president of his youth, Woodrow Wilson, but he was determined to apply the lessons of his failure to ratify the League of Nations. He would pursue the opposite approach in creating the United Nations and passing the Marshall Plan.

In October 1945, a month after the surrender of Japan, President Truman began to change the national conversation from victory to responsibility, summed up in a speech dubbed "The Golden Rule for World Peace."

"We conclusively proved that free government is the most efficient government in every emergency," he crowed to a packed crowd at the American Legion Fair in Caruthersville, Missouri. They had won the war, but the hard work of winning the peace had just begun.

"We understand that the road to peace is just as difficult and may be more difficult as was the road to victory during the war," Truman said. "We may make mistakes. We may have difficulties, but I am asking you to exercise that admonition which we will find in the Gospels and which Christ told us was the way to get along in the world: 'Do by your neighbor as you would be done by.' And that applies to you and you just as it applies to Great Britain and France and China and Russia and Czechoslovakia and Poland and Brazil . . . We are going to accept that Golden Rule, and we are going forward to meet our destiny, which I think Almighty God intended us to have—and we are going to be the leaders."[2]

The ultimate postwar expression of the Golden Rule in action was the Marshall Plan.

By 1947, Army chief of staff George Marshall, who oversaw Eisenhower and MacArthur in the Second World War, had been elevated to serve as secretary of state. The resident of Leesburg, Virginia—related to Robert E. Lee's aide Charles Marshall—responded to economic chaos in postwar Europe and the growing threat of communist expansion by announcing an unprecedented policy of postwar reconstruction and investment.

Winston Churchill would be widely credited with calling it "the least sordid act in human history."[3] But it was really an act of enlightened self-interest; Lincoln's vision of winning the peace applied on a global scale.

The plan was announced in front of 15,000 people on a bright June day at Harvard's graduation ceremony. Marshall had traded his dark green uniform and chest full of medals for a light gray suit and navy blue tie. Onstage alongside him sat the poet T. S. Eliot, author of "The Waste Land," who was receiving an honorary degree. Marshall presented the graduates his own bleak vision of the future—but then offered a way out.

The war was not yet won, Marshall told the students, many of whom were veterans attending college on the GI Bill. Europe was poor and insecure, devastated by war, and now under threat of the Soviets.

Europe "must have substantial additional help, or face economic, social and political deterioration of a very grave character," Marshall said in his calm, courtly voice. "The remedy lies in breaking the vicious circle and restoring the confidence of the European people in the economic future of their own countries and of Europe as a whole . . . It is logical that the United States should do whatever it is able to do to assist in the return of normal economic health in the world, without which there can be no political stability and no assured peace."

Addressing the bear in the room, Marshall said that the goal of the program was not simply to counter Russia in the emerging Cold War. "Our policy is directed not against any country or doctrine but against hunger, poverty, desperation and chaos. Its purpose should be the revival of a working economy in the world so as to permit the emergence of political and social conditions in which free institutions can exist. Such assistance, I am convinced, must not be on a piece-meal basis as various crises develop. Any assistance that this Government may render in the future should provide a cure rather than a mere palliative."[4]

This was the opposite of reparations. It was an investment in peace. Marshall was not a great orator, but he had the charisma of common sense. Announcing the plan was the easy part. What secured its passage was the way it was pursued by Truman and Marshall.

Learning from Woodrow Wilson's mistakes, they were decidedly bipartisan in their approach from the start.

Truman insisted the plan be named after his secretary of state, who was far more popular than he was on Capitol Hill at the time, telling one aide that if the Truman name was on it, it would "quiver a couple of times and die"[5] in the Republican-controlled Congress.

Together, they cultivated Senator Arthur Vandenberg, the powerful Republican chairman of the Senate Committee on Foreign Relations. The former Michigan newspaper editor—whose grandfather was a Lincoln delegate at the 1860 convention—had been a staunch isolationist before Pearl Harbor. But he'd come to embrace the necessity of American leadership in the world, serving as a Truman-appointed U.S. representative to the creation of the United Nations, famously declaring that "we must stop partisan politics at the water's edge." The treaty to join the U.N. passed the Senate almost unanimously, and even in an election year, competing against the Truman-led Democrats, Vandenberg said, "Politics are important, but peace is indispensable."[6]

But when Vandenberg first heard of the Marshall Plan, he objected on fiscal grounds. It was far too expensive: 11 cents out of every dollar in the federal budget. Congress would never appropriate that kind of money to be used overseas, Vandenberg assured reporters.

But by bringing Vandenberg in early and adopting his suggestions, Truman and Marshall created a sense of personal investment that led the senator to influence his committee and withstand the slings and arrows from the far right of his own party. "I have to sit up and be called a Benedict Arnold," he groused to Marshall.[7]

Vandenberg insisted on creating a bipartisan blue-ribbon panel comprised of business, labor, and academic leaders to debate the program in public. There were short films making the case for the Marshall Plan using Hollywood stars. Republican support for humanitarian aid was boosted when Truman drafted former president Herbert Hoover to coordinate international food relief efforts on behalf of the administration in a high-profile global tour. The transparency and trans-partisan nature of the policy and the public relations campaign helped win Americans over.

Their effort was aided by world events. A surge in Soviet aggression across Eastern Europe created a sense of urgency that built bipartisan bridges between hawkish Republicans and anti-communist Democrats. In quick succession, the Russians moved to control states on its western border under the "iron curtain" and were threatening governments in Greece and Turkey. So the Marshall Plan was sold—as, in fact, it was—as a bulwark against Bolshevism by stabilizing western democracy. It was the olive branch that complemented the arrows of the Truman Doctrine: "to support free peoples who are resisting attempted subjugation by armed minorities or by outside pressures."[8]

To help address concerns that the plan would be a global extension of the heavy spending of the New Deal, Vandenberg insisted the Marshall Plan be a partnership with participating European nations and run like a business, rather than a government program, with strict accounting for its expenses.

To achieve that end, Vandenberg recruited Paul Hoffman, the fifty-six-year-old president of the Studebaker Corporation and a fellow Republican, to run the cornerstone of Truman's foreign policy. At the outset, Hoffman declared, "Today there can be no thing as a Republican foreign policy or a Democratic foreign policy. There can only be an American foreign policy."[9]

The Economic Recovery Act of 1948—which encompassed the Marshall Plan—passed the Republican-controlled Senate by a vote of 69 to 17 and the House by an overwhelming margin. The whole effort took ten months.

The war-weary American people had been convinced along bipartisan lines to forgo any peace dividend and instead spend one-tenth of the total federal budget—some $7 billion per year for the next three years—to secure the gains made in the Second World War.

With his salesman's persuasion, Hoffman built on bipartisan support by tapping Democratic ambassador Averell Harriman as his second-in-command, who brought in a deputy named Abraham Lincoln Gordon. Hoffman saw his mission with the sweep of history, correcting the opportunities lost after the Civil War and the First World War.

"If, after the Civil War, the North had accepted Lincoln's precept of 'malice towards none; with charity for all' and waged the peace by promoting recovery in the South, it could have quickly restored goodwill, understanding and prosperity," Hoffman wrote in his memoir, *Peace Can Be Won*. "A few million dollars loaned to the Southern states, to help them acquire feed and livestock and plows for farms and plantations would have added hundreds of millions to the wealth of the nation. With such assistance the South could have staged a faster comeback in 10 years than it did in 30 . . . But instead of economic aid the North sent carpetbaggers. And more than 50 years after the Civil War had ended, I could personally testify as a Northern recruit in a Southern camp, to the resentment and bitterness that were the result of the North's blindness in not waging the peace.[10]

"In the immediate period after World War I we might have also won the peace if we had worked at it with vigor and imagination," Hoffman continued. "From Stockholm to Seattle to Samarkand, the people wanted peace. But we didn't work at it. Instead, we in the United States spurned the League of Nations. We returned to the 'normalcy' of our isolationism. Great Britain and France reverted to the normalcy of that mutual distrust which gave Hitler the greenlight to build his war machine." But he said, "It would not be fair to say that we didn't work at waging peace, at least to some extent, after World War II."[11]

Within days of the Marshall Plan's passage, dozens of ships were sailing across the Atlantic, full of grain, fertilizer, and equipment, to ports across Europe. For the second time in a decade, Americans were greeted as saviors. "It is fitting that the people of Western Europe should attempt to renew their capacity for wonder," a reporter for *The Economist* wrote, describing the outreach as "an act without peer in history."[12] It gave a boost of confidence and matériel to the citizens of struggling postwar countries who suddenly found themselves hopeful about the future, a sentiment buoyed by high employment.

With the aim of exorcising the ghosts of history, a system of economic interdependence was instituted by linking French and German coal and steel production, making the prospect of war impractical if not impossible. "Germany knows that its fate is bound up with that of Western Europe as a whole," said German chancellor Konrad Adenauer, while marveling at the uniquely American approach to winning the peace: "Probably for the first time in history, a victorious country held out its hand so that the vanquished might rise again."[13]

Americans' charitable impulse inspired them to chip in beyond their tax dollars. In 1948, a train rolled out from Omaha, Nebraska, to collect food from midwestern farmers to help feed European families in need. It was called the Abraham Lincoln Friendship Train[14] and, as boxcars painted with Lincoln's profile rolled across the prairie, it collected more than 2,000 cars full of food to aid the Marshall Plan's efforts.

By 1951, steel production in Europe had doubled from four years before, while industrial and agricultural output were well above pre-war levels. There were new power plants in France and Italy, new dams in the Netherlands and Austria. Humanitarian aid led to new low-cost housing, food for schoolchildren, and the eradication of tuberculosis. Germany in particular was a beneficiary, gaining $3 billion in direct aid from the Marshall Plan, as wartime rubble was turned into concrete for new construction. It was, as Churchill once wrote of Lincoln, a prime example of adding "to the triumph of armies those lasting victories which are gained over the hearts of men."[15]

In the end, the security of Western Europe was strengthened by the creation of NATO, while trade agreements created the foundation for the European Union. Europe was stabilized by economic interdependence, spurring growth while taming inflation. Political moderates rose in parliaments rather than more ideologically extreme parties. It was a mammoth task, spanning sixteen partner nations, made more difficult by the Soviet Union's constant attempts to undermine its effectiveness while sowing the seeds of distrust with disinformation campaigns. But the Cold War did not turn hot, and the countries of Western Europe did not fall into the tyrannical communist trap.

It was bold, balancing idealism with realism. But the ultimate test of any strategy is its success. As General Eisenhower said at the outset: "The success of this occupation can only be judged fifty years from now. If the Germans at that time have a stable, prosperous democracy, then we shall have succeeded."[16]

We now know the answer. In the end, liberal democracy was saved, western Europe united, and the next world war prevented by a proactive investment to win the peace. As Truman said decades later, "We completely defeated our enemies and made them surrender. And then we helped them to recover, to become democratic, and to rejoin the community of nations. Only America could have done that."[17]

Lincoln might have smiled.

Conclusion

As he traveled to his first inauguration, Abraham Lincoln gave a speech at the New Jersey state capitol in Trenton. With the Civil War looming, he surprised the assembled state senators by ruminating on American history, how stories from the Revolutionary War inspired him as a child. He pointed out that they met just a few miles from where George Washington and his troops famously crossed the Delaware River in a daring midnight raid on Christmas 1776.

"I recollect thinking then, boy even though I was, that there must have been something more than common that those men struggled for," Lincoln said, "something even more than National Independence; that something that held out a great promise to all the people of the world for all time to come."[1]

America had a meaning beyond itself, Lincoln believed. Our patriotism is more than mere nationalism and our success is not for ourselves alone. Americans—whom he called "God's almost chosen people"—had a sacred trust to save democracy, to find redemption for the original sin of slavery, and to secure "a just, and a lasting peace, between ourselves and with all nations."

Because of Lincoln's moral courage, moderation, and subsequent martyrdom, the United States survived the Civil War and grew stronger. He showed us that despite the deepest divisions, a diverse democracy could reunite and find a new birth of freedom, however flawed.

Today, almost 250 years from our founding, it's sometimes said that America feels more divided than at any point since the Civil

War. Bitter partisanship; tribal politics; regional, racial, and economic divides have turned fellow citizens against one another while trust in our institutions declines. The idea of the Good America that rebuilt Europe can seem distant while the rise of demagogues and dictators in our time strains the belief that right makes might.

Lincoln's example offers us a path away from polarization. His commitment to reconciliation retains the force of revelation. Even during the Civil War, he refused to back down from his belief that there is more that unites us than divides us. And he showed us that defending democracy is a cause that can be just as heroic as winning it in the first place.

Lincoln's plan to win the peace is his unfinished symphony; but in its existing notes, we can find an anthem that can begin to bridge our divisions.

"Those who can win a war well can rarely make a good peace," Winston Churchill said, "and those who make a good peace would never have won the war."[2] Lincoln was the exception to this rule.

Combining magnanimity with power, he confronted the most difficult task a statesman can face—and though he did not live to see its success, Lincoln's prescription for winning the peace was vindicated over time.

His insistence on unconditional surrender—rejecting offers of ceasefire and negotiated settlement—was controversial. Peace activists clamored for an end to war at any cost, even the perpetuation of slavery and the permanent division of the nation. Lincoln's desire for a liberal postwar Reconstruction put him in conflict with radical Republican allies who wanted vengeance after victory. But unconditional surrender followed by a magnanimous peace was precisely the policy pursued by the United States after the Second World War, rebuilding Germany and Japan into enduring allies and liberal democracies.

After winning the war and securing the rule of law, Lincoln understood that political reform was needed to reseed democracy in the South while addressing the root causes of the conflict: abolishing slavery and renouncing secession. He believed that states must feel a sense of ownership in their own Reconstruction after accepting defeat; rebel leaders would not be executed but they should not be allowed to run for office or regain power.

Lincoln understood that postwar economic expansion could help reunite the nation. Even in the darkest days of the war, he looked forward, signing legislation that would connect the continent by railroad, providing incentives for westward expansion, opening the doors to new immigrants, and establishing what would become more than one hundred new colleges throughout the United States. He believed these policies would help de-emphasize postwar divisions between the North and South by moving the nation's focus West, creating a sense of personal investment in a shared, prosperous future.

It worked. The population and per capita income of the United States more than doubled between the beginning of the Civil War and the end of the century, while the gross domestic product (GDP) of the United States grew fourfold from $69 billion to $320 billion.[3] By 1900, there were more railways connecting the United States than in all of Europe, and steel production surged as America surpassed Britain as the world's leading industrial nation, without the burdens of empire.

Winning the peace through economic investment was also carried out after the Second World War, stabilizing local economies and creating an increasingly interconnected Europe through the Marshall Plan. Americans learned that investing in peace was far less expensive than fighting another war. In the process, they contained communism and expanded democracy amid decades of unprecedented economic growth, leading to the longest period of continental peace in recorded history.

The final step in Lincoln's prescription to win the peace proved the most challenging. The reintegration of the South into a common American culture, the changing of hearts and minds, would take time and education, equal opportunity, and national migration. Even General Sherman recognized this: "No matter what change we may desire in the feelings and thoughts of the people [in the] South, we cannot accomplish it by force."[4] Lincoln placed great hope in the Freedmen's Bureau to help refugees achieve self-sufficiency. If it had been allowed to continue its work without political interference from Andrew

Johnson, it may have had a more lasting positive effect, cultivating a land-owning class of free black farmers. Instead, Black Codes were imposed, denying equal rights while perpetuating white supremacy. Lincoln's hope that a practical system could be devised where "the two races could gradually live themselves out of their old relation to each other, and both come out better prepared for the new," was not pursued. Confederate leaders were allowed to regain power, the myth of the Lost Cause was allowed to proliferate, and civil rights were denied for another century. The failures of Reconstruction after Lincoln's death remains a stain on American democracy.

But in the broader arena, Lincoln's insights on how to win the peace have been proven correct.

Among contemporary peacekeepers, it's now considered settled wisdom that civil wars that end in a decisive military victory rather than a negotiated settlement are less likely to slip back into violence.[5] After the failures of the Treaty of Versailles—with an armistice that preceded negotiations, followed by punishing reparations—the "good occupations" in Germany and Japan continue to "serve as models for modern post-combat stability operations" for the U.S. Army.[6]

Conflict transformation is what the military now calls Lincoln's vision of Reconstruction, seeking "to resolve the root causes of conflict and instability while building the capacity of local institutions to forge and sustain effective governance, economic development and the rule of law," according to the U.S. Army.[7] In addition, comprehensive international studies show that economic growth reduces the likelihood of civil war.[8] The United Nations' peacebuilding strategy is likewise predicated on "long-term political, economic and social provisions to address the root causes of a conflict."[9] It's now commonly understood that after stabilization, it's essential to strengthen basic government services, invest in economic development, educate people, and establish democratic institutions, so citizens can trust in fair and representative elections. Lincoln anticipated it all.

Lincoln did not, of course, get everything right. His vision for reconciliation and reunification was necessarily incomplete. Arguably, his worst decision was selecting Andrew Johnson to be his 1864 running mate. It was politically inspired: breaking outside the party system to broaden the appeal of the National Union Party, and balancing his profile with a Southern Democrat. But the short-term benefits were outweighed by the long-term costs: it did not adequately occur to Lincoln that he could be choosing a presidential successor. He trusted too much in their ties as young congressmen. The essential difference between the two men came down to character—and character is the single most important quality in a president.

It can fairly be suggested that Lincoln's forgiving view of human nature and people's capacity for change underestimated how quickly the South would try to reinstate the structures of white supremacy after slavery. It's impossible to know exactly how Lincoln would have responded, but given that equality under the law was a bedrock principle, it is reasonable to assume that—like President Grant—he would have insisted on enforcement of federal law, which Andrew Johnson refused to do, bolstered by his bigotry.

There also remains a robust debate about whether the radical Republican plan for Reconstruction, aggressively pursued from the start, might have been more successful in securing equal rights than Lincoln's liberal vision. Having won the war, it's argued that there was a narrow window within which to force the newly defeated South to accept the need to adjust to a new reality rather than giving them room to retrench. Likewise, Lincoln's opening bid for black suffrage focused on the "very intelligent" as well as veterans—could be accused of opening the door to literacy tests that were among the tools used to suppress the vote in the South. The radical Republicans were more uncompromising in their immediate commitment to interracial democracy in ways that put them squarely on the right side of history as seen from the early decades of the twenty-first century.

But history needs to be fairly understood in the context of its time rather than solely in retrospect. Lincoln's insistence on a magnanimous peace was designed to lead people in his desired direction—but not too far, too fast—so as to avoid a self-defeating backlash. That's what Frederick Douglass essentially acknowledged at the dedication of the emancipation memorial in 1876: "Had he put the abolition of slavery before the salvation of the Union, he would have inevitably driven from him

a powerful class of the American people and rendered resistance to rebellion impossible. Viewed from the genuine abolition ground, Mr. Lincoln seemed tardy, cold, dull, and indifferent. But measuring him by the
sentiment of his country, a sentiment he was bound as a statesman to
consult, he was swift, zealous, radical, and determined."[10]

We can never definitively know the right answer to these historical "what-ifs." We can only contrast Lincoln's intended direction
with the results of the reactionary reconstruction pursued by Andrew
Johnson. We know its value in part because when Lincoln's vision was
betrayed, it brought misery that delayed justice even as it preserved an
uneasy peace. But whether the sin is slavery or segregation, we know
that the violation of our deepest values corrodes our collective soul.

The debates of history do not end. They play out in our politics to this
day. The party of Lincoln now finds its political base in the states of
the former Confederacy, which switched their allegiance after President Lyndon Johnson—a southern Democrat—signed civil rights
legislation precisely one hundred years after the Civil War. Not coincidentally, the two parties have also switched political identities, with
Republicans the party of conservative populism and Democrats the
party of moderate progressivism.

The first African-American U.S. president, Barack Obama, kicked
off his 2008 campaign at the old Illinois statehouse in Springfield,
where Lincoln had given his "House Divided" speech 150 years before.
Summoning the spirit of Lincoln, the forty-five-year-old Democratic
senator said, "Through his will and his words, he moved a nation and
helped free a people . . . because men and women of every race, from
every walk of life, continued to march for freedom long after Lincoln
was laid to rest, today we have the chance to face the challenges of this
millennium together, as one people—as Americans."[11]

The historian David Blight has written, "as long as we have a politics of race in America, we will have a politics of Civil War memory."[12]
Recently we've seen an unwelcome uptick in talk about a "second
Civil War."[13] It's grown from self-styled militia members to extremists online, crossing over into conservative populist protests, fueled by

conservative commentators and even a few members of Congress.[14] The rhetoric of "aggressive defensiveness" is again being used in reaction to an overdue reckoning about Confederate statues that have become culture war flashpoints; even some statues of Lincoln have been toppled. President Donald Trump retweeted warnings about a second civil war to enflame his base during his first impeachment.[15] Trump then refused to accept the legitimacy of his defeat in 2020, manufacturing baseless claims of fraud and inciting insurrection. Some of the pro-Trump rioters who stormed the U.S. Capitol—trying to stop the counting of electoral votes to certify the victory of Joe Biden and Kamala Harris—were wearing T-shirts proclaiming "civil war"[16] while others wielded Confederate flags.[17] Threatening civil war is the politics of incitement, an insult to our democracy and our history. But it did not emerge from a vacuum.

Decades earlier, Newt Gingrich, Georgia congressman and future speaker of the house, began to describe politics as an extension of civil war. In 1988, he said, "The left at its core understands in a way Grant understood after Shiloh that this is a Civil War, that only one side will prevail, and the other side will be relegated to history." This was not an idle reference, he explained. "This war has to be fought with the scale and duration and savagery that is only true of Civil Wars. While we are lucky in this country that our Civil Wars are fought at the ballot box, not on the battlefields, nonetheless it is a Civil War."[18] If you keep telling people they are engaged in a civil war, sooner or later they start to believe you.

In recent years, we've seen partisan politics deepen their divide along regional, racial, and ideological lines, loudly denying the legitimacy of the opposition. We have watched distrust escalate as hate proliferates. This is dangerous for a democracy. As Ulysses S. Grant warned a decade after Appomattox, "If we are to have another [civil war], I predict that the dividing line will not be Mason and Dixon's, but between patriotism and intelligence on the one side, and superstition, ambition, and ignorance on the other."[19]

We should not have to learn these lessons again. The memory of three quarters of a million American dead—even 150 years ago—should be enough to calm overheated emotions, especially among people who claim to revere the Constitution.

Still, we must find a way to de-escalate and depolarize. "We are not enemies, but friends," as Lincoln said, "though passion may have strained, it must not break our bonds of affection." A renewed appreciation for our shared history can help, as Lincoln suggested in his first inaugural: "The mystic chords of memory will swell when again touched, as surely they will be, by the better angels of our nature." But perspective is the thing we have least of in our politics.

We can take some courage and comfort from the fact that we have been through far worse as a nation. Whatever challenges we face, they are small compared to those our country confronted in Lincoln's time.

The lessons of Lincoln's leadership can still guide us. He was a soulful centrist, "principled without being fanatical," as Robert Penn Warren said, "flexible without being opportunistic."[20] He showed us how to bridge divides by reaching out with humor and humility, recognizing that moral courage does not confer moral superiority, and empathy is a pathway to persuasion. His reputation for honesty allowed him to rebuild trust among adversaries, while he reminds us that kindness is consistent with effective leadership. Most of all, Lincoln demonstrated that the ideals of a diverse liberal democracy can galvanize more people than any demagogue preaching the skin-deep comforts of tribal divides.

If these qualities seem almost extinct in our politics today, they were rare in Lincoln's time as well. After all, our greatest president was bookended by two of our worst—James Buchanan's weakness opened the door to war while Andrew Johnson's bitter impulses undermined the peace. Still, the republic survived. We will not find another Lincoln—but he can inspire individuals with a similar spirit to carry forward his vision of reconciliation.

"Human-nature will not change," Lincoln said after winning reelection in 1864. "In any future great national trial, compared with the men of this, we shall have as weak, and as strong, as silly and as wise, as bad and good. Let us, therefore, study the incidents of this, as philosophy to learn wisdom from, and none of them as wrongs to be revenged."[21]

This is the essence of applied history—it is not simply the study of what happened but why it happened and how the answers to those questions can guide us now. *Useful* wisdom is the goal. We do not learn history to cultivate resentments and pass them on to the next generation in a spirit of revenge. That is how wars never really end.

When General George Marshall accepted his Nobel Peace Prize in 1953, he reflected on the need to study history for the purpose of peace. He'd grown up in a time when school textbooks in the North presented "a strikingly different picture of our Civil War from those written in the South." Marshall believed that education based on common facts was essential to stopping future wars before they start: "Our students must first seek to understand the conditions, as far as possible without national prejudices, which have led to past tragedies and should strive to determine the great fundamentals which must govern a peaceful progression toward a constantly higher level of civilization."[22]

While the art of war is endlessly studied, the art of peace is comparatively ignored. Peace is, of course, not a static state. But the process of securing peace after war requires the systemic study of what has worked—and what has not—throughout history, distilled into best practices and then implemented by wise leaders through determined policy. It requires responsibility and humility, a willingness to invest in the preservation of peace from a position of strength, because weakness invites aggression. This process will not end war and it will not abolish human error. But it is a necessary step toward the goal of securing civilization and stopping senseless bloodshed.

There have been efforts in this direction, from the creation of the ill-fated League of Nations after the First World War to the more durable United Nations after the Second World War. The United Nations was built by a generation tempered by two world wars, whose balance of realism and idealism was captured by President John F. Kennedy: "Let us focus on a more practical, more attainable peace, based not on a sudden revolution in human nature but on a gradual evolution in human institutions."[23]

But the hard-won lessons of history can be forgotten. Progress is not inevitable. In the early years of the twenty-first century, the United States invaded Iraq without a plan to win the peace.[24] It's not that such a plan didn't exist—it had been developed by officers at the Pentagon[25]—but it was disregarded by ideologically driven civilian leaders who believed they could remake the Middle East with a small footprint of soldiers who would be greeted as liberators. A decade later, after engaging in an international intervention in Libya designed to stop a looming slaughter, no plan for securing the peace was implemented after displacing the dictator, which created even more chaos. And so, a new generation saw that blundering out of wars is as much a mistake as blundering into them.

We need to wage peace with the same intensity as war, recognizing as Lincoln did that the two cannot be understood in isolation. War and peace are interconnected. One of the most important roles a leader can play after winning a war is to provide freedom from fear, on both sides of the divide. The defeated must feel that they will be treated fairly as long as they accept the legitimacy of the outcome. Victory is, ironically, a time for humility and resolve. The preservation of peace with justice requires an active commitment. As Lincoln once cautioned, "The victor will soon be the vanquished, if he relax in his exertion."[26]

Through the power of his example, Lincoln helped establish an art of peace rooted in reconciliation—and that has made him an enduring inspiration for peacemakers around the world.

A half century after Lincoln's death, Mahatma Gandhi—the founder of the philosophy of nonviolence—wrote that he was "the greatest President of America. It may safely be said that Lincoln sacrificed his life in order to put an end to the sufferings of others. But Lincoln can be said to be still alive; for the changes he made in the American Constitution are still in force. And Lincoln's name will be known as long as America endures. It will thus be seen that Lincoln has become immortal, for his greatness consisted not in his talent or his wealth, but in his innate goodness."[27] Gandhi's admiration for Lincoln showed how the pursuit of unconditional surrender and magnanimous peace could apply to the arena of civil resistance.

During the Cold War, the mayor of West Berlin, Willy Brandt—who would go on to become German chancellor and win a Nobel Peace Prize—made a pilgrimage to Springfield and declared: "This man does not belong to you alone, my friends. He belongs to all of us, above all to our young people, and he lives in the hearts of mankind everywhere. In Abraham Lincoln, intellectual force was matched with moral strength. He understood the spirit as well as the needs of his time; and he was possessed of that pragmatic way of thinking which is conducive to successful action and which always stands the test if it is anchored in firm convictions."[28]

A century after the Civil War, another Nobel Peace Prize winner, Dr. Martin Luther King Jr., found inspiration in Lincoln, mentioning him dozens of times in speeches and sermons.[29] In his most celebrated address, the "I Have a Dream" speech in 1963, Dr. King stood on the steps of the Lincoln Memorial and declared, "Five score years ago, a great American in whose symbolic shadow we stand today, signed the Emancipation Proclamation . . . It came as a joyous daybreak to end the long night of their captivity. But one hundred years later, the Negro still is not free." By invoking Lincoln along with the Declaration of Independence and the Constitution, King challenged the country to live up to its ideals in a spirit of reconciliation without retreat from full equality, to "transform the jangling discords of our nation into a beautiful symphony of brotherhood." His assassination five years later in Memphis placed him in the pantheon of American martyrs alongside Lincoln.

Nelson Mandela, the Nobel Peace Prize–winning political-prisoner-turned-president of South Africa, was similarly inspired by Lincoln's leadership while overturning apartheid. In 1991, Mandela said, "We can find a resonance and a relevance to our situation in the words of Abraham Lincoln's Gettysburg Address . . . We, too, must say that our nation 'shall have a new birth of freedom—and that government of the people, by the people, for the people, shall not perish from the earth.' We must say this because indeed our nation is having a new birth, having engaged in its own great Civil War—which, also dedicated to the proposition that all men are created equal, unhappily is not yet concluded."[30]

Mandela would be eulogized as "Africa's Lincoln" by his biographer John Carlin. "The big truth is that Mandela, like Lincoln, achieved the historically rare feat of uniting a fiercely divided country," Carlin wrote. "The feat is rare because what ordinary politicians have always done is seek power by highlighting differences and fueling antagonisms. Mandela sought it by appealing to people's common humanity."[31]

That is what reconciling leaders do. They rise above tribal divides by focusing on our common humanity. They restore harmony by confronting contradictions, with the goal of making a divided system whole and consistent. They move forward with an absence of malice, secure in the belief that right ultimately makes might. In the process, they can help create the conditions for a just and lasting peace.

We are all the children of Abraham, guided by the light of history. Lincoln's vision for winning the peace and his example of reconciling leadership were integrated. They flowed from his character and his understanding of human nature, with its ever-upward aspirations, adding a spiritual dimension to democracy.

Lincoln's almost mystical attachment to the Union was far more than a constitutional obligation adopted with his oath of office. Fused with the abolition of slavery, it was a broader assertion of the underlying unity of humanity, embodied by the essential diversity of the United States, reflected in his declaration that "the theory of our government is universal freedom."[32]

In his greatest speeches, Lincoln broke down the barriers of time, invoking the past to illuminate the present while setting a direction for the future. In the last six weeks of his life, he reached the pinnacle of his powers, moving by instinct born of experience, viewing the shattered landscape with perspective.

All the diverse strains of Lincoln's life—the prairie lawyer and the politician; the poet and the lay preacher; the wartime president and the peacemaker—culminated in the final paragraph of his Second Inaugural Address. Its message was reinforced by all that he saw and did over the final forty-one days of his life, from his walk through the ruins of Richmond holding Tad's hand while greeting newly freed men and women, to consoling wounded Union and Confederate soldiers alike, to joy over Lee's surrender at Appomattox, to the guidance of his last speech from the White House—offering not just a glimpse of victory, but a glimpse of grace.

As the sun shone through the clouds at the start of his Second Inaugural, Lincoln offered up his own Sermon on the Mount, speaking from the place where all divisions fall away to reveal the transcendent truth:

America is both North and South, White and Black, Republican and Democrat. We are laughter and loss, Saturday night and Sunday morning, Old Testament and New. Liberty and equality are not opposites in inevitable conflict, but act in concert under the practical balance of the Union. In the end, even war and peace are intimately entwined.

Lincoln's vision of the fight for peace was crystalized in the final paragraph of his Second Inaugural Address. Read it again, out loud:

> With malice toward none; with charity for all; with firmness in the right, as God gives us to see the right, let us strive on to finish the work we are in; to bind up the nation's wounds; to care for him who shall have borne the battle, and for his widow and his orphan—to do all which may achieve and cherish a just, and a lasting peace, among ourselves, and with all nations.

Those seventy-four words remain the best sentence in our democracy. There is poetry and rhythm but more than that: there is durable wisdom, pointing imperfect people toward a more perfect union.

It is a place of forgiveness and love: "with malice toward none; with charity for all."

It is a place where determination does not slip into self-righteousness: "with firmness in the right, as God gives us to see the right, let us strive on to finish the work we are in."

It is a place where compassion meets action: "to bind up the nation's wounds; to care for him who shall have borne the battle and for his widow and his orphan."

Most of all, it is a place where we have the courage to reconcile and reunite: "to do all which may achieve and cherish a just, and a lasting peace, among ourselves, and with all nations."

Lincoln showed us the way.

Appendix

LINCOLN'S SECOND INAUGURAL ADDRESS

March 4, 1865

Fellow Countrymen:

At this second appearing to take the oath of the presidential office there is less occasion for an extended address than there was at the first. Then a statement somewhat in detail of a course to be pursued seemed fitting and proper. Now, at the expiration of four years during which public declarations have been constantly called forth on every point and phase of the great contest which still absorbs the attention and engrosses the energies of the nation little that is new could be presented.

The progress of our arms, upon which all else chiefly depends is as well known to the public as to myself and it is, I trust, reasonably satisfactory and encouraging to all. With high hope for the future no prediction in regard to it is ventured.

On the occasion corresponding to this four years ago all thoughts were anxiously directed to an impending civil war. All dreaded it ~ all sought to avert it. While the inaugural address was being delivered from this place devoted altogether to saving the Union without war insurgent agents were in the city seeking to destroy it without war ~ seeking to dissolve the Union and divide effects by negotiation.

Both parties deprecated war but one of them would make war

rather than let the nation survive, and the other would accept war rather than let it perish. And the war came.

One eighth of the whole population were colored slaves not distributed generally over the union but localized in the southern part of it. These slaves constituted a peculiar and powerful interest. All knew that this interest was somehow the cause of the war. To strengthen perpetuate and extend this interest was the object for which the insurgents would rend the Union even by war while the government claimed no right to do more than to restrict the territorial enlargement of it.

Neither party expected for the war the magnitude or the duration which it has already attained. Neither anticipated that the cause of the conflict might cease with or even before the conflict itself should cease. Each looked for an easier triumph and a result less fundamental and astounding.

Both read the same Bible and pray to the same God and each invokes His aid against the other. It may seem strange that any men should dare to ask a just God's assistance in wringing their bread from the sweat of other men's faces but let us judge not that we be not judged. The prayers of both could not be answered ~ that of neither has been answered fully. The Almighty has His own purposes. "Woe unto the world because of offenses for it must needs be that offenses come but woe to that man by whom the offense cometh." If we shall suppose that American slavery is one of those offenses which in the providence of God must needs come but which having continued through His appointed time He now wills to remove and that He gives to both North and South this terrible war as the woe due to those by whom the offense came shall we discern therein any departure from those divine attributes which the believers in a living God always ascribe to Him. Fondly do we hope ~ fervently do we pray ~ that this mighty scourge of war may speedily pass away. Yet, if God wills that it continue until all the wealth piled by the bondsman's two hundred and fifty years of unrequited toil shall be sunk and until every drop of blood drawn with the lash shall be paid by another drawn with the sword as was said three thousand years ago so still it must be said "the judgments of the Lord are true and righteous altogether."

With malice toward none; with charity for all; with firmness in the right as God gives us to see the right, let us strive on to finish the work we are in; to bind up the nation's wounds; to care for him who shall have borne the battle and for his widow and his orphan—to do all which may achieve and cherish a just, and a lasting peace, among ourselves, and with all nations.

LINCOLN'S FINAL SPEECH

April 11, 1865

We meet this evening, not in sorrow, but in gladness of heart. The evacuation of Petersburg and Richmond, and the surrender of the principal insurgent army, give hope of a righteous and speedy peace whose joyous expression can not be restrained. In the midst of this, however, He from whom all blessings flow, must not be forgotten. A call for a national thanksgiving is being prepared, and will be duly promulgated. Nor must those whose harder part gives us the cause of rejoicing, be overlooked. Their honors must not be parceled out with others. I myself was near the front, and had the high pleasure of transmitting much of the good news to you; but no part of the honor, for plan or execution, is mine. To Gen. Grant, his skillful officers, and brave men, all belongs. The gallant Navy stood ready, but was not in reach to take active part.

By these recent successes the re-inauguration of the national authority—reconstruction—which has had a large share of thought from the first, is pressed much more closely upon our attention. It is fraught with great difficulty. Unlike a case of a war between independent nations, there is no authorized organ for us to treat with. No one man has authority to give up the rebellion for any other man. We simply must begin with, and mould from, disorganized and discordant elements. Nor is it a small additional embarrassment that we, the loyal people, differ among ourselves as to the mode, manner, and means of reconstruction.

As a general rule, I abstain from reading the reports of attacks upon myself, wishing not to be provoked by that to which I can not properly offer an answer. In spite of this precaution, however, it comes to my knowledge that I am much censured for some supposed agency in setting up, and seeking to sustain, the new State government of Louisiana. In this I have done just so much as, and no more than, the public knows. In the Annual Message of Dec. 1863 and accompanying Proclamation, I presented *a* plan of re-construction (as the phrase goes) which, I promised, if adopted by any State, should be acceptable to, and sustained by, the Executive government of the nation. I distinctly stated that this was not the only plan which might possibly be acceptable; and I also distinctly protested that the Executive claimed no right to say when, or whether members should be admitted to seats in Congress from such States. This plan was, in advance, submitted to the then Cabinet, and distinctly approved by every member of it. One of them suggested that I should then, and in that connection, apply the Emancipation Proclamation to the theretofore excepted parts of Virginia and Louisiana; that I should drop the suggestion about apprenticeship for freed-people, and that I should omit the protest against my own power, in regard to the admission of members to Congress; but even he approved every part and parcel of the plan which has since been employed or touched by the action of Louisiana. The new constitution of Louisiana, declaring emancipation for the whole State, practically applies the Proclamation to the part previously excepted. It does not adopt apprenticeship for freed-people; and it is silent, as it could not well be otherwise, about the admission of members to Congress. So that, as it applies to Louisiana, every member of the Cabinet fully approved the plan. The message went to Congress, and I received many commendations of the plan, written and verbal; and not a single objection to it, from any professed emancipationist, came to my knowledge, until after the news reached Washington that the people of Louisiana had begun to move in accordance with it. From about July 1862, I had corresponded with different persons, supposed to be interested, seeking a reconstruction of a State government for Louisiana. When the message of 1863, with the plan before mentioned, reached New-Orleans, Gen. Banks wrote me that he was confident the people, with his military co-operation, would reconstruct, substantially on that plan. I wrote him, and some of them to try it; they tried it, and the result is known. Such only has been my agency in getting up the Louisiana government. As to sustaining it, my promise is out, as before stated. But, as bad promises are better broken than kept, I shall treat this as a bad promise, and break it, whenever I shall be convinced that keeping it is adverse to the public interest. But I have not yet been so convinced.

I have been shown a letter on this subject, supposed to be an able one, in which the writer expresses regret that my mind has not seemed to be definitely fixed on the question whether the seceding States, so called, are in the Union or out of it. It would perhaps, add astonishment to his regret, were he to learn that since I have found professed Union men endeavoring to make that question, I have *purposely* forborne any public expression upon it. As appears to me that question has not been, nor yet is, a practically material one, and that any discussion of it, while it thus remains practically immaterial, could have no effect other than the mischievous one of dividing our friends. As yet, whatever it may hereafter become, that question is bad, as the basis of a controversy, and good for nothing at all—a merely pernicious abstraction.

We all agree that the seceded States, so called, are out of their proper relation with the Union; and that the sole object of the government, civil and military, in regard to those States is to again get them into that proper practical relation. I believe it is not only possible, but in fact, easier to do this, without deciding, or even considering, whether these States have ever been out of the Union, than with it. Finding themselves safely at home, it would be utterly immaterial whether they had ever been abroad. Let us all join in doing the acts necessary to restoring the proper practical relations between these States and the Union; and each forever after, innocently indulge his own opinion whether, in doing the acts, he brought the States from without, into the Union, or only gave them proper assistance, they never having been out of it.

The amount of constituency, so to speak, on which the new Louisiana government rests, would be more satisfactory to all, if it contained fifty, thirty, or even twenty thousand, instead of only about twelve thousand, as it does. It is also unsatisfactory to some that the elective franchise is not given to the colored man. I would myself prefer that it were now conferred on the very intelligent, and on those who serve our cause as soldiers. Still the question is not whether the Louisiana government, as it stands, is quite all that is desirable. The question is, "Will it be wiser to take it as it is, and help to improve it; or to reject, and disperse it?" "Can Louisiana be brought into proper practical relation with the Union *sooner* by *sustaining*, or by *discarding* her new State government?"

Some twelve thousand voters in the heretofore slave-state of

Louisiana have sworn allegiance to the Union, assumed to be the rightful political power of the State, held elections, organized a State government, adopted a free-state constitution, giving the benefit of public schools equally to black and white, and empowering the Legislature to confer the elective franchise upon the colored man. Their Legislature has already voted to ratify the constitutional amendment recently passed by Congress, abolishing slavery throughout the nation. These twelve thousand persons are thus fully committed to the Union, and to perpetual freedom in the state—committed to the very things, and nearly all the things the nation wants—and they ask the nations recognition and it's assistance to make good their committal. Now, if we reject, and spurn them, we do our utmost to disorganize and disperse them. We in effect say to the white men "You are worthless, or worse—we will neither help you, nor be helped by you." To the blacks we say "This cup of liberty which these, your old masters, hold to your lips, we will dash from you, and leave you to the chances of gathering the spilled and scattered contents in some vague and undefined when, where, and how."

If this course, discouraging and paralyzing both white and black, has any tendency to bring Louisiana into proper practical relations with the Union, I have, so far, been unable to perceive it. If, on the contrary, we recognize, and sustain the new government of Louisiana the converse of all this is made true. We encourage the hearts, and nerve the arms of the twelve thousand to adhere to their work, and argue for it, and proselyte for it, and fight for it, and feed it, and grow it, and ripen it to a complete success. The colored man too, in seeing all united for him, is inspired with vigilance, and energy, and daring, to the same end. Grant that he desires the elective franchise, will he not attain it sooner by saving the already advanced steps toward it, than by running backward over them? Concede that the new government of Louisiana is only to what it should be as the egg is to the fowl, we shall sooner have the fowl by hatching the egg than by smashing it? Again, if we reject Louisiana, we also reject one vote in favor of the proposed amendment to the national Constitution.

To meet this proposition, it has been argued that no more than three fourths of those States which have not attempted secession are necessary to validly ratify the amendment. I do not commit myself against this, further than to say that such a ratification would be questionable, and sure to be persistently questioned; while a ratification by three-fourths of all the States would be unquestioned and unquestionable.

I repeat the question, "Can Louisiana be brought into proper practical relation with the Union *sooner* by *sustaining* or by *discarding* her new State Government?"

What has been said of Louisiana will apply generally to other States. And yet so great peculiarities pertain to each state, and such important and sudden changes occur in the same state; and withal, so new and unprecedented is the whole case, that no exclusive, and inflexible plan can be safely prescribed as to details and collaterals. Such exclusive, and inflexible plan, would surely become a new entanglement. Important principles may, and must, be inflexible.

In the present *"situation"* as the phrase goes, it may be my duty to make some new announcement to the people of the South. I am considering, and shall not fail to act, when satisfied that action will be proper.

Acknowledgments

In some ways, the seeds of this book were sown in 1937, when my grandfather—a young, orphaned Greek immigrant named John Avlon—was given a framed photo of Abraham Lincoln by a man named Frederick H. Meserve, a prominent New York collector of all things Lincoln. A handwritten note on the matted border said it was printed directly from a negative taken by Mathew Brady in Washington, D.C., in 1864. It was an act of kindness, a further welcoming to America, and it carried forward, hanging on the wall of our apartment when I was a child. Dropped into a story well underway, I wanted to know more about the man in black with the leather boots.

We are guided by the light of history. As a journalist, I use history to bring perspective to current events. As a writer, my books have all focused on how to overcome hyper-partisanship and polarization—attacking the problem from different angles—mindful that those forces have led to the decline of democracies in the past. But, as my son, Jack, is quick to remind me, "Books have no influence on anything except the mind."

This book was written primarily during the presidency of Donald Trump and completed during the Covid pandemic. Having Lincoln to return to, day after day, was medicine. Lincoln is that rare person who does not disappoint upon closer study. For all his very human flaws, there is nothing small or mean or petty about him. He does not tear other people down to get ahead or allow ideology, partisanship, or religion to excuse amoral behavior. He reminds us that character is destiny and kindness can be consistent with effective leadership.

Embarking on a Lincoln book is daunting given that more than

16,000 volumes have already been written. As I developed this idea, I ran it by several Lincoln scholars—Harold Holzer, Louis Masur, Tom Schwartz, and Daniel Weinberg—to see if it had been already done or whether I was reaching beyond where the facts might lead. I was happy to find that Lincoln the Peacemaker was open territory.

My agent, Sloan Harris, was champion of this book from the beginning. He is everything an author could want in an agent: intelligent, insightful, and energetic with an empathetic understanding of what makes an author and a specific book really tick. He's deservedly risen to the top ranks of ICM and I look forward to working with him for a long time to come.

A year into the work, the world of literary history lost a legend in Alice Mayhew. In addition to being my editor, Alice was a neighbor in Sag Harbor. But I am grateful to Jonathan Karp for directing me to Priscilla Painton as her successor and editor of this book. Priscilla's background as a journalist and her renowned work as an editor of political history made her the obvious fit. Her insights made the book better, and so many thanks are due to her and Hana Park, Phil Metcalf, and everyone at Simon & Schuster.

Jesse Rifkin was a tireless research assistant throughout this project. He was thorough and enterprising, helping find obscure articles that I'd flagged, formatting the voluminous endnotes, and organizing the photo permissions. I owe him a debt of gratitude with appreciation for his talents.

Early readers of a manuscript are invaluable, especially at those times when you run the risk of missing the forest for the trees, and both Margaret and my mother were beyond helpful in this process. One of the joys in life is becoming friends with your teachers, and my high school English teacher from Milton, David Dunbar, gave the book its first full read outside my family. Lincoln studies guru Harold Holzer took the time for a close read early in the process, and his feedback was clarifying and encouraging. It's not often that you can call on a former Pentagon historian and Civil War expert to make sure you're getting all military details right, but that's what I was able to get from retired general David Armstrong. Shamil Idriss of Search for Common Ground gave valuable feedback on the book's application to current peace-making efforts, and it was an honor to have John Paul Lederach, author of *The Moral Imagination: The Art and Soul of Building Peace*, and *Reconcile*, to take the time to read the manuscript and make suggestions that helped to validate Lincoln's intuition of many principles that have become best practices for peace builders around the world. His faith-inspired approach also helped me appreciate how Lincoln was following the path prescribed in the Book of Micah: "Do justice, love kindness, walk humbly with your God." There were also key conversations during the book's composition, especially with Dr. Conrad Crane of the U.S. Army War College and Nadia Schadlow—two of America's premier experts on securing peace after war. Finally, thanks are always due to Errol Louis and Matt Pottinger for their insights and, most important, for their friendship.

The crafting and research of a book is part of the fun for me, but few cold calls could ever result in more on the ground generosity than Richmond U.S. Park Ranger and historian Michael D. Gorman, who took time from his busy schedule to lead a small band of Avlons—including my son, Jack, and mother, Dianne—on a walk from the location where Lincoln landed by Shockoe Creek (not Rockett's Landing, as often misreported) up to the Virginia State Capitol, allowing us to trace the steps of Lincoln's uphill walk into Richmond. His ninety-page essay on Lincoln in Richmond is also a definitive assessment of history from a local perspective. On the same visit, Ana Edwards was also kind to give us a tour of the Confederate White House and its environs.

I should note here a stylistic decision in this book that relates especially to the quotes from the scenes after the fall of Richmond. I've chosen to take most of the quotations from freedmen and -women from the crude, often confusing, and definitely dehumanizing racial dialect that was often used in contemporary accounts and turned it into a faithful clarification of the words they spoke, consistent with contemporary English. Good people can disagree, but I think this is the right course, consistent with dignity and clarity.

There is a fascinating back story to the cover image of this book. It is a painting by N. C. Wyeth of Abraham Lincoln, commissioned by the John C. Morrell meat packing company for its 1940 calendar, "America in the Making." Selected as the image for the month of December, Wyeth's conception was Lincoln reading his second inaugural address—specifically the lines "With Malice Toward None; With Charity for All." Wyeth often worked with American myths, but in this painting he uncharacteristically placed his subject in an atmospheric and elemental background, the sun at his face, as storm clouds gathered—or receded—behind him. It's believed that the choice was inspired by the sense that the Second World War would soon engulf the United States—as it did. After this inspired commission, the John C. Morrell Company graciously gave all the paintings in the series to Iowa State University. I'm grateful to Allison Sheridan, at the University Museums of Iowa State University, for helping secure the rights for republication. But crucial final hurdles were cleared thanks to the beyond-the-call-of-duty assistance from Courtney Stanton, vice president of Smithfield Bioscience, and Jeff Porter of the Smithfield Law Department. Given that Smithfield Foods purchased John C. Morrell more than a decade ago, their help in clearing up a copyright question was invaluable to bring about the perfect cover image for this book. N. C. Wyeth was a giant of American illustration—a great tradition that is being carried forward by artists like Cathie Bleck, who drew the Lincoln profile icon throughout the book. Thanks also to the supremely talented, supernaturally cool, and completely hilarious Lynsey Addario for taking my author photo.

This book was sold when I was Editor in Chief of *The Daily Beast* and researched and written during nights, weekends, and vacations since I joined CNN full-time in the summer of 2018. I am proud to be part of this global independent news organization committed to breaking news and accountability journalism—especially at a time when freedom of the press is under attack. I want to thank Jeff Zucker for his exemplary leadership along with the rest of his senior team: Amy Entelis, Michael Bass, Ken Jautz, Andrew Morse, Allison Gollust, Rick Davis, Calvin Sims, Ramon Escobar, Rebecca Kutler, Sam Fiest, and my friend Matt Dornic. The New Day team has been a blast to work with, especially our EPs—Eric Hall, Javi Morgado, Jim Murphy, and Izzy Povich; our on-air early AM family—John Berman, Brianna Keilar, Laura Jarret, and Christine Romans; and the crew (including Bruce, Brad, Dean, Lou, Bookman, Phil, Joe, Rob, and many more) who make everything happen with efficiency and humor.

The on-air friendships you see at CNN are real off camera, and

I'd like to thank Don Lemon, Poppy Harlow, Alisyn Camerota, Chris Cuomo, Erin Burnett, Kate Bolduan, Mark Preston, Harry Enten, Fareed Zakaria, Dana Bash, Bakari Sellers, Ana Cabrerra, Jake Tapper, Jim Sciutto, Christiane Amanpour, Anderson Cooper, Abby Phillip, Jim Acosta, Bill Weir, Donie O'Sullivan, Sanjay Gupta, Brian Stelter, Oliver Darcy, Marshall Cohen, Sarah Sidner, Bianna Golodryga, Van Jones, Erica Hill, Elie Honig, SE Cupp, Michael Holmes, Andrew Kaczynski, Neel Khairzada, Jon Auerbach, Jon Adler, Susie Xu, and Margaret Dawson. It's an honor and a pleasure to work with such a talented group. Participating in CNN's Lincoln series, *Divided We Stand*, gave me a chance to air some of the ideas in this book on camera. I look forward to working with that team more in the future.

In researching this book, I've been struck by how relatively thin the study of peace and postwar stabilization is compared to the study of war. The two are of course connected, but narrative histories are overwhelmingly (and perhaps understandably) weighted toward winning the war—rather than winning the peace. This needs to be recalibrated. There are some organizations that are dedicated to this subject, from the relatively new Jackson Institute at Yale University and Columbia University's International Center for Cooperation and Conflict Resolution to the century-old Hoover Institution on War, Revolution, and Peace, which has invaluable archives and fellows—including the late, great Charlie Hill. Professor Daniel Lieberfeld's work on "reconciliation-oriented leadership" deserves to be more widely known, particularly his paper comparing the leadership styles of Lincoln and Mandela. The Gilder-Lehrman Institute, led by the dynamic Jim Basker, also plays a key role in ensuring that civic education and American history remain core to public education. It's an essential role that helps advance a civil society.

Lincoln believed that "the better part of one's life consists of his friendships," and on that front I have been blessed with too many to name comprehensively from every stage of life. You know who you are. Love to my godparents and my godchildren—Benji, Flora, Matilda, Catherine, Alex, Miles & Cole—and, of course, their parents: The Damons, the Vanderzees, the Catlins, and the Pottingers. Thanks to the Grace Church School community, the RTR team (Bill, Mickey, Maya, Jon, Paul, and Kahlil), Citizens Union of New York, YPO, and all our friends in Charleston. Shout-out to all my fellow Beasts with love and respect for the memory of Chris Dickey, Ed Victor, and Harry Evans. This book was researched in part while on vacation with our friends Lynn and Evelyn as well as Bill and Zoe, with much of it written at the National Arts Club and the third floor of John Jermain Library. And especially after the Covid year, I want to thank our Sag Harbor crew: Elise and Mike, Emma and David, Jenny and Scott, James and Jillian, Annie and Soumi, Mark and Vimla (Everest & Paloma!), Sally and Robin, Don and Tim, Henrick and Bita, Jordan and Robert, Joy, Tuna, Camilla, Julian and Meg, Jimmy and Jane, Nicole and Joel, Michael and Cathie, Jeff and Michelle, Suzanne and Peter, Jeff and Kelly, Libby and Chris, Max and Kaileigh, Jim and Angela. It's a magic place.

To my family, I owe everything. To my mother and father for instilling a love of history and debate and appreciation for our county, reinforced by the example of my beloved grandparents from Youngstown, Ohio, whose spirit flows on in the whole Phillips family—Joan, Lexa and David, and Alex—and down to the next generation with Reynolds and Alex Timbers and all our extended family, especially Rebekah. Thanks are always due to my amazing outlaw Hoover family—Andy, Jeanie, Alex, Margaret (aka Dos Equis), McKenna, and Sophie. Nothing can be achieved without a supportive spouse, and I am blessed to have found a beautiful, loving, and dynamic mate in Margaret. She is bright and shining in every way—that's why I call you LOML.

When you have children, all the mysteries of the universe are revealed: our two beautiful children, Jack and Toula Lou—now eight and six—are pure joy and wonder. In the happy chaos of our home, they amaze, delight, and inspire, reminding us every day of the true meaning of life and love. In return, we try to tell them every day that we love them unconditionally and eternally—which means forever and ever, never ever stopping, no matter what. This is for them.

—Sag Harbor, New York, 2021

Selected Bibliography

American Antislavery Writings: Colonial Beginnings to Emancipation. Ed. James G. Basker. New York: Library of America, 2012.

Armitage, David. *Civil Wars: A History in Ideas*. New York: Alfred A. Knopf, 2017.

Arnold, Isaac N. *The Life of Abraham Lincoln*. Chicago, IL: Jansen, McClurg & Company, 1885.

Battles and Leaders of the Civil War, Vol. IV. Eds. Clarence Clough Buel Johnson and Robert Underwood. New York: Castle Books, 1982.

Belz, Herman. *Reconstructing the Union: Theory and Policy during the Civil War*. Ithaca, NY: Cornell University Press, 1969.

Blight, David W. *Frederick Douglass: Prophet of Freedom*. New York: Simon & Schuster, 2020.

———. *Race and Reunion: The Civil War in American Memory*. Cambridge, MA: Belknap Press, 2001.

Brooks, Noah. *Washington, D.C., in Lincoln's Time: A Memoir of the Civil War Era by the Newspaperman Who Knew Lincoln Best*. Ed. Herbert Mitgang. Athens: University of Georgia Press, 1989.

Burlingame, Michael. *Abraham Lincoln: A Life Vol. 2*. Baltimore: Johns Hopkins University Press, Reprint edition, November 6, 2012.

Carwardine, Richard. *Lincoln: A Life of Purpose and Power*. New York: Alfred A. Knopf, 2006.

Catton, Bruce. *A Stillness at Appomattox*. New York: Random House, 1953.

Cox, LaWanda. *Lincoln and Black Freedom*. University of South Carolina Press, 1981.

Current, Richard N. and J. G. Randall. *Lincoln the President, Volume 2: Midstream to the Last Full Measure*. New York: Da Capo Press, Inc., 1997.

de Chambrun, Adolphe. *Impressions of Lincoln and the Civil War: A Foreigner's Account.* Trans. Aldebert de Chambrun. New York: Random House, 1952.

Donald, David Herbert. *Lincoln.* New York: Simon & Schuster, 1996.

Foner, Eric. *The Fiery Trial: Abraham Lincoln and American Slavery.* New York: W.W. Norton, 2011.

———. *Politics and Ideology in the Age of the Civil War.* New York: Oxford University Press, 1980.

———. *Reconstruction: America's Unfinished Revolution.* New York: Harper Perennial, 2014.

Gaddis, John Lewis. *On Grand Strategy.* New York: Penguin Press, 2018.

The Global Lincoln. Ed. Richard Carwardine and Jay Sexton. New York: Oxford University Press, 2011.

Goodwin, Doris Kearns. *Team of Rivals: The Political Genius of Abraham Lincoln.* New York: Simon & Schuster, 2006.

Grant, Ulysses S. *Personal Memoirs of Ulysses S. Grant, Volumes One and Two.* New York: Charles L. Webster and Company, 1885.

Hatcher, Edmund N. *The Last Four Weeks of the War.* Columbus: J. Wiggins & Co., 1891.

Hay, John and John G. Nicolay. *Abraham Lincoln: A History, Vol. 9.* New York: The Century Co., 1917.

Hesseltine, William B. *Lincoln's Plan of Reconstruction.* Ed. Wm Stanley Hoole. Gloucester: The Confederate Publishing Company, Inc., 1963.

Holzer, Harold. *Lincoln and the Power of the Press.* New York: Simon & Schuster, 2014.

Holzer, Harold, and Norton Garfinkle. *A Just and Generous Nation: Abraham Lincoln and the Fight for American Opportunity.* New York: Basic Books, 2015.

Hoover, Herbert and Hugh Gibson. *The Problems of Lasting Peace.* New York: Doubleday, Doran and Company, Inc., 1942.

Janey, Caroline E. *Remembering the Civil War.* Chapel Hill, NC: UNC Press, 2013.

Lawson, Melinda. *Patriot Fires: Forging a New American Nationalism in the Civil War North.* Lawrence: University Press of Kansas, 2002.

Lieberfeld, Daniel. "Lincoln, Mandela, and Qualities of Reconciliation-Oriented Leadership," *Peace and Conflict: Journal of Peace Psychology* (January 1, 2009).

The Lincoln Anthology: Great Writers on His Life and Legacy from 1860 to Now. Ed. Harold Holzer. New York: The Library of America, 2008.

Lincoln Observed: Civil War Dispatches of Noah Brooks. Ed. Michael Burlingame. Baltimore: Johns Hopkins University Press, 1998.

Lincoln on War: Our Greatest Commander-in-Chief Speaks to America. Ed. Harold Holzer. Chapel Hill, NC: Algonquin Books of Chapel Hill, 2011.

Lincoln's Own Yarns and Stories. Ed. Alexander K. McClure. Philadelphia: The John C. Winston Company, 1940.

Lincoln Stories . . . . Told By Him in the Military Office in the War Department During the Civil War. Trans. David Homer Bates. New York: William Edwin Rudge, Inc., 1926.

Masur, Louis P. *The Civil War: A Concise History.* New York: Oxford University Press, 2011.

————. *Lincoln's Last Speech.* New York: Oxford University Press, 2015.

McPherson, James M. *Abraham Lincoln and the Second American Revolution.* New York: Oxford University Press, 1992.

An Oral History of Abraham Lincoln: John G. Nicolay's Interviews and Essays. Ed. Michael Burlingame. Carbondale: Southern Illinois University Press, 1996.

Peterson, Merrill D. *Lincoln in American Memory.* New York: Oxford University Press, 1995.

Pfanz, Donald C. *The Petersburg Campaign: Abraham Lincoln at City Point, March 20-April 9, 1865.* Lynchburg: H. E. Howard, Inc., 1989.

Randall, J.G. *Lincoln the Liberal Statesman.* New York: Dodd, Mead & Company, 1947.

Reck, W. Emerson. *A. Lincoln: His Last 24 Hours.* Jefferson, NC: McFarland & Company, Inc., Publishers, 1994.

Reconstruction: Voices from America's First Great Struggle for Racial Equality. Ed. Brooks D. Simpson. New York: The Library of America, 2018.

Reynolds, John S. *Reconstruction in South Carolina 1865–1877.* Columbia: The State Co. Publishers, 1905.

Rummel, R. J. *Understanding Conflict and War, Volume 5: The Just Peace.* Beverly Hills, CA: Sage Publications, Inc., 1981.

Schadlow, Nadia. *War and the Art of Governance.* Washington, D.C.: Georgetown University Press, 2017.

Seitz, Don C. *Lincoln the Politician: How the Rail-Splitter and Flatboatman Played the Great American Game.* New York: Coward-McCann, Inc., 1931.

Sherman, William T. *Memoirs of General William T. Sherman.* New York: D. Appleton & Co., 1875.

Simpson, Brooks D. *Let Us Have Peace: Ulysses S. Grant and the Politics of*

War & Reconstruction, 1861–1868. Chapel Hill: University of North Carolina Press, 1991.

Stoddard, William Osborn. *The Lives of the Presidents: Abraham Lincoln and Andrew Johnson.* New York: Frederick A. Stokes & Brother, 1888.

Temple, Wayne C. *Lincoln's Travels on the River Queen During the Last Days of His Life.* Mahomet, IL: Mayhaven Publishing, 2007.

Thomas Morris Chester, Black Civil War Correspondent: His Dispatches from the Virginia Front. Ed. R.J.M. Blackett. New York: Da Capo Press, 1989.

Thomas, Benjamin P. *Abraham Lincoln: A Biography.* New York: Alfred A. Knopf, 1952.

Trueblood, Elton. *Abraham Lincoln: Theologian of American Anguish.* New York: Harper & Row Publishers, Inc., 1973.

Varon, Elizabeth R. *Appomattox: Victory, Defeat, and Freedom at the End of the Civil War.* New York: Oxford University Press, 2014.

Waugh, John C. *Re-electing Lincoln: The Battle for the 1864 Presidency.* New York: Crown Publishers, Inc., 1997.

White, Richard. *The Republic for Which It Stands.* New York: Oxford University Press, 2017.

Wills, Garry. *Lincoln at Gettysburg.* New York: Simon & Schuster, 1992.

Wilson, Douglas L. *Lincoln's Sword: The Presidency and the Power of Words.* New York: Alfred A. Knopf, 2006.

Wood, Forrest G. *Black Scare: The Racist Response to Emancipation and Reconstruction.* Berkeley: University of California Press, 1970.

The Works of Abraham Lincoln, Vol. 7. Ed. Arthur Brooks Lapsley. New York: The Knickerbocker Press, 1906.

Zornow, William Frank. *Lincoln & the Party Divided.* Norman: University of Oklahoma Press, 1954.

Notes

INTRODUCTION

1 David Dixon Porter. *Incidents and Anecdotes of the Civil War.* New York: D. Appleton and Company, 1886, p. 295.

2 R. J. M. Blackett, ed. *Thomas Morris Chester, Black Civil War Correspondent: His Dispatches from the Virginia Front.* Baton Rouge, LA: Louisiana State University Press, 1989, pp. 295-296.

3 William H. Crook, "Lincoln's Last Day," *Harper's Monthly Magazine.* September 1907.

4 Charles Coffin. *The Boys of '61; or, Four Years of Fighting.* Boston, MA: Estes and Lauriat, 1884, p. 512.

5 R. J. M. Blackett, ed. *Thomas Morris Chester, Black Civil War Correspondent: His Dispatches from the Virginia Front.* Baton Rouge, LA: Louisiana State University Press, 1989, p. 295.

6 Thomas Thatcher Graves. "The Fall of Richmond II: The Occupation," *Battles and Leaders of the Civil War, vol 4.* New York, 1887, reprint, Robert Underwood Johnson and Clarence Clough Buel, ed. 1956; 4:728.

7 Horace Greeley. *Greeley on Lincoln.* New York: The Baker & Taylor Co., 1893, p. 75.

8 James Conroy. *Our One Common Country: Abraham Lincoln and the Hampton Roads Peace Conference of 1865.* Guilford, CT: Lyons Press, 2014, p. 174. Quote by Elizabeth Peabody.

9 Shakespeare, William. *Henry V:* Act 3, Scene 6-1600.

10 J. J. Hill. *A Sketch of the 29th Regiment of Colored Troops.* Baltimore: Dougherty, McGuire & Co., 1867, p. 27.

11 David D. Ryan. *Four Days in 1865: The Fall of Richmond.* Richmond, VA: Cadmus Marketing, 1993, pp. 124-125.

12   Civil War Sites Advisory Commission Report on the Nation's Civil
     War Battlefields. National Park Service and U.S. Department of In-
     terior, 1993. http://npshistory.com/publications/battlefield/cwsac
     /report.pdf.

13   Guy Gugliotta. "New Estimate Raises Civil War Death Toll," *New York
     Times*. April 3, 2012.

14   Author's calculation using the average length of a coffin: six feet, six
     inches times 750,000 equals 923 miles.

15   David Armitage. *Civil Wars: A History in Ideas*. New York: Alfred A.
     Knopf, 2017, p. 165.

16   "Our Rebellion Abroad: Effect of the Rebellion on Public Senti-
     ment in France—Loss of American Prestige," *New York Times*, April 16,
     1861.

17   "A Leaden Headed Lord On Democracy," *New York Times*, Novem-
     ber 19, 1861.

18   Abraham Lincoln, Letter to James C. Conkling, August 26, 1863.

19   John Hay. *Inside Lincoln's White House: The Complete Civil War Diary
     of John Hay*. Carbondale, IL: Southern Illinois University Press, 1997,
     p. 69.

20   Rufus Rockwell Wilson. *Intimate Memories of Lincoln*. Elmira, NY: Pri-
     mavera Press, 1945, p. 610.

21   Alfred John Church and William Jackson Brodribb, eds. *The Agricola
     and Germany of Tacitus*. London: MacMillan and Co., 1877, p. 29.

22   William Tecumseh Sherman. *Memoirs of General William T. Sherman*.
     New York: D. Appleton and Company, 1904, p. 327.

23   Abraham Lincoln, First Annual Message, December 3, 1861.

24   Daniel Lierberfeld. "Lincoln, Mandela, and Qualities of Reconciliation-
     oriented Leadership," *Peace and Conflict*, 15: 27–47, 2009.

25   Author interview with Daniel Weinberg, proprietor of the Abraham
     Lincoln Bookshop, Chicago, Illinois, August 2020.

26   David Dixon Porter. *Incidents and Anecdotes of the Civil War*. New York:
     D. Appleton and Company, 1886, p. 314.

27   Ken Lawrence. "Yes, John Wilkes Booth Did Speak Those Notorious
     Words at Lincoln's Last Speech," *History News Network*, May 10, 2020.

28   Judge David Davis, quoted in Merrill D. Peterson, *Lincoln in American
     Memory*. New York: Oxford University Press, 1994, p. 99.

29   William H. Herndon and Jesse W. Weik, ed. Douglas L. Wilson and
     Rodney O. Davis. *Herndon's Lincoln*. Urbana: University of Illinois
     Press, 2006, p. 138.

30 Roy P. Basler, ed. *The Collected Works of Abraham Lincoln* 8 vols. New Brunswick, NJ: Rutgers University Press, 1953, 2:220-21.

31 "Lifelong Friend of Lincoln Draws Picture of Lincoln as He Saw Him," *New York Times*, March 22, 1908, p. 38.

32 Lincoln's speech on the House floor, January 12, 1848. Roy P. Basler, ed. *The Collected Works of Abraham Lincoln* 8 vols. New Brunswick, NJ: Rutgers University Press, 1953-55, 1: 439.

33 Douglas L. Wilson and Rodney O. Davis, eds., *Herndon's Informants: Letters, Interviews, and Statements about Abraham Lincoln* (Urbana, IL: University of Illinois Press, 1998), p. 357.

34 George H. Haynes. "The Causes of Know-Nothing Success in Massachusetts." *The American Historical Review*, vol. 3, no. 1, 1897, pp. 67–82.

35 "Party Division," Senate.gov

36 "Party Divisions of the House of Representatives, 1789 to Present," history.house.gov

37 Harold Holzer. *Lincoln and the Power of the Press: The War for Public Opinion*. New York: Simon & Schuster, 2014, p. 186.

38 Roy P. Basler, ed. *Collected Works of Abraham Lincoln*, p. 323.

39 Ibid., pp. 322–323.

40 Lincoln letter to Henry L. Pierce and others: April 6, 1859. Roy P. Basler, ed. *The Collected Works of Abraham Lincoln* 8 vols. New Brunswick, NJ: Rutgers University Press, 1953, 3: 375.

41 *Complete Works of Abraham Lincoln, Volume 12*. New York: Francis D. Tandy Company, 1905, p. 3.

42 Lincoln speech on March 6, 1860, referring to Douglas. Roy P. Basler, ed. *The Collected Works of Abraham Lincoln* 8 vols. New Brunswick, NJ: Rutgers University Press, 1953, 4: 18.

43 Lincoln speech at New Haven, Connecticut: March 6, 1860. Roy P. Basler, ed. *The Collected Works of Abraham Lincoln* 8 vols. New Brunswick, NJ: Rutgers University Press, 1953, 4: 20.

44 First Debate with Stephen A. Douglas at Ottawa, Illinois. Roy P. Basler, ed. *The Collected Works of Abraham Lincoln* 8 vols. New Brunswick, NJ: Rutgers University Press, 1953, 3: 14.

45 *Complete Works of Abraham Lincoln, Volume 12*. New York: Francis D. Tandy Company, 1905, p. 4.

46 Jenkin Lloyd Jones. *Love and Loyalty*. Chicago, IL: The University of Chicago Press, 1907, p. 378.

47 Lincoln, remarks at Springfield, Illinois, November 20, 1860. Roy P.

Basler, ed. *The Collected Works of Abraham Lincoln* 8 vols. New Brunswick, NJ: Rutgers University Press, 1953, 4: 142-3.

48 1860 Census: Population of the United States. https://www.census.gov/library/publications/1864/dec/1860a.html.

49 Abraham Lincoln, Message to Congress, July 4, 1861.

50 Ibid.

51 U.S. Census: Population of the United States in 1860—South Carolina. https://www2.census.gov/library/publications/decennial/1860/population/1860a-32.pdf.

52 Joanne B. Freeman. *The Field of Blood: Violence in Congress and the Road to Civil War.* New York: Farrar, Straus and Giroux, 2018, p. 5.

53 John C. Calhoun Senate floor speech, January 10, 1838. Richard K. Crallé, ed. *Speeches of John C. Calhoun.* New York: D. Appleton and Company, 1859, p. 180.

54 Lincoln speech at Leavenworth, Kansas, December 3, 1859. Roy P. Basler, ed. *The Collected Works of Abraham Lincoln* 8 vols. New Brunswick, NJ: Rutgers University Press, 1953, 3: p. 502.

55 "The Republican Party Going to the Right House," Lithograph by Louis Maurer for Currier and Ives, 1860. Reprinted in Bernard F. Reilly, Jr., *American Political Prints 1776–1876: A Catalogue of the Library of Congress.* Boston: G.K. Hall, 1991, p. 443.

56 Abraham Lincoln, Cooper Union Speech, February 27, 1860.

57 James Buchanan, Fourth Annual Message to Congress on the State of the Union, December 3, 1860.

58 Alexander H. Stephens, Cornerstone Speech, March 21, 1861.

59 Lincoln Inaugural Address, March 4, 1861.

60 Abraham Lincoln, Letter to Charles D. Drake, October 5, 1863. Roy P. Basler, ed. *The Collected Works of Abraham Lincoln* 8 vols. New Brunswick, NJ: Rutgers University Press, 1953, 6: 500.

61 "Evidence for The Unpopular Mr. Lincoln: The People at the Polls 1860–1864." American Battlefield Trust at battlefields.org. Accessed February 23, 2021.

62 John Niven, ed. *The Salmon P. Chase Papers, Vol. 1.* Kent, OH: The Kent State University Press, 1993, p. 476.

63 Wilmer C. Harris. *Public Life of Zachariah Chandler.* Lansing: Michigan Historical Commission, 1917, p. 61.

64 W. M. Dickson to Friedrich Hassaurek, Cincinnati, Hassaurek Papers, September 27, 1861, Ohio Historical Society.

65 Abraham Lincoln, Letter to Edwin M. Stanton, July 14, 1864. Roy P. Basler, ed. *The Collected Works of Abraham Lincoln* 8 vols. New Brunswick, NJ: Rutgers University Press, 1953, 7: 440.

66 Ward Hill Lamon. *Recollections of Abraham Lincoln 1847–1865*. Chicago: A. C. McClurg and Company, 1895, p. 188.

67 "The Right Man in the Right Place." *New York Times*, September 7, 1863.

68 James Russell Lowell. "The President's Policy." *North American Review*, January 1864.

69 Abraham Lincoln, Letter of instruction to John G. Nicolay, c. July 16, 1860. Roy P. Basler, ed. *The Collected Works of Abraham Lincoln* 8 vols. New Brunswick, NJ: Rutgers University Press, 1953, 4: 83.

70 Abraham Lincoln, Speech at Peoria, Illinois, October 16, 1854. Roy P. Basler, ed. *The Collected Works of Abraham Lincoln* 8 vols. New Brunswick, NJ: Rutgers University Press, 1953, 2:248.

71 Lincoln-Douglas first debate, August 21, 1858. Roy P. Basler, ed. *The Collected Works of Abraham Lincoln* 8 vols. New Brunswick, NJ: Rutgers University Press, 1953, 3:14.

72 *Complete Works of Abraham Lincoln, Volume 12*. New York: Francis D. Tandy Company, 1905, p. 19.

73 William H. Seward, Letter to Charles Francis Adams, April 10, 1861, written "in the name of the President." Marion Mills Miller, ed. *Letters and Telegrams: Adams to Garrison*. New York: The Current Literature Publishing Co., 1907, p. 3.

74 David Homer Bates. *Lincoln in the Telegraph Office: Recollections of the United States Military Telegraph Corps During the Civil War*. New York: Century Co., 1907, p. 205.

75 Ida Tarbell. *The Life of Abraham Lincoln, Volume Four*. New York: Lincoln Historical Society, 1909, p. 21.

76 "Lincoln on the execution of a slave trader, 1862," The Gilder Lehrman Institute of American History. Accessed February 23, 2021.

77 Abraham Lincoln telegraph to Grant, August 17, 1864. Roy P. Basler, ed. *The Collected Works of Abraham Lincoln* 8 vols. New Brunswick, NJ: Rutgers University Press, 1953, 7: 499.

78 Lynda Lasswell Crist and Suzanne Scott Gibbs, eds. *The Papers of Jefferson Davis: 1880–1889*. Baton Rouge, LA: Louisiana State University Press, 2015, p. 223.

79 John W. Forney. *Anecdotes of Public Men, Volume II*. New York: Harper & Brothers, 1873, p. 179.

80 Elizabeth Keckley. *Behind the Scenes: Or, Thirty Years a Slave, and Four Years in the White House.* New York: G. W. Carleton & Co., Publishers, 1868, p. 131.

81 Francis Bicknell Carpenter, *Six Months at the White House.* New York: Hurd and Houghton, 1866, p. 150.

82 Philip B. Kunhardt II and Peter W. Kunhardt. *Looking for Lincoln: The Making of an American Icon.* New York: Alfred A. Knopf, 2008. p. 98.

83 Allen Thorndike Rice. *Reminiscences of Abraham Lincoln: By Distinguished Men of his Time.* New York: North American Publishing Company, 1886, p. 427–428.

84 Wayne Whipple. "Abraham Lincoln: The Great American Humorist," *The Hampton Magazine*, February 1912.

85 Quoted in Don E. Fehrenbacher and Virginia Fehrenbacher, *Recollected Words of Lincoln.* Stanford, CA: Stanford University Press, 1996, 18. See also *New York Times*, May 10, 1885.

86 Michael Burlingame, ed. *An Oral History of Abraham Lincoln: John G. Nicolay's Interviews and Essays.* Carbondale: Southern Illinois University Press, 1996, 2. Conversation with Hon. O. H. Browning at Leland Hotel Springfield, June 17, 1875.

87 Frederick Douglass. "Oration by Frederick Douglass, delivered on the occasion of the unveiling of the Freedman's monument in memory of Abraham Lincoln," Digital Public Library of America. April 14, 1876.

88 Abraham Lincoln. Address to the New Jersey State Senate, Trenton, New Jersey, February 21, 1861.

89 Elizabeth Keckley. *Behind the Scenes: Or, Thirty Years a Slave, and Four Years in the White House.* New York: G. W. Carleton & Co., Publishers, 1868, p. 136.

90 Abraham Lincoln, "The Perpetuation of Our Political Institutions: Address Before the Young Men's Lyceum of Springfield, Illinois," January 27, 1838.

91 Abraham Lincoln, Letter to Erastus Corning, June 12, 1863. Roy P. Basler, ed. *The Collected Works of Abraham Lincoln* 8 vols. New Brunswick, NJ: Rutgers University Press, 1953, 6:267.

92 Abraham Lincoln, Cooper Union Address, New York, February 27, 1860.

93 Elizabeth Keckley. *Behind the Scenes: Or, Thirty Years a Slave, and Four Years in the White House.* New York: G. W. Carleton & Co., Publishers, 1868, p. 136.

94   Abraham Lincoln, Speech in United States House of Representatives on Internal Improvements, June 20, 1848. Roy P. Basler, ed. *The Collected Works of Abraham Lincoln* 8 vols. New Brunswick, NJ: Rutgers University Press, 1953, 1: 484.

95   Noah Webster. 1758–1843: *An American Dictionary of the English Language*, vol. 2. New York: S. Converse, 1828.

96   Michael Burlingame and John R. Turner Ettlinger, eds. *Inside Lincoln's White House: The Complete Civil War Diary of John Hay*, p. 135.

97   Richard Carwardine. *Lincoln: A Life of Purpose and Power.* New York City: Alfred A. Knopf, 2006, p. 242.

98   Noah Brooks. "Personal Recollections of Abraham Lincoln," *Harper's Monthly Magazine*, May 1865.

99   Frederick Douglass. *Life and Times of Frederick Douglass.* Boston: De Wolfe & Fiske Co., 1892, p. 594.

100   Abraham Lincoln, Letter to Zachariah Chandler, November 20, 1863. Roy P. Basler, ed. *The Collected Works of Abraham Lincoln* 8 vols. New Brunswick, NJ: Rutgers University Press, 1953, 7: 24.

101   "The Message of the Governor of Missouri," the contents of Abraham Lincoln's pockets on the evening of his assassination. n.d. Retrieved from the Library of Congress.

102   Roy P. Basler, ed. *The Collected Works of Abraham Lincoln* 8 vols. New Brunswick, NJ: Rutgers University Press, 1953, 2: 532.

103   Charles Lincoln Van Doren. *A History of Knowledge: Past, Present, and Future.* New York: Ballantine Books, 1991, 275.

104   Gideon Welles. *Diary of Gideon Welles, Secretary of the Navy Under Lincoln and Johnson.* Boston: Houghton Mifflin Company, 1911, 2:279.

105   Abraham Lincoln letter to George F. Shepley, November 21, 1862. Roy P. Basler, ed. *The Collected Works of Abraham Lincoln* 8 vols. New Brunswick, NJ: Rutgers University Press, 1953, 5: 504.

106   "Pacific Railway Act." Library of Congress.

107   Homestead Act of 1862 (12 Stat. 392).

108   Morrill Act of 1862, Section 4 (12 Stat. 503).

109   W. Emerson Reck. *A. Lincoln: His Last 24 Hours.* Jefferson, NC: McFarland & Company, Inc., Publishers, 1987, p. 20.

110   Yosemite Act of 1864 (13 Stat. 325).

111   Abraham Lincoln, Letter to Nathaniel Banks, August 5, 1863.

112   Henry J. Raymond to Simon Cameron. August 19 and August 21, 1864. Simon Cameron Papers, Library of Congress, Washington, D.C.

113   David E. Johnson and Johnny R. Johnson. *A Funny Thing Happened*

on the Way to the White House. Lanham, MD: Taylor Trade Publishing, 1983, p. 37.

114 George Templeton Strong. *The Diary of George Templeton Strong,* September 5, 1864, entry. New York: Macmillan, 1952.

115 *New-York Tribune,* September 8, 1864.

116 John Hay and John G. Nicolay. *Abraham Lincoln: A History, Vol. 9.* New York: The Century Co., 1917, p. 353.

117 John C. Waugh. *Reelecting Lincoln: The Battle for the 1864 Presidency.* Cambridge, MA: De Capo Press, 1997, p. 21.

118 *Harper's Weekly,* "The Eighth of November." November 12, 1864.

119 John Hay and John G. Nicolay. *Abraham Lincoln: A History, Vol. 9.* New York: The Century Co., 1917, p. 376.

120 Noah Brooks. *Washington, D.C., in Lincoln's Time: A Memoir of the Civil War Era by the Newspaperman Who Knew Lincoln Best.* Herbert Mitgang, ed. Athens: University of Georgia Press, 1989, p. 143.

121 J. G. Randall. *Lincoln the Liberal Statesman.* New York: Dodd, Mead & Company, 1947, p. 260.

122 Jonathan W. White. "How Lincoln Won the Soldier Vote." *New York Times,* November 7, 2014.

123 "Presidential Election of 1860: A Resource Guide." Presidential Election of 1860: A Resource Guide. Virtual Programs & Services, Library of Congress. Accessed September 19, 2020. https://www.loc.gov/rr/program/bib/elections/election1860.html. "Presidential Election of 1864: A Resource Guide." Presidential Election of 1864: A Resource Guide. Virtual Programs & Services, Library of Congress. Accessed September 19, 2020. https://www.loc.gov/rr/program/bib/elections/election1864.html.

124 "Lincoln on the 1864 Election," Lincoln Home (National Park Service).

125 "Administration of Abraham Lincoln," *The Galaxy,* volume XXIV. New York: Sheldon & Company, 1877, p. 617.

126 Abraham Lincoln speech at Peoria, Illinois, October 16, 1854. Roy P. Basler, ed. *The Collected Works of Abraham Lincoln* 8 vols. New Brunswick, NJ: Rutgers University Press, 1953, 2: 282. http://quod.lib.umich.edu/l/lincoln/.

127 Merrill D. Peterson. *Lincoln in American Memory.* New York: Oxford University Press, 1994, p. 8.

128 Naphtali J. Rubinger. *Abraham Lincoln and the Jews.* New York: Jonathan David Publishers, 1962, p. 69.

129 Jane Addams. *Twenty Years at Hull House.* New York: The MacMillan Company, 1911, p. 23.

130 "A Talk with Jeff. Davis," *Ventura Signal.* Originally published, *Lynchburg Virginian*, May 9, 1884.

131 Winston Churchill. *History of the English-Speaking Peoples.* CA: Dodd, Mead, 1958, p. 263.

132 Count S. Stakelberg. "Tolstoy Holds Lincoln World's Greatest Hero," *New York World.* February 7, 1909.

133 Richard Carwardine and Jay Sexton, eds. *The Global Lincoln.* New York City: Oxford University Press, 2011, p. 10.

134 Count S. Stakelberg. "Tolstoy Holds Lincoln World's Greatest Hero," *New York World*, February 7, 1909.

135 John Steele Gordon, "Forgotten Viceroy," *American Heritage*, February/March 1992, vol. 43, issue 1.

Section I
WITH MALICE TOWARD NONE

1 "The Inauguration," *Evening Star.* March 4, 1865.

2 *New York Tribune.* March 6, 1865.

3 Michael Burlingame, ed. *Lincoln Observed: Civil War Dispatches of Noah Brooks.* Baltimore, MD: The Johns Hopkins University Press, 1998, p. 165.

4 Walt Whitman. *Prose Works.* Philadelphia: David McKay, 1892.

5 *Washington Evening Star.* March 4, 1865.

6 John Sherman. *John Sherman's Recollections of Forty Years in the House, Senate and Cabinet.* Chicago: The Werner Company, 1895, p. 298.

7 Gideon Welles. *Diary of Gideon Welles, Secretary of the Navy Under Lincoln and Johnson.* Boston: Houghton Mifflin Company, 1911, p. 252.

8 *New York World.* March 7, 1865.

9 Elena Popchock. "A Great Coat and a Great Tragedy: The Life of Lincoln's Brooks Brothers Overcoat." Ford's Theater website at Fords.org.

10 Abraham Lincoln, Address to the New Jersey Senate at Trenton, New Jersey. February 21, 1861. Roy P. Basler, ed. *The Collected Works of Abraham Lincoln* 8 vols. New Brunswick, NJ: Rutgers University Press, 1953, 4: 236.

11 Abraham Lincoln, Farewell Address. Springfield, Illinois, February 11, 1861.

12 Michael Burlingame, ed. *Lincoln Observed: Civil War Dispatches of Noah Brooks.* Baltimore, MD: The Johns Hopkins University Press, 1998, p. 168.

13 Elizabeth Keckley. *Behind the Scenes: Or, Thirty Years a Slave, and Four Years in the White House.* New York: G.W. Carleton & Co., Publishers, 1868, p. 156.

14 *Washington Evening Star*, March 18, 1865.

15 James Grant. *Bagehot: The Life and Times of the Greatest Victorian.* New York: W.W. Norton & Company, 2019, p. 135.

16 Roy P. Basler, ed. *The Collected Works of Abraham Lincoln* 8 vols. New Brunswick, NJ: Rutgers University Press, 1953, 7: 301.

17 Noel Rae. "How Christian Slaveholders Used the Bible to Justify Slavery," *Time*, February 23, 2018.

18 *New York Times*, February 25, 1864.

19 Abraham Lincoln, second lecture on discoveries and inventions, February 11, 1859. Roy P. Basler, ed. *The Collected Works of Abraham Lincoln* 8 vols. New Brunswick, NJ: Rutgers University Press, 1953-55, 3: 360.

20 Merwin Roe, ed. *Speeches & Letters of Abraham Lincoln, 1832–1865.* London: J.M. Dent & Sons, 1907, p. 153.

21 Harold Holzer. *Lincoln and the Power of the Press: The War for Public Opinion.* New York: Simon & Schuster, 2014, p. 482-483.

22 Alexander McClure. *Abraham Lincoln and Men of War-Times.* Philadelphia: The Times Publishing Company, 1892, p. 338.

23 Isaiah 1:17–18.

24 Eddy W. Davison and Daniel Foxx. *Nathan Bedford Forrest: In Search of the Enigma.* Gretna, LA: Pelican Publishing Company, Inc., 2007, p. 242.

25 Frederick Douglass. *Life and Times of Frederick Douglass, Written by Himself.* Boston: De Wolfe & Fiske Co., 1892, p. 442.

26 Frederick Douglass, Speech at the Brooklyn Union League for Lincoln's Birthday, February 13, 1893.

27 Isaac N. Arnold. *The Life of Abraham Lincoln.* Chicago: Jansen, McClurg & Company, 1885, p. 404.

28 *New York Herald*, March 5 and 6, 1865.

29 *New York World*, March 6, 1865.

30 *New York Herald*, March 6, 1865, p. 5.

31 *Boston Evening Transcript*, March 6, 1865.

32 Walt Whitman. *Memoranda During the War.* Bedford, MA: Applewood Books, 1990, p. 55.

33 Allen Thorndike Rice. *Reminiscences of Abraham Lincoln: By Distinguished Men of His Time* (New York: North American Publishing Company, 1886), p. 193.

34 Frederick Douglass. *Life and Times of Frederick Douglass.* Boston: De Wolfe & Fiske Co., 1892, p. 444.

35 Ibid, p. 453.

36 Adelaide W. Smith. *Reminiscences of an Army Nurse During the Civil War.* New York: Graves Publishing Company, 1911, p. 221.

37 Margarita Spalding Gerry, ed. *Through Five Administrations: Reminiscences of Colonel William H. Crook, Body-Guard to President Lincoln.* New York: Harper & Brothers Publishers, 1910, p. 26.

38 Ibid., p. 27.

39 Abraham Lincoln, Letter to Thurlow Weed, March 15, 1865. Roy P. Basler, ed. *The Collected Works of Abraham Lincoln* 8 vols. New Brunswick, NJ: Rutgers University Press, 1953, 8: 53.

Section II:
UNCONDITIONAL SURRENDER: LINCOLN AT WAR

1 Abraham Lincoln, Annual message to Congress, December 6, 1864. Roy P. Basler, ed. *The Collected Works of Abraham Lincoln* 8 vols. New Brunswick, NJ: Rutgers University Press, 1953, 8: 151.

2 Frederick Douglass, Letter to Theodore Tilton, October 15, 1864.

3 Abraham Lincoln, Letter to Isaac M. Schermerhorn, September 12, 1864. Roy P. Basler, ed. *The Collected Works of Abraham Lincoln* 8 vols. New Brunswick, NJ: Rutgers University Press, 1953, 8: 1.

4 Abraham Lincoln, Speech in U. S. House of Representatives on the Presidential Question, July 27, 1848. Roy P. Basler, ed., *The Collected Works of Abraham Lincoln* 8 vols. New Brunswick, NJ: Rutger's University Press, 1953–55, 1: 510.

5 Michael Beschloss. *Presidents of War.* New York: Crown, 2018, p. 195.

6 Abraham Lincoln, Letter to Don C. Buell, January 13, 1862. Roy P. Basler, ed. *The Collected Works of Abraham Lincoln* 8 vols. New Brunswick, NJ: Rutgers University Press, 1953, 5: 98.

7 "The Civil War: 150 Years—Legacy—Page 2 of 5: The Legacy of the Civil War," National Parks Service, nps.gov.

8 Abraham Lincoln, Annual message to Congress, December 6, 1864.

Roy P. Basler, ed. *The Collected Works of Abraham Lincoln* 8 vols. New Brunswick, NJ: Rutgers University Press, 1953, 8: 151.

9 Abraham Lincoln, Letter to Cuthbert Bullitt, July 28, 1862.

10 Roy P. Basler, ed. *The Collected Works of Abraham Lincoln* 8 vols. New Brunswick, NJ: Rutgers University Press, 1953, 6:79.

11 Abraham Lincoln, Letter to Joseph Hooker, January 6, 1863. Roy P. Basler, ed. *The Collected Works of Abraham Lincoln* 8 vols. New Brunswick, NJ: Rutgers University Press, 1953, 6:79.

12 Abraham Lincoln, Letter to George G. Meade, July 14, 1863 (unsent). Roy P. Basler, ed. *The Collected Works of Abraham Lincoln* 8 vols. New Brunswick, NJ: Rutgers University Press, 1953, 6:328.

13 U.S. Grant to Jesse Root Grant, April 21, 1861.

14 Adam Badeau. *Grant in Peace: From Appomattox to Mount McGregor. A Personal Memoir.* Hartford, CT: S.S. Scranton & Company, 1887.

15 Horace Porter. *Campaigning with Grant.* New York City: The Century Company, 1897, p. 70.

16 Francis Lieber. *Instructions for the Government of Armies of the United States in the Field.* April 24, 1863, Art. 5(2).

17 Francis Lieber, General Orders No. 100, April 24, 1863.

18 Ibid.

19 Abraham Lincoln response to a serenade, February 1, 1865. Roy P. Basler, ed. *The Collected Works of Abraham Lincoln* 8 vols. New Brunswick, NJ: Rutgers University Press, 1953, 8: 254.

20 Michael Burlingame. *Abraham Lincoln: A Life.* Baltimore, MD: The Johns Hopkins University Press, 2008, p. 756.

21 Washington correspondence, February 22, by Van [D. W. Bartlett], Springfield, Massachusetts, Republican, February 25, 1865.

22 Alexander H. Stephens. *A Constitutional View of the Late War Between the States* 2 vols. Philadelphia: National Publishing Company, 1870, 2: 601.

23 William C. Harris. "The Hampton Roads Peace Conference: A Final Test of Lincoln's Presidential Leadership," *Journal of the Abraham Lincoln Association*, volume 21, issue 1, Winter 2000.

24 The Trial of Hon. Clement L. Vallandigham. Cincinnati, OH: Rickey and Carroll, 1863, p. 11.

25 James B. Conroy. *Our One Common Country: Abraham Lincoln and the Hampton Roads Peace Conference of 1865.* Guilford, CT: Lyons Press, 2014, p. 195.

26 Ibid.

27 Ibid.

28 William C. Harris. "The Hampton Roads Peace Conference: A Final Test of Lincoln's Presidential Leadership," *Journal of the Abraham Lincoln Association*, volume 21, issue 1, Winter 2000.

29 Ibid.

30 Doris Kearns Goodwin. *Team of Rivals: The Political Genius of Abraham Lincoln*. New York: Simon & Schuster, 2006, p. 693.

31 William C. Harris. "The Hampton Roads Peace Conference: A Final Test of Lincoln's Presidential Leadership," *Journal of the Abraham Lincoln Association*, volume 21, issue 1, Winter 2000.

32 Ibid.

33 LaWanda Cox. *Lincoln and Black Freedom: A Study in Presidential Leadership*. Columbia, SC: University of South Carolina Press, 1981, p. 142.

34 Beverly Wilson Palmer and Holly Byers Ochoa, eds., *The Selected Papers of Thaddeus Stevens*, Volume 1: January 1814–March 1865 (Pittsburgh, PA: University of Pittsburgh Press, 1997), 317.

35 Abraham Lincoln, Letter to General Nathaniel Banks, August 5, 1863.

36 Herman Belz. *Reconstructing the Union*. Ithica, NY: Cornell University Press, 1969, p. 108.

37 William O. Stoddard. *Inside Lincoln's White House in Wartime*. 1892, p. 35.

38 Sara Norton, ed. *Letters of Charles Eliot Norton*. Boston: Houghton Mifflin Company, 1913, p. 422.

39 William C. Harris. *With Charity For All: Lincoln and the Restoration of the Union*. Lexington: The University Press of Kentucky, 1997, p. 243.

40 Shelby Foote. *The Civil War: A Narrative, Vol. 1*. New York: Penguin Random House, 1958, p. 242.

41 Abraham Lincoln, letter to Erastus Corning and others, June 12, 1863. Roy P. Basler, ed. *The Collected Works of Abraham Lincoln* 8 vols. New Brunswick, NJ: Rutgers University Press, 1953-55, 6: 267-8.

42 "The Inauguration Ball," *New York Times*, March 8, 1865.

43 Megan Gambino. "Document Deep Dive: The Menu From President Lincoln's Second Inaugural Ball," *Smithsonian Magazine*, January 15, 2013.

44 "The Inauguration Ball," *New York Times*, March 8, 1865.

45 Allen Thorndike Rice, ed. *Reminiscences of Abraham Lincoln by distinguished men of his time*. New York: Harper and New Brothers Publishers, 1888, p. 222.

46 "The President's Health," *New York Tribune,* March 17, 1865.

BLACK IN BLUE AND GRAY

1 Howell Cobb, Letter to James A. Seddon, January 8, 1865. *The War of the Rebellion: A Compilation of the Official Records of the Union and Confederate Armies.* Washington, D.C.: Government Printing Office, 1900, series 4, vol. 3, pp. 1,009–1,010.

2 Ella Lonn. *Desertion During the Civil War.* Lincoln: University of Nebraska Press, 1998, p. 28.

3 "Black Soldiers in the U.S. Military During the Civil War," National Archives. https://www.archives.gov/education/lessons/blacks-civil-war.

4 Don C. Seitz. *Lincoln the Politician: How the Rail-Splitter and Flatboatman Played the Great American Game.* New York: Coward-McCann, Inc., 1931, p. 349.

5 Rebecca Onion. "Lincoln's Promise: We'll Take an Eye for an Eye to Protect Our Black Troops," *Slate,* August 6, 2013.

6 "First to Serve." National Park Service, website.

7 Ibid.

8 R.J. M. Blackett, ed. *Thomas Morris Chester, Black Civil War Correspondent: His Dispatches from the Virginia Front.* Baton Rouge: Louisiana State University Press, 1989, p. 294-295.

9 Abraham Lincoln, Letter to Ulysses S. Grant, August 9, 1863. Roy P. Basler, ed. *The Collected Works of Abraham Lincoln* 8 vols. New Brunswick, NJ: Rutgers University Press, 1953, 6: 374.

10 David Williams. *Rich Man's War: Class, Caste, and Confederate Defeat in the Lower Chattahoochee Valley.* Athens: University of Georgia Press, 1998, p. 163.

11 Congressional Medal of Honor Society, "Honoring the African American Recipients of the Civil War." February 11, 2020.

12 Abraham Lincoln, Letter to James C. Conkling, August 26, 1863. Roy P. Basler, ed. *The Collected Works of Abraham Lincoln* 8 vols. New Brunswick, NJ: Rutgers University Press, 1953, 6: 408.

13 Abraham Lincoln, Speech to One Hundred Fortieth Indiana Regiment, March 17, 1865. Roy P. Basler, ed. *The Collected Works of Abraham Lincoln* 8 vols. New Brunswick, NJ: Rutgers University Press, 1953, 8: 361.

14 Abraham Lincoln, Letter to James S. Wadsworth, January 1864. Roy P. Basler, ed. *The Collected Works of Abraham Lincoln* 8 vols. New Brunswick, NJ: Rutgers University Press, 1953, 1: 191.

FATHER ABRAHAM ON THE FRONT LINES

1 Robert O. Zinnen, Jr. "City Point: The Tool That Gave General Grant Victory," *Quartermaster Professional Bulletin,* Spring 1991.

2 "African-Americans at City Point, 1864–1865," National Park Service.

3 Abraham Lincoln, Telegram to Ulysses S. Grant, March 20, 1865. Roy P. Basler, ed. *The Collected Works of Abraham Lincoln* 8 vols. New Brunswick, NJ: Rutgers University Press, 1953, 8: 367.

4 John S. Barnes. "With Lincoln from Washington to Richmond in 1865," *Appleton's Magazine,* May 1907, 9: 5.

5 Wayne C. Temple. *Lincoln's Travels on the River Queen During the Last Days of His Life.* Mahomet, IL: Mayhaven Publishing, 2007, p. 9.

6 "The Explosion at City Point: Particulars of the Disaster—List of Casualties," *New York Times,* August 13, 1864.

7 Michael Burlingame. *Abraham Lincoln: A Life.* Baltimore: The Johns Hopkins University Press, 2008, p. 807.

8 John S. Barnes. "With Lincoln from Washington to Richmond in 1865," *Appleton's Magazine,* May 1907, 9: 5.

9 Margarita Spalding Gerry, ed. *Through Five Administrations: Reminiscences of Colonel William H. Crook Body Guard to President Lincoln.* New York: Harper & Brothers, 1907, p. 23.

10 "The South Strikes Back—The Battle of Fort Stedman." National Park Service. https://www.nps.gov/parkhistory/online_books/hh/13/hh13i.htm

11 Michael Burlingame. *Abraham Lincoln: A Life.* Baltimore, MD: The Johns Hopkins University Press, 2008, p. 785. Original source: *Letters of Colonel Theodore Lyman from the Wilderness to Appomattox* (Boston: Atlantic Monthly Press, 1922), 325. Lyman to his wife, 26 Mar. 1865, in George R. Agassiz, ed., Meade's Headquarters, 1863–1865.

12 E. R. Hutchins, ed. *The War of the Sixties.* New York: The Neale Publishing Company, 1912, p. 225. Chapter by R. D. Funkhouser, "Storming of Fort Steadman, on Hares Hill, Front of Petersburg, Va., March 25, 1865."

13 J. A. Watrous. "Lincoln's Last Review: An Interesting Reminiscence of the Civil War," *National Tribune.* August 13, 1903.

14 Doris Kearns Goodwin. *Team of Rivals: The Political Genius of Abraham Lincoln.* New York City: Simon & Schuster, 2006, p. 710.

15 Ibid.

LINCOLN AND THE KITTENS

1 Roy P. Basler, ed. *The Collected Works of Abraham Lincoln* 8 vols. New Brunswick, NJ: Rutgers University Press, 1953, 8: 374. http://quod.lib.umich.edu/l/lincoln/.

2 David Dixon Porter. *Incidents and Anecdotes of the Civil War.* New York City: D. Appleton and Company, 1886, p. 318.

3 Horace Porter. *Campaigning with Grant.* New York: The Century Company, 1897, p. 410.

4 Ibid.

5 John S. Barnes. "With Lincoln from Washington to Richmond in 1865," *Appleton's Magazine,* May 1907, vol. 9, no. 5.

6 Michael Burlingame. *Abraham Lincoln: A Life.* Baltimore, MD: The Johns Hopkins University Press, 2008, p. 781.

7 Ibid., p. 782.

8 Jesse R. Grant. *In the Days of My Father, General Grant.* New York: Harper & Brothers Publishers, 1925, p. 23.

9 Adam Badeau. *Grant in Peace: From Appomattox to Mount McGregor. A Personal Memoir.* Hartford, CT: S.S. Scranton & Company, 1887, p. 359.

10 Ibid., p. 360.

11 Michael Beschloss, *Presidents of War,* New York: Crown, 2018, p. 212.

12 John S. Barnes. "With Lincoln from Washington to Richmond in 1865," *Appleton's Magazine,* May 1907, vol. 9, no. 5.

13 Ibid.

14 Ibid.

15 Noah Andre Trudeau. *Lincoln's Greatest Journey: Sixteen Days that Changed a Presidency, March 24–April 8, 1865.* El Dorado Hills, CA: Savas Beatie, 2016, pp. 70–71.

16 Edmund N. Hatcher. *The Last Four Weeks of the War.* Columbus, OH: J. Wiggins & Co., 1891, p. 98.

17 John F. Marszalek. *Sherman: A Soldier's Passion for Order.* Carbondale, IL: Southern Illinois University Press, 1993, pp. 476–477.

18 Linus Pierpont Brockett. *Our Great Captains.* New York City: Charles B. Richardson, 1865, p. 162.

19 Burke Davis. *Sherman's March.* New York: Random House, 1980, p. 244.

20 Robert Tilney. *My Life in the Army.* Philadelphia: Ferris & Leach, 1912. p. 196.

PEACEMAKERS ON THE *RIVER QUEEN*

1 Carl Sandburg. *Storm Over the Land: A Profile of the Civil War.* New York: Harcourt, Brace and Company, 1939, p. 377.
2 President Harry S. Truman news conference, February 13, 1947.
3 General Sherman, Letter to George Healy, January 13, 1868.
4 William Tecumseh Sherman. *Memoirs of General William T. Sherman, Written by Himself.* New York: D. Appleton and Company, 1875, p. 328.
5 Horace Porter. "Lincoln and Grant," *The Century Illustrated Monthly Magazine*, 1885, vol. 30, p. 945.
6 John Russell Young. *Around the World with General Grant.* New York: American News Company, 1879, p. 301.
7 Ulysses S. Grant. *Personal Memoirs of U.S. Grant.* New York: Charles L. Webster & Company, 1886, p. 424.
8 William Tecumseh Sherman. *Memoirs of General William T. Sherman.* New York: D. Appleton and Company, 1904, p. 329.
9 David Dixon Porter. *The Naval History of the Civil War.* New York: The Sherman Publishing Company, 1886, p. 795.
10 David Dixon Porter. *Incidents and Anecdotes of the Civil War.* New York: D. Appleton and Company, 1886, p. 324.
11 William Tecumseh Sherman. *Memoirs of General William T. Sherman.* New York: D. Appleton and Company, 1875, p. 326.
12 Horace Porter. *Campaigning with Grant.* New York: The Century Company, 1897, pp. 423–424.
13 William Tecumseh Sherman. *Memoirs of General William T. Sherman.* New York: D. Appleton and Company, 1904, p. 327.
14 Ibid., p. 326.
15 David Dixon Porter, *Incidents and Anecdotes of the Civil War* (New York City: D. Appleton and Company, 1886), p. 314.
16 William Tecumseh Sherman. *Memoirs of General William T. Sherman, Written by Himself.* New York: D. Appleton and Company, 1875, p. 327.
17 Ibid.
18 Ibid., p. 328.

THE GHOSTS OF PETERSBURG

1 J. R. Hamilton, Letter, March 29, 1865. Quoted in Harry Butowsky. *Appomattox Manor—City Point: A History.* National Parks Service, 1978, p. 265.

2 Horace Porter. *Campaigning with Grant*. New York: The Century Company, 1897, p. 425.

3 Ibid.

4 Albert D. Richardson. *A Personal History of Ulysses S. Grant*. Hartford, CT: American Publishing Company, 1885, p. 467.

5 Horace Porter. "Lincoln and Grant," *The Century*, vol. 30, p. 946.

6 Horace Porter. *Campaigning with Grant*. New York: The Century Company, 1897, p. 426.

7 Ida Tarbell. "The Life of Abraham Lincoln," vol. II, pp. 231–232.

8 Noah Andre Trudeau. *Lincoln's Greatest Journey: Sixteen Days that Changed a Presidency, March 24–April 8, 1865*. El Dorado Hills, CA: Savas Beatie, 2016, p. 103.

9 *The Maine Bugle*, vol. 1. Rockland, ME: The Maine Association, 1894, p. 802.

10 John Y. Simon, ed. *The Papers of Ulysses S. Grant: February 21–April 30, 1865*. Carbondale, IL: Southern Illinois University Press, 1985, p. 273.

11 Phillip Henry Sheridan. *Personal Memoirs of P. H. Sheridan, General, United States Army, Volume 2*. New York City: Charles L. Webster & Company, 1888, p. 145.

12 Septima M. Collis. *A Woman's War Record, 1861–1865*. New York: The Knickerbocker Press, 1889, p. 60.

13 Edwin Stanton, Telegraph to Abraham Lincoln, March 31, 1865. Roy P. Basler, ed. *The Collected Works of Abraham Lincoln* 8 vols. New Brunswick, NJ: Rutgers University Press, 1953, 8: 378.

14 "Abraham Lincoln's Favorite Poem." Abraham Lincoln Online, accessed February 23, 2021. http://www.abrahamlincolnonline.org/lincoln/education/knox.htm

15 William H. Crook. "Lincoln's Last Day," *Harper's Monthly Magazine*. September 1907.

16 *Southern Historical Society Papers, Volume XI: January to December, 1883*. Richmond, VA: Southern Historical Society, p. 184. Written by an anonymous "Courier" of the Artillery Second Corps: March 21, 1884.

17 Benjamin P. Thomas and Sylvanus Cadwallader. "Three Years with Grant," *American Heritage*, October 1955.

18 Ibid.

19 Noah Andre Trudeau. *Lincoln's Greatest Journey: Sixteen Days that Changed a Presidency, March 24–April 8, 1865*. El Dorado Hills, CA: Savas Beatie, 2016, p. 142.

20   Ward Hill Lamon. *Recollections of Abraham Lincoln 1847–1865*. Chicago: A.C. McClurg and Company, 1895, pp. 115-16.

21   Abraham Lincoln, Message to Ulysses S. Grant, April 2, 1865. Roy P. Basler, ed. *The Collected Works of Abraham Lincoln* 8 vols. New Brunswick, NJ: Rutgers University Press, 1953, 8: 383.

22   Michael Burlingame. *Abraham Lincoln: A Life*. Baltimore, MD: The Johns Hopkins University Press, 2008, p. 788.

23   Charles Carleton Coffin. *Abraham Lincoln*. New York: Harper and Brothers, 1893, p. 501.

24   Jacob Buch. "Lincoln at City Point," *National Tribune*. October 23, 1890.

25   Allen D. Albert, ed., *History of the Forty-fifth Regiment Pennsylvania Veteran Volunteer Infantry, 1861–1865*. Williamsport, PA: Grit Publishing Company, 1912, 176.

26   Michael Burlingame. *Abraham Lincoln: A Life*. Baltimore, MD: The Johns Hopkins University Press, 2008, p. 170.

27   William H. Crook. "Lincoln's Last Day." *Harper's Monthly Magazine,* September 1907.

28   Ulysses S. Grant. *Personal Memoirs of U.S. Grant*. New York City: Charles L. Webster & Company, 1886, p. 612.

29   R. J. M. Blackett, ed. *Thomas Morris Chester, Black Civil War Correspondent: His Dispatches from the Virginia Front*. Baton Rouge: Louisiana State University Press, 1989, p. 314.

30   Horace Porter. *Campaigning with Grant*. New York: The Century Company, 1897, p. 451.

31   Adam Badeau. *Military History of Ulysses S. Grant: From April 1861 to April 1865, vol. 3*. New York City: D. Appleton and Company, 1881, p. 536.

32   *An Act to establish a Bureau for the Relief of Freedmen and Refugees.* March 3, 1865.

33   David Homer Bates. "Lincoln's Last Days," *The Century Illustrated Monthly Magazine,* vol. LXXIV. New York: The Century Co., 1907, p. 770.

34   Noah Brooks. "The Close of Lincoln's Career," *The Century Illustrated Monthly Magazine*, May 1895, pp. 18-26.

35   Noah Andre Trudeau. *Lincoln's Greatest Journey: Sixteen Days that Changed a Presidency, March 24–April 8, 1865*. El Dorado Hills, CA: Savas Beatie, 2016, p. 174.

36   Edmund N. Hatcher. *The Last Four Weeks of the War*. Columbus, OH: J. Wiggins & Co., 1891, p. 118.

37 Francis Fisher Browne, ed. *The Every-day Life of Abraham Lincoln: A Biography from an Entirely New Standpoint, with Fresh and Invaluable Material*. New York: n.d. Thompson Publishing Co., 1887, p. 689.

38 Edwin M. Stanton to Abraham Lincoln, April 3, 1865. Roy P. Basler, ed. *The Collected Works of Abraham Lincoln* 8 vols. New Brunswick, NJ: Rutgers University Press, 1953, 8: 384–385.

39 Abraham Lincoln, Telegram to Edwin M. Stanton, April 3, 1865. Roy P. Basler, ed. *The Collected Works of Abraham Lincoln* 8 vols. New Brunswick, NJ: Rutgers University Press, 1953, 8: 385.

40 Donald C. Pfanz. *The Petersburg Campaign: Abraham Lincoln at City Point, March 20–April 9,* 1865. Lynchburg, VA: H.E. Howard, 1989, p. 58.

Section III:
A MAGNANIMOUS PEACE:
LINCOLN AND THE FALL OF RICHMOND

1 David D. Ryan. *Four Days in 1865: The Fall of Richmond.* Richmond, VA: Cadmus Marketing, 1993, p. 51.

2 *Medal of Honor, 1863–1968: "In the Name of the Congress of the United States,"* vols. 11-12. Washington, D.C.: U.S. Government Printing Office, 1968, p. 912.

3 Edmund N. Hatcher. *The Last Four Weeks of the War.* Columbus, OH: J. Wiggins & Co., 1891, p. 136-137.

4 R. J. M. Blackett, ed. *Thomas Morris Chester, Black Civil War Correspondent: His Dispatches from the Virginia Front.* Baton Rouge: Louisiana State University Press, 1989, p. 292.

5 Ibid., p. 290.

6 Ibid.

7 David D. Ryan. *Four Days in 1865: The Fall of Richmond.* Richmond, VA: Cadmus Marketing, 1993. p. 94.

8 *The Century Illustrated Monthly Magazine,* 1890, vol. 40, p. 307.

9 David Dixon Porter papers, Library of Congress: Container 23, Private Journal No 2, pp. 46–55.

10 Noah Andre Trudeau. *Lincoln's Greatest Journey: Sixteen Days That Changed a Presidency, March 24–April 8, 1865.* El Dorado Hills, CA: Savas Beaties, 2016, p. 183.

11 Michael D. Gorman. "A Conqueror or a Peacemaker?: Abraham Lincoln in Richmond," *The Virginia Magazine of History and Biography,* January 2015, vol. 123, no. 1.

12 David Dixon Porter. *Incidents and Anecdotes of the Civil War.* New York: D. Appleton and Company, 1886, p. 294-295.

13 "Late Scenes in Richmond," Charles Coffin, *The Atlantic,* June 1865.

14 David Herbert Donald. *Lincoln.* New York: Simon & Schuster, 1995, p. 576.

15 David Dixon Porter papers, Library of Congress: Container 23, Private Journal No. 2, pp. 46–55.

16 David Dixon Porter. *Incidents and Anecdotes of the Civil War.* New York: D. Appleton and Company, 1886, p. 295.

17 Ibid., p. 296.

18 Ibid.

19 R. J. M. Blackett, ed. *Thomas Morris Chester, Black Civil War Correspondent: His Dispatches from the Virginia Front.* Baton Rouge: Louisiana State University Press, 1989, pp. 294-295.

20 David Dixon Porter. *Incidents and Anecdotes of the Civil War.* New York City: D. Appleton and Company, 1886, p. 297.

21 William H. Crook. "Lincoln's Last Day," *Harper's Monthly Magazine,* September 1907.

22 Allen Thorndike Rice. *Reminiscences of Abraham Lincoln: By Distinguished Men of His Time.* New York: North American Publishing Company, 1886, p. 182.

23 William A. Sinclair. *The Aftermath of Slavery: A Study of the Condition and Environment of the American Negro.* Boston: Small, Maynard & Company, 1905, p. 52.

24 William H. Crook. "Lincoln's Last Day," *Harper's Monthly Magazine,* September 1907.

25 David Dixon Porter papers, Library of Congress: Container 23, Private Journal No. 2, pp. 46–55.

26 David Dixon Porter. *Incidents and Anecdotes of the Civil War.* New York: D. Appleton and Company, 1886, p. 301.

27 George T. Dudley. "Lincoln in Richmond," *National Tribune,* October 1, 1896.

28 Clarence Buel and Robert U. Johnson, eds., *Battles and Leaders of the Civil War,* Vol. IV (New York: The Century Co., 1888), 727.

29 George F. Shepley. "Incidents of the Capture of Richmond," *The Atlantic Monthly,* July 1880, vol. 46, issue 273, pp. 26-27.

30 Michael Burlingame. *Abraham Lincoln: A Life.* Baltimore, MD: The Johns Hopkins University Press, 2008, p. 807.

31 R. J. M. Blackett, ed. *Thomas Morris Chester, Black Civil War*

Correspondent: His Dispatches from the Virginia Front. Baton Rouge, LA: Louisiana State University Press, 1989, pp. 294–295.

INSIDE THE CONFEDERATE WHITE HOUSE

1 John S. Barnes. "With Lincoln from Washington to Richmond in 1865," *Appleton's Magazine,* May 1907, vol. 9, no. 5.

2 Ibid.

3 Michael D. Gorman. "A Conqueror or a Peacemaker?: Abraham Lincoln in Richmond," *The Virginia Magazine of History and Biography*, January 1, 2015, p. 36.

4 *New York Herald*, April 9, 1865.

5 Ibid.

6 *Washington Daily Morning Chronicle*, April 10, 1865.

7 *New York Times*, January 28, 1885.

8 John Campbell. *Recollections of the evacuation of Richmond*, April 2d, 1865. Baltimore: John Murphy & Co., 1880, p. 6.

9 Ibid., p. 7.

10 Ibid., p. 8.

11 Ibid.

12 Clarence Buel and Robert U. Johnson, eds., *Battles and Leaders of the Civil War*, Vol. IV (New York: The Century Co., 1888), 727.

13 Michael D. Gorman. "A Conqueror or a Peacemaker?: Abraham Lincoln in Richmond," *The Virginia Magazine of History and Biography*, January 1, 2015.

14 William Jewett Tenney. *The Military and Naval History of the Rebellion in the United States. With Biographical Sketches of Deceased Officers.* New York: D. Appleton & Company, 1865, p. 693.

15 "Incidents of the Capture of Richmond," *The Atlantic Monthly*, Volume 46. Boston: Houghton, Mifflin and Company, 1880, p. 28.

16 William H. Crook. "Lincoln's Last Day," *Harper's Monthly Magazine*, September 1907.

17 R. J. M. Blackett, ed. *Thomas Morris Chester, Black Civil War Correspondent: His Dispatches from the Virginia Front.* Baton Rouge: Louisiana State University Press, 1989, p. 288.

18 Ibid., p. 42.

19 Sara Agnes Rice Pryor. *Reminiscences of Peace and War.* New York: Grosset & Dunlap Publishers, 1904, p. 357.

20 Charles Carleton Coffin. *Freedom Triumphant: The Fourth Period of the*

War of the Rebellion from September, 1864, to Its Close, Volume 7. New York: Harper Brothers, 1891, p. 436.

21 R. J. M. Blackett, ed. *Thomas Morris Chester, Black Civil War Correspondent: His Dispatches from the Virginia Front.* Baton Rouge: Louisiana State University Press, 1989, p. 298.

22 Ibid., pp. 304–305.

23 Clarence Buel and Robert U. Johnson, ed. *Battles and Leaders of the Civil War: Volume IV.* New York: The Century Co., 1888, p. 728.

24 Judith White McGuire. *Diary of a Southern Refugee, During the War, By a Lady of Virginia.* New York: E. J. Hale & Son, 1868, p. 349.

25 Charles Coffin. "The President's Entry into Richmond," *Boston Journal,* April 10, 1865.

CONVERSATIONS WITH THE ENEMY

1 Don E. Fehrenbacher and Virginia Fehrenbacher, eds. *Recollected Words of Abraham Lincoln.* Stanford, CA: Stanford University Press, 1996, p. 172.

2 David Dixon Porter. *Incidents and Anecdotes of the Civil War.* New York: D. Appleton and Company, 1886, p. 338.

3 Edward H. Ripley. "Final Scenes at the Capture and Occupation of Richmond, April 3, 1865," *New York Mollus,* December 5, 1906.

4 Ervin S. Chapman. *Latest Light on Lincoln, and War-time Memories.* New York: Fleming H. Revell Company, 1917, 2:500.

5 Edward H. Ripley. "Final Scenes at the Capture and Occupation of Richmond, April 3, 1865," *New York Mollus,* December 5, 1906.

6 Michael D. Gorman. "A Conqueror or a Peacemaker?: Abraham Lincoln in Richmond," *The Virginia Magazine of History and Biography,* January 1, 2015.

7 Abraham Lincoln to John A. Campbell, April 5, 1865. Roy P. Basler, ed. *The Collected Works of Abraham Lincoln* 8 vols. New Brunswick, NJ: Rutgers University Press, 1953, 8: 386.

8 John W. Bell. *Memoirs of Governor William Smith, of Virginia: His Political, Military, and Personal History.* New York: Moss Engraving Company, 1891, p. 213.

9 Noah Andre Trudeau. *Lincoln's Greatest Journey: Sixteen Days That Changed a Presidency, March 24–April 8, 1865.* El Dorado Hills, CA: Savas Beatie, 2016, p. 204.

10 Charles M. Segal, ed. *Conversations with Lincoln: Lincoln's Thoughts and*

Actions as Expressed in his Conversations with His Contemporaries in the Years 1860–1865. New York: G. Putnam & Sons, 1961, p. 390.

11 John A. Campbell, Letter to James S. Speed, August 31, 1865. (Papers of John A. Campbell).

12 Allan B. Magruder. "Lincoln's Plans of Reconstruction," *The Atlantic*, January 1876.

13 Charles M. Segal, ed. *Conversations with Lincoln: Lincoln's Thoughts and Actions as Expressed in his Conversations with His Contemporaries in the Years 1860–1865.* New York: G. Putnam & Sons, 1961, p. 389.

14 John A. Campbell, Letter to Horace Greeley, April 26, 1865. Southern Historical Society. Southern Historical Society Papers, Volume 42. Richmond, VA: Wm. Ellis Jones' Sons, Inc., 1917, p. 61.

15 Caroline Myers. *Events Which Befell Us.* Chapel Hill: Phillips-Myers Papers, University of North Carolina, p. 4.

16 David Dixon Porter. *The Naval History of the Civil War.* New York: The Sherman Publishing Company, 1886, p. 800.

17 Ibid.

18 David D. Porter. "Lincoln at Richmond: Admiral Porter Recalls Some Striking Scenes," *New York Tribune*, January 18, 1885.

19 William H. Crook. "Lincoln's Last Day," *Harper's Monthly Magazine*, September 1907.

20 David D. Porter. "Lincoln at Richmond: Admiral Porter Recalls Some Striking Scenes," *New York Tribune*, January 18, 1885.

21 David Dixon Porter papers, Library of Congress: Container 23, Private Journal No. 2, pp. 46–55.

22 David Dixon Porter. *Incidents and Anecdotes of the Civil War.* New York: D. Appleton and Company, 1885, p. 312.

23 Septima Maria Collis. *A Woman's War Record, 1861–1865.* New York: G.P. Putnam's Sons, 1889, p. 63.

24 Charles H. T. Collis, "Mr. Lincoln's Magnanimity." From Septima Maria Levy Collis, *A Woman's War Record, 1861–1865* (1889).

25 Septima Maria Collis. *A Woman's War Record, 1861–1865.* New York: G.P. Putnam's Sons, 1889, p. 67.

26 Charles H. T. Collis, "Mr. Lincoln's Magnanimity." From Septima Maria Levy Collis, *A Woman's War Record, 1861–1865* (1889).

27 Septima Maria Collis. *A Woman's War Record, 1861–1865.* New York: G.P. Putnam's Sons, 1889, p. 69.

28 William H. Crook. "Lincoln's Last Day," *Harper's Monthly Magazine*, September 1907.

29 Marquis de Chambrun. "Personal Recollections of Mr. Lincoln," *The Century Magazine*, January 1893.

30 Abraham Lincoln to Ulysses S. Grant, April 6, 1865. Roy P. Basler, ed. *The Collected Works of Abraham Lincoln* 8 vols. New Brunswick, NJ: Rutgers University Press, 1953, 8: 388.

31 David Dixon Porter. *Incidents and Anecdotes of the Civil War.* New York: D. Appleton and Company, 1886, p. 287.

32 Journal of Admiral David Dixon Porter, Library of Congress.

33 Elizabeth Keckley. *Behind the Scenes: Or, Thirty Years a Slave, and Four Years in the White House.* New York: G. W. Carleton & Co., 1868, p. 163.

34 Ibid., p. 166.

35 Abraham Lincoln to Ulysses S. Grant, April 7, 1865. Roy P. Basler, ed. *The Collected Works of Abraham Lincoln* 8 vols. New Brunswick, NJ: Rutgers University Press, 1953, 8: 392.

36 Marquis de Chambrun. "Personal Recollections of Mr. Lincoln," *The Century Magazine*, January 1893.

37 Ibid.

38 Marquis Adolphe de Chambrun. *Impressions of Lincoln and the Civil War: A Foreigner's Account.* New York: Random House, 1952, p. 81.

39 Elizabeth Keckley. *Behind the Scenes: Or, Thirty Years a Slave, and Four Years in the White House.* New York: G. W. Carleton & Co., 1868, p. 170.

40 Allen Thorndike Rice, ed. *Reminiscences of Abraham Lincoln*, pp. 43–44.

DIXIE AND MACBETH

1 Cornelia Hancock. *Letters of a Civil War Nurse: Cornelia Hancock, 1863–1865.* Lincoln: University of Nebraska Press, 1998, p. 170.

2 Macomber. "Honoring Lincoln's Memory," *San Francisco Call*, May 29, 1897, p. 2.

3 Joseph Wheelan. *Their Last Full Measure: The Final Days of the Civil War.* Boston: De Capo Press, 2015, p. 267.

4 Adelaide W. Smith. *Reminiscences of an Army Nurse During the Civil War.* New York: Greaves Publishing Company, 1911, p. 224.

5 Carl Sandburg. *Abraham Lincoln: The War Years.* New York: Harcourt, Brace & Company, 1939, p. 171.

6 Marquis de Chambrun. "Personal Recollections of Mr. Lincoln," *The Century Magazine*, January 1893.

7 Miles Hoffman. "If Abraham Lincoln Had An iPod." NPR, February 16, 2009.

8 Marquis de Chambrun. "Personal Recollections of Mr. Lincoln," *The Century Magazine*, January 1893.

9 David Herbert Donald. *Lincoln*. New York: Simon & Schuster, 1995, p. 580.

10 Julia Dent Grant. *Personal Memoirs of Julia Dent Grant*. New York: G.P. Putnam's Sons, 1975, p. 119.

11 Marquis de Chambrun. "Personal Recollections of Mr. Lincoln," *The Century Magazine*, January 1893.

12 Robert E. Lee, Letter to Ulysses S. Grant, April 8, 1865.

13 Ron Chernow. *Grant*. New York: Penguin Books, 2017, p. 502.

14 Ulysses S. Grant, Letter to Robert E. Lee, April 9, 1865.

15 William Shakespeare, *Macbeth*, Act III, Scene II.

16 Marquis Adolphe de Chambrun. *Impressions of Lincoln and the Civil War: A Foreigner's Account*. New York: Random House, 1952.

Section IV
APPOMATTOX AND THE ART OF PEACE

1 Isaac N. Arnold. *The Life of Abraham Lincoln*. Chicago: Jansen, McClurg & Company, 1885, p. 375.

2 Shelby Foote. *The Civil War: A Narrative: Volume 3: Red River to Appomattox*. New York: Vintage Civil War Library, 1986, p. 942.

3 Ibid.

4 Edwin Porter Alexander. *Military Memoirs of a Confederate*. New York: Charles Scribner's Sons, 1907, p. 605.

5 Benjamin P. Thomas, ed. *Three Years with Grant: As Recalled by War Correspondent*. New York: Alfred A. Knopf, 1955.

"WE ARE ALL AMERICANS"

1 Kristi Finefield. "A Tale of Two Houses and the U.S. Civil War." Library of Congress, April 9, 2015.

2 Brooks D. Simpson, *Let Us Have Peace: Ulysses S. Grant and the Politics of War & Reconstruction, 1861–1868*. Chapel Hill: University of North Carolina Press, 1991, p. 84.

3 Arthur C. Parker. *The Life of General Ely S. Parker: Last Grand Sachem of the Iroquois and General Grant's Military Secretary*. Buffalo, NY: Buffalo Historical Society, 1919, p. 133.

4   Ulysses S. Grant. *Personal Memoirs of U.S. Grant: Two Volumes in One.* New York: Charles L. Webster & Company, 1886, p. 630.

5   "Narrative of Ely S. Parker re: Robert E. Lee's Surrender at Appomattox," Library of Congress, 1893.

6   Ulysses S. Grant. *Personal Memoirs of U.S. Grant.* New York: Charles L. Webster & Company, 1886, p. 631.

7   Ibid., pp. 629–630.

8   Horace Porter, *Campaigning with Grant.* New York: The Century Company, 1897, pp. 482–483.

9   Ibid., p. 483.

10 Bruce Catton. *A Stillness at Appomattox: The Army of the Potomac Trilogy.* New York City: Knopf Doubleday Publishing Group, 2010.

11 Horace Porter. *Campaigning with Grant.* New York City: The Century Company, 1897, p. 486.

12 Marquis Adolphe de Chambrun. *Impressions of Lincoln and the Civil War: A Foreigner's Account.* New York: Random House, 1952, p. 83.

13 Ibid.

14 Ibid., pp. 82–86.

15 Ibid., p. 84.

16 Frederick William Seward. *Reminiscences of a War-time Statesman and Diplomat, 1830–1915.* New York: G.P. Putnam's Sons, 1916, p. 253.

17 Frank Abial Flower. *Edwin McMasters Stanton: The Autocrat of Rebellion, Emancipation, and Reconstruction.* Akron, OH: The Saalfield Publishing Company, 1905, 278.

18 Benjamin Franklin Morris, ed. *Memorial Record of the Nation's Tribute to Abraham Lincoln.* Washington, D.C.: W.H. & O.H. Morrison, 1865, p. 18.

19 Gideon Welles. *Diary of Gideon Welles, Secretary of the Navy Under Lincoln and Johnson.* Boston: Houghton Mifflin Company, 1911, p. 278.

20 Noah Brooks. *Washington in Lincoln's Time.* New York: The Century Company, 1895, p. 252.

21 Abraham Lincoln, Speech, April 10, 1865. Roy P. Basler, ed. *The Collected Works of Abraham Lincoln* 8 vols. New Brunswick, NJ: Rutgers University Press, 1953, 8: 393.

22 *New York Times,* July 25, 1885.

23 Michael R. Ridderbusch. "The Lincoln Reminiscence Manuscript in the Francis Harrison Pierpont Papers," *West Virginia History: A Journal of Regional Studies,* Spring 2007, p. 87.

24 Ibid.

25 Abraham Lincoln, First debate with Stephen A. Douglas at Ottawa, Illinois, August 21, 1858. Roy P. Basler, ed. *The Collected Works of Abraham Lincoln* 8 vols. New Brunswick, NJ: Rutgers University Press, 1953, 3: 27.

26 William H. Gilman, ed. *The Journals and Miscellaneous Notebooks of Ralph Waldo Emerson*, 16 vols. Cambridge, MA: Harvard University Press, 1960-1982, 15: 459.

27 William H. Crook. *Lincoln's Last Day*. *Harper's Monthly Magazine,* September 1907.

28 Noah Brooks. *Washington in Lincoln's Time*. New York: The Century Company, 1895, p. 255.

LINCOLN'S LAST SPEECH

1 Noah Brooks. *Washington DC in Lincoln's Time*, Herbert Mitgang, ed. University of Georgia Press, 1952, p. 263.

2 Elizabeth Keckley. *Behind the Scenes, Or, Thirty Years a Slave and Four Years in the White House.* New York City: G. W. Carleton & Co., 1868, p. 175.

3 Ibid., p. 177.

4 Michael R. Ridderbusch. "The Lincoln Reminiscence Manuscript in the Francis Harrison Pierpont Papers," *West Virginia History: A Journal of Regional Studies.* Spring 2007, p. 87.

5 Louis P. Masur. *Lincoln's Last Speech: Wartime Reconstruction and the Crisis of Reunion.* New York: Oxford University Press, 2015.

6 Eric Foner. *The Fiery Trial: Abraham Lincoln and American Slavery.* New York: W. W. Norton, 2011, p. 330.

7 Gideon Welles, *Diary of Gideon Welles, Secretary of the Navy Under Lincoln and Johnson.* Boston: Houghton Mifflin Company, 1911, p. 522.

8 Abraham Lincoln to Michael Hahn, March 13, 1864. Roy P. Basler, ed. *The Collected Works of Abraham Lincoln* 8 vols. New Brunswick, NJ: Rutgers University Press, 1953, 7: 243.

9 Doris Kearns Goodwin. *Team of Rivals: The Political Genius of Abraham Lincoln.* New York: Simon & Schuster, 2006, p. 728.

10 Elizabeth Keckley. *Behind the Scenes: Or, Thirty Years a Slave, and Four Years in the White House.* New York: G. W. Carleton & Co., Publishers, 1868, p. 178.

11 John G. Nicolay and John Hay. *Abraham Lincoln: A History Volume 10.* New York: The Century Co., 1909, p. 147.

12 Marquis Adolphe de Chambrun. *Impressions of Lincoln and the Civil War: A Foreigner's Account.* New York: Random House, 1952, p. 93.

13 Noah Brooks. "Personal Reminiscences of Lincoln," *Scribner's Monthly.* 15 (March 1878), p. 567.

14 Ruth Painter Randall. *Lincoln's Sons.* Boston: Little, Brown & Co., 1955, p. 161.

15 Louis P. Masur. *Lincoln's Last Speech: Wartime Reconstruction and the Crisis of Reunion.* New York: Oxford University Press, 2015, p. 166.

16 Ibid.

17 Ibid., p. 168.

18 Ibid., p. 167.

19 Ibid., p. 166.

20 Ibid., p. 169.

21 Abraham Lincoln letter to James H. Van Alene, April 14th, 1865. Roy P. Basler, ed., *The Collected Works of Abraham Lincoln* 8 vols. New Brunswick, NJ: Rutgers University Press, 1953-55, Vol. 8: p. 413.

22 Ibid., p. 180.

23 "The Legacy of the Civil War," National Park Service, p. 2.

24 Ibid.

25 Recollections of William Pitt Kellogg, University of Michigan Library, *The Abraham Lincoln Quarterly,* Vol. 3, No. 7. 1945.

26 "Lincoln's Last Day: New Facts Now Told for the First Time," William Crook, *Harper's Monthly Magazine,* September 1907.

27 Michael Burlingame. *Abraham Lincoln: A Life, Volume 2.* Baltimore: The Johns Hopkins University Press, 2008, p. 794.

28 Gideon Welles. *Diary of Gideon Welles, Secretary of the Navy Under Lincoln and Johnson.* Boston, MA: Houghton Mifflin Company, 1911, 2:280.

29 Southern Historical Society Papers, vol. XXXII. Richmond, Va., January-December 1904.

30 Marquis Adolphe de Chambrun. *Impressions of Lincoln and the Civil War: A Foreigner's Account.* New York: Random House, 1952, pp. 92-93.

31 Mansuell B. Field. *Memories of Many Men and of Some Women.* London: Sampson Low, Marston, Low, & Searle, 1874, p. 321.

GOOD FRIDAY, 1865

1 Elizabeth Keckley. *Behind the Scenes, Or, Thirty Years a Slave and Four Years in the White House.* New York City: G. W. Carleton & Co., 1868, pp. 137–138.

2 W. Emerson Reck. *A. Lincoln: His Last 24 Hours.* Jefferson, NC: McFarland & Company, Inc., Publishers, 1987, p. 9.

3 *Harper's Weekly,* April 22, 1865.

4 W. Emerson Reck. *A. Lincoln: His Last 24 Hours.* Jefferson, NC: McFarland & Company, Inc., Publishers, 1987, p. 20.

5 Edward Winslow Martin. *The Life and Public Services of Schuyler Colfax.* New York: United States Publishing Company, 1868, pp. 187–188.

6 W. Emerson Reck. *A. Lincoln: His Last 24 Hours.* Jefferson, NC: McFarland & Company, Inc., Publishers, 1987, p. 20.

7 Ovando James Hollister. *Life of Schuyler Colfax.* New York: Funk & Wagnalls, 1886, p. 253.

8 Ibid.

9 Richmond Morcom. "They All Loved Lucy," *American Heritage.* October 1970, vol. 21, issue 6.

10 Ward Lemon Hill. *Recollections of Abraham Lincoln,* 1864–1875. Washington, D.C.: 1911, p. 247.

11 Jim Bishop. *The Day Lincoln Was Shot.* New York: Harper and Brothers, 1955, p. 117.

12 W. Emerson Reck. *A. Lincoln: His Last 24 Hours.* Jefferson, NC: McFarland & Company, 1987, p. 44.

13 Ibid., p. 26.

14 Gideon Welles. *Diary of Gideon Welles, Secretary of the Navy Under Lincoln and Johnson.* Boston: Houghton Mifflin Company, 1911, 2:283.

15 Ibid.

16 Frederick W. Seward. *Seward at Washington, As Senator and Secretary of State.* New York: Derby and Miller, 1891, p. 275.

17 Ibid.

18 Courtlandt Canby, ed. *Lincoln and the Civil War: A Profile and a History.* New York: George Braziller Inc., 1958, p. 166.

19 W. Emerson Reck. *A. Lincoln: His Last 24 Hours.* Jefferson, NC: McFarland & Company, Inc., Publishers, 1987, p. 32.

20 William A. Spicer. *History of the Ninth and Tenth Regiments Rhode Island Volunteers, and the Tenth Rhode Island Battery, in the Union Army in 1862.* Providence: Snow & Farnham Printers, 1892, p. 358.

21 Jim Bishop. *The Day Lincoln Was Shot.* New York: Harper and Brothers, 1955, p. 115.

22 Ibid.

23 David S. Shields. "Nat Fuller's Feast," *Commonplace: The Journal of Early American Life.*

24 Gideon Welles. "Lincoln and Johnson," *The Galaxy*, April 1872.

25 Ibid.

26 Ibid.

27 Doris Kearns Goodwin. *Team of Rivals: The Political Genius of Abraham Lincoln*. New York: Simon & Schuster, 2006, p. 732.

28 Ida Tarbell. *The Life of Abraham Lincoln, Volume Four.* New York: Lincoln Historical Society, 1909, p. 28.

29 Abraham Lincoln letter to James H. Van Alen, April 14th, 1865. Roy P. Basler, ed., *The Collected Works of Abraham Lincoln* 8 vols., New Brunswick, NJ: Rutgers University Press, 1953-55, Vol. 8: p. 413.

30 Charles A. Dana. *Recollections of the Civil War.* New York City: D. Appleton and Company, 1913, p. 237-238.

31 W. Emerson Reck. *A. Lincoln: His Last 24 Hours.* Jefferson, NC: McFarland & Company, Inc., Publishers, 1987, p. 46.

32 Mary Todd Lincoln, Letter to Francis B. Carpenter, November 15, 1865.

33 William H. Herndon and Jesse W. Wierk. *Abraham Lincoln: The True Story of a Great Life.* New York: D. Appleton and Company, 1923, 194.

34 W. Emerson Reck. *A. Lincoln: His Last 24 Hours.* Jefferson, NC: McFarland & Company, Inc., Publishers, 1987, p. 49.

35 David Ross Locke. *Divers Views, Opinions, and Prophecies of Yoors Trooly Petroleum V. Nasby.* Cincinnati: R.W. Carroll & Co., 1867, p. 300.

36 W. Emerson Reck. *A. Lincoln: His Last 24 Hours.* Jefferson, NC: McFarland & Company, Inc., Publishers, 1987, p. 52.

37 William H. Crook. "Lincoln's Last Day," *Harper's Monthly Magazine.* September 1907.

38 Ibid.

Section V
RECONSTRUCTION:
A TRAGEDY IN THREE ACTS

1 Rev. Henry Ward Beecher letter to Abraham Lincoln, February 4, 1865. Roy P. Basler, ed. *The Collected Works of Abraham Lincoln* 8 vols. New Brunswick, NJ: Rutgers University Press, 1953–55, 8: p. 318.

2 Naphtali J. Rubinger. *Abraham Lincoln and the Jews.* New York: Jonathan David Publishers, 1962, p. 69.

3 Richard Wightman Fox. "The President Who Died For Us," *New York Times.* April 14, 2006.

4 Theodore Hamm, ed., *Frederick Douglass in Brooklyn*. New York: Akashic Books, 2017, p. 99.

5 William C. Harris. *With Charity For All: Lincoln and the Restoration of the Union*. Lexington: The University Press of Kentucky, 1997, p. 265. *Washington Daily Morning Chronicle*, April 17, 1865.

6 Ibid., p. 267. *Little Rock Unconditional Union*, April 20, 1865. *Little Rock Unconditional Union*, April 22, 1865.

7 "Glorious News. Lincoln and Seward Assassinated! Lee Defeats Grant. Andy Johnson Inaugurated President," *Alabama Beacon*, April 21, 1865.

8 Emma LeConte diary entry, April 21-22, 1865.

9 William Tecumseh Sherman, Letter to Henry Wagner Halleck, April 18, 1865. Reprinted, War Department, et al., *The War of the Rebellion: A Compilation of the Official Records of the Union and Confederate Armie; Series 1 - Volume XLVII, Part 3*. Washington, D.C.: Government Printing Office, 1896, p. 245.

10 James Grant. *The Life and Times of the Greatest Victorian*. New York: W.W. Norton, 2019.

11 Herman Melville. "The Martyr." Faith Barrett and Cristanne Miller, eds., *Words for the Hour: A New Anthology of American Civil War Poetry*. University of Massachusetts Press, 2005. Reprint.

12 William C. Harris. *With Charity For All: Lincoln and the Restoration of the Union*. Lexington: The University Press of Kentucky, 1997, p. 266. Henry L. Dawes to Electra Dawes, April 16, 1865. "The Reconstruction Period, 1865-1869," unpublished manuscript in Dawes Papers.

13 "The Disaffection Among the Southern Soldiers," *Toledo Blade*. *The contents of Abraham Lincoln's pockets on the evening of his assassination*. n.d. Retrieved from the Library of Congress.

14 "A Conscript's Epistle to Jeff. Davis." *The contents of Abraham Lincoln's pockets on the evening of his assassination*. n.d. Retrieved from the Library of Congress.

15 "John Bright on the Presidency." *The contents of Abraham Lincoln's pockets on the evening of his assassination*. n.d. Retrieved from the Library of Congress.

16 "President Lincoln's Letter to Mr. Hackett," *Liverpool Post*. October 1, 1864.

17 "President Lincoln." n.d. Retrieved from Library of Congress.

THE ANTI-LINCOLN

1 "The Johnson Party," *The Atlantic.* September 1866.

2 Carl Schurz. *The Reminiscences of Carl Schurz: Volume 3.* London: John Murray, 1908, pp. 95–6.

3 Eric Foner. *Reconstruction: America's Unfinished Revolution.* New York: Harper Perennial, 2014, p. 282.

4 Ibid., p. 281.

5 R. J. M. Blackett, ed. *Thomas Morris Chester, Black Civil War Correspondent: His Dispatches from the Virginia Front.* Baton Rouge: Louisiana State University Press, 1989, p. 313.

6 Carl Schurz, "Report on the Condition of the South," December 19, 1865. *Teaching American History* website.

7 "MISSISSIPPI; Message of Gov. Humphreys to the Legislature on Negro Troops He Holds that the Courts Should be Open to the Negro," *New York Times.* December 3, 1865.

8 Ulysses S. Grant, *Personal Memoirs and Selected Letters 1839–1865.* New York: Library of America, 1990, p. 752.

9 The first seven ex-Confederates elected to Congress took their seats in July 1868: Nelson Tift, William P. Edwards, Pierce M. B. Young, Oliver H. Dockery, Christopher C. Bowen, Manuel S. Corely, and James H. Gross.

10 James M. McPherson. "War and Peace in the post-Civil War South," *The Making of Peace: Rulers, States and the Aftermath of War,* eds. Williamson Murray and Jim Lacey. New York: Cambridge University Press, 2009, p. 163.

11 Eric L. McKitrick. *Andrew Johnson and Reconstruction.* Chicago: University of Chicago Press, 1960, p. 84.

12 David W. Blight. *Frederick Douglass: Prophet of Freedom.* New York: Simon & Schuster, 2018, p. 475.

13 "Down in the Cinnabar Mines," *Harper's New Monthly Magazine,* October 1865.

14 W. E. B. Du Bois, *Black Reconstruction in America, 1860–1880.* New York: Oxford University Press, 2007, p. 323.

15 W. E. B. Du Bois. "The Freedmen's Bureau," *The Atlantic Monthly,* March 1901.

16 Andrew Johnson: Veto of the Freedmen's Bureau Bill, February 19, 1866.

17 Paul H. Bergeron, ed. *The Papers of Andrew Johnson: Volume 10,*

February–July 1866. Knoxville: The University of Tennessee Press, 1967, p. 152.

18 Andrew Johnson's veto message for the Civil Rights bill, March 27, 1866.

19 Ulysses S. Grant, Letter to his wife, Julia, September 9, 1866. Gerard W. Gawalt, ed. *My Dear President: Letters Between Presidents and Their Wives.* New York: Black Dog & Leventhal Publishers, 2006, p. 103.

20 Burke A. Hinsdale, ed. *The Works of James Abram Garfield.* Boston: James R. Osgood and Co., 1882, p. 249.

21 William Stoddard. *Abraham Lincoln and Andrew Johnson.* New York: Frederick A. Stokes & Brother, 1888, p. 40 of Andrew Johnson section.

22 Andrew Johnson, Veto of the First Reconstruction Act, March 2, 1867.

23 Theodore Hamm, ed. *Frederick Douglass in Brooklyn.* New York: Akashic Books, 2007, p. 109.

24 Andrew Johnson, "Proclamation 179—Granting Full Pardon and Amnesty for the Offense of Treason Against the United States During the Late Civil War," December 25, 1868.

USA VS. KKK

1 *Cincinnati Commercial*, August 28, 1868.

2 John S. Reynolds. *Reconstruction in South Carolina, 1865 to 1877.* South Carolina: The State Co. Publishers, 1905, p. 495.

3 William C. Davis. *Crucible of Command: Ulysses S. Grant and Robert E. Lee—The War They Fought, the Peace They Forged.* Boston: Da Capo Press, 2014, pp. 478-479.

4 Nick Sacco. "A Free Country for White Men: The Legacy of Frank Blair Jr. and His Statue in St. Louis," *The Journal of the Civil War Era.* July 28, 2017.

5 James D. McCabe. *The Life and Public Services of Horatio Seymour: Together with a Complete and Authentic Life of Francis P. Blair, Jr.* New York City: United States Publishing Company, 1868, pp. 311–312.

6 "Inauguration," *New York Times.* March 5, 1869.

7 Ulysses S. Grant, First Inaugural Address, March 4, 1869.

8 Jean Edward Smith. *Grant.* New York: Simon & Schuster, 2001, p. 545.

9 Campbell Robertson. "Over 2,000 Black People Were Lynched From 1865 to 1877, Study Finds," *New York Times.* June 16, 2020.

10 Allen C. Guelzo. *Reconstruction: A Concise History.* New York: Oxford University Press, 2018, p. 77.

11 James M. McPherson. "War and Peace in the Post–Civil War South," *The Making of Peace: Rulers, States and the Aftermath of War*, eds. Williamson Murray and Jim Lacey. Cambridge University Press, 2009, p. 173.

12 Forrest G. Wood. *Black Scare: The Racist Response to Emancipation and Reconstruction*. University of California Press, 1970, p. 122.

13 Gideon Welles. *Diary of Gideon Welles, Secretary of the Navy Under Lincoln and Johnson*. Boston, MA: Houghton Mifflin Company, 1911, 2:279.

14 John Y. Simon, ed. *The Papers of Ulysses S. Grant: November 1, 1870–May 31, 1871*. Carbondale, IL: Southern Illinois University Press, 1998, p. 246.

15 Ibid., p. 336.

16 "Able Letter from Honorable Amos T. Akerman of Georgia," *New York Times.* September 12, 1868.

17 "POLITICAL AFFAIRS.; Address of the Tennessee Legislative Committee to the President," *New York Times.* September 12, 1868.

18 Stephen Cresswell. *Mormons and Cowboys, Moonshiners and Klansman: Federal Law Enforcement in the South and West, 1870–1893*. Tuscaloosa: University of Alabama Press, 2002, p. 49.

19 Jean Edward Smith. *Grant.* New York: Simon & Schuster, 2001, p. 547.

20 Charles Lane. *The Day Freedom Died: The Colfax Massacre, the Supreme Court, and the Betrayal of Reconstruction*. New York: Henry Holt and Company, 2008, p. 4.

21 Ron Chernow. *Grant.* New York: Penguin Books, 2017, p. 710.

22 Henry Louis Gates. *Reconstruction: America After the Civil War*, PBS documentary, 2019.

23 Jean Edward Smith. *Grant.* New York: Simon & Schuster, 2001, p. 547.

THE STAR-SPANGLED BETRAYAL

1 James M. McPherson. "War and Peace in the post-Civil War South," *The Making of Peace: Rulers, States and the Aftermath of War,* eds. Williamson Murray and Jim Lacey. Cambridge University Press, 2009, p. 171.

2 "Forty-Fourth Congress: March 4, 1875, to March 3, 1877." List of members from House.gov.

3 C. Van Woodward. *Reunion and Reaction: The Compromise of 1877 and the End of Reconstruction*. New York: Oxford University Press, 1966, p. 4.

4   Ibid., p. 9.

5   Caitlin McCarthy. "The 'lessons' of the United Daughters of the Con-
    federacy still have influence today in the Mid-South." LocalMemphis
    .com / WATN-TV ABC 24, September 8, 2020.

6   Susan Cianci Salvatore, ed., *Civil Rights in America: A National Historic
    Landmarks Theme Study* (2009), 14.

7   Glenn Feldman. *The Disfranchisement Myth: Poor Whites and Suffrage
    Restriction in Alabama.* Athens: University of Georgia Press, 2004,
    p. 136.

8   Eric Foner ed. *Freedom's Lawmakers: A Directory of Black Officeholders
    During Reconstruction Revised Edition.* Baton Rouge: Louisiana State
    University Press, 1996.

9   "A Talk with Jeff. Davis," *Ventura Signal.* Originally published in the
    Lynchburg Virginian, May 9, 1884.

10 Jeffrey Martin. "Alabama Lawmakers Call for End to Jefferson Davis
    Holiday in Only State to Still Give Confederate President Own Day,"
    Newsweek. June 4, 2020.

11 Frederick Douglass. "Composite Nation," Lecture in the Parker Frater-
    nity Course, Boston—Folder 1 of 3. 1867. Manuscript/Mixed Mate-
    rial. Retrieved from the Library of Congress, www.loc.gov/item/mfd
    .22016/.

12 "Lincoln's Diplomacy." Kogoro Takahira. *Abraham Lincoln: The Tribute
    of a Century: 1809–1909.* AC. McClurg & Co., 1910, p. 243.

13 R. J. M. Blackett, ed. *Thomas Morris Chester, Black Civil War Correspon-
    dent: His Dispatches from the Virginia Front.* Baton Rouge: Louisiana
    State University Press, 1989, p. 73.

14 Walt Whitman. *Prose Works 1892, Volume 2.* New York: New York UP,
    1963, p. 508.

15 Merrill D. Peterson. *Lincoln in American Memory.* New York: Oxford
    University Press, 1995, p. 258.

16 Harold Holzer. *Monument Man: The Life and Art of Daniel Chester
    French.* New York, Princeton Architectural Press, 2019, pp. 284-285.

Section VI
THE FIGHT FOR PEACE

1   Letter from President Herbert Hoover to Emanuel Hertz, June 17,
    1929.

WOODROW WILSON'S LOST CAUSE

1 Woodrow Wilson. "Robert E. Lee: An Interpretation." Speech at the University of North Carolina, January 19, 1909.

2 Woodrow Wilson, "Abraham Lincoln: A Man of the People," speech in Chicago, February 12, 1909.

3 Joseph R. Wilson. *Mutual Relations of Master and Slave as Taught in the Bible.* Augusta, GA: Steam Press of Chronicle & Sentinel, 1861.

4 August Heckscher. *Woodrow Wilson: A Biography.* New York: Scribner, 1991, p. 13.

5 Woodrow Wilson. "Essay on John Bright," *Virginia University Magazine*, 19:354–370, March 1880.

6 Woodrow Wilson. "The Reconstruction of the Southern States," *The Atlantic.* January 1901.

7 Ibid.

8 Woodrow Wilson. Speech to National Press Club. May 15, 1916. Ray Stannard Baker and William E. Dodd, eds. *The New Democracy: Presidential Messages, Addresses, and Other Papers (1913–1917).* New York: 1926, 2:171.

9 Arthur S. Link. *Wilson the Diplomatist: A Look at His Major Foreign Policies.* New York: The Johns Hopkins Press, 1968, p. 7.

10 Woodrow Wilson. Speech to Senate, "Peace Without Victory." January 22, 1917.

11 "Lloyd George on Lincoln," *New York Times*, February 13, 1917.

12 Merrill D. Peterson. *Lincoln in American Memory.* New York: Oxford University Press, 1994, p. 199.

13 "George and Lincoln," *The Cambrian.* September 1, 1917, p. 11.

14 Baker And Blink, and Carol Hirsch. "Abraham Lincoln What Would You Do?" Milwaukee: Metropolitan Music Pub. Co., 1918. [Monographic.] Notated Music. https://www.loc.gov/item/2013567030/.

15 Arthur S. Link, ed. *The Papers of Woodrow Wilson*, 69 vols. Princeton, N.J.: Princeton University Press, 1966–1994, 49:485.

16 Joseph E. Persico. "Nov. 11, 1918: Wasted Lives on Armistice Day," *Army Times.* November 9, 2017.

17 Patricia O'Toole. *The Moralist: Woodrow Wilson and the World He Made.* New York: Simon & Schuster, 2018, p. 341.

18 Ibid., p. 347.

19 David Lloyd George. *The Truth About the Peace Treaties.* London: Victor Gollancz Ltd., 1938, p. 225.

20 Henry Wickham Steed. *Through Thirty Years, 1892–1922: A Personal Narrative.* London: William Heinemann, Ltd., 1924, 2:310.

21 Isabelle de Pommereau, "Germany finishes Paying WWI Reparations, Ending Century of 'Guilt,'" *Christian Science Monitor*, October 4, 2010.

22 Harry S. Truman, Letter to Bess Wallace. October 30, 1918.

23 Robert H. Ferrell, ed. *Dear Bess: The Letters from Harry to Bess Truman, 1910–1959.* Columbia: University of Missouri Press, 1983, p. 281.

24 John Meynard Keynes. *The Economic Consequences of the Peace.* London: Macmillan and Co., 1919, p. 51.

25 Herbert Hoover. *The Problems of Lasting Peace.* New York: Doubleday, Doran and Company, 1942, p. 121.

26 Herbert Hoover. *Years of Adventure: 1874–1920.* New York: Macmillan, 1952, p. 462.

27 Spencer Tucker, ed. *World War I: Encyclopedia, Vol 1.* Santa Barbara: ABC-CLIO, 2005 p. 426.

DEPLOYING THE LINCOLN LEGEND

1 Richard F. Weingroff. "The Lincoln Highway," *Highway History*. Federal Highway Administration. April 7, 2011.

2 Edgar DeWitt Jones. *Lincoln and the Preachers.* Books for Libraries Press, 1970, p. 154.

3 "Silent Films featuring Abraham Lincoln," IMDb, January 28, 2018. https://www.imdb.com/list/ls021683164/.

4 Franklin D. Roosevelt. "Address at the Dedication of the Memorial on the Gettysburg Battlefield, Gettysburg, Pennsylvania," July 3, 1938.

5 Ibid.

6 Barry Schwartz. "Memory as a Cultural System: Abraham Lincoln in World War II," *International Journal of Sociology and Social Policy*, December 1997.

7 Robert Sherwood, *Abe Lincoln in Illinois* (play), 1938.

8 Merrill D. Peterson. *Lincoln in American Memory.* New York: Oxford University Press, 1994, p. 322.

9 Mark Harris. *Five Came Back: A Story of Hollywood and the Second World War.* New York: Penguin Books, 2014, p. 136.

10 Barry Schwartz, "Memory as a Cultural System: Abraham Lincoln in World War II," *International Journal of Sociology and Social Policy*, December 1997.

11 King George VI, Christmas message, December 25, 1942.

12 "Lincoln Day Broadcast Will Cover the World; Wallace, Archbishop of Canterbury on Radio," *New York Times*, February 6, 1944.

13 Barry Schwartz. "Memory as a Cultural System: Abraham Lincoln in World War II," *International Journal of Sociology and Social Policy*. December 1997.

14 Kaylyn Sawyer. "Belonging to the Ages: The Enduring Relevance of Aaron Copland's *Lincoln Portrait*," *Journal of the Abraham Lincoln Association*, vol. 40: 1, Winter 2019, pp. 25–45.

15 Howard Taubman. "Copland on Lincoln," *New York Times*. February 1, 1953.

16 Carl Sandburg's contribution to the Radio Script for CBS, "Coca Cola . . . 'The Pause That Refreshes on the Air,'" August 16, 1942.

A PLAN TO WIN THE PEACE

1 Irwin L. Hunt. *American Military Government of Occupied Germany, 1918–1920* (1943), p. viii.

2 Michael R. Beschloss. *The Conquerors: Roosevelt, Truman and the Destruction of Hitler's Germany, 1941–1945*. New York City: Simon & Schuster, 2002, p. 15.

3 Franklin D. Roosevelt, Speech to Congress. September 14, 1943.

4 Franklin Delano Roosevelt, "Memorandum for the Secretary of State," October 20, 1944.

5 *Public Papers of the Presidents of the United States: F. D. Roosevelt, 1944–1945, vol. 13*, pp. 209-210. (Franklin D. Roosevelt's July 29, 1944, press conference.)

6 Irwin L. Hunt. *American Military Government of Occupied Germany, 1918–1920*. March 4, 1920, p. 64.

7 Rebecca Patterson. *Revisiting a School of Military Government: How Reanimating a World War II–Era Institution Could Professionalize Military Nation Building*. Kauffman Foundation Research Series, June 2011, pp. 10, 17.

8 Ibid., pp. 8–9.

DENAZIFICATION AND DEMOCRATIZATION

1 Michael R. Beschloss. *The Conquerors: Roosevelt, Truman and the Destruction of Hitler's Germany, 1941–1945*. New York: Simon & Schuster, 2002, p. 255.

2   Robert J. Donovan. *The Second Victory: The Marshall Plan and the Post-war Revival of Europe.* New York: Madison Books, 1987, p. 17.

3   Michael R. Beschloss. *The Conquerors: Roosevelt, Truman and the Destruction of Hitler's Germany, 1941–1945.* New York: Simon & Schuster, 2002, pp. 229–230.

4   Jean Edward Smith. *Lucius D. Clay: An American Life.* New York City: Henry Holt and Company, 1990, p. 6.

5   "Lucius Clay Dies; Led Berlin Airlift," *New York Times.* April 17, 1978, A1.

6   U.S. Army. *Handbook for Military Government,* "Supreme Commander's Area of Control," part I.

7   Jean Edward Smith. *Lucius D. Clay: An American Life.* New York: Henry Holt and Company, 1990, p. 6.

8   Ibid., p. 238.

9   John Steele Gordon. "Forgotten Viceroy," *American Heritage*, February/March 1992, vol. 43, issue 1.

10   Lucius Clay. *Decision in Germany.* New York: Doubleday & Co., 1950, p. ix.

11   Directive to the Commander in Chief of the U.S. Occupation Forces (JCS 1067) (April 1945).

12   Lucius Clay. *Decision in Germany.* New York: Doubleday & Co., 1950, pp. 67–68.

13   "Patton Belittles Denazification; Holds Rebuilding More Important," *New York Times.* September 23, 1945, p. 26.

14   "Interview with General Lucius D. Clay," *Senior Officers Debriefing Program*, p. 18.

15   David W. Ellwood. *Rebuilding Europe: Western Europe, America and Postwar Reconstruction.* New York: Routledge, 1992, p. 54.

16   Robert Murphy. *Diplomat Among Warriors: The Unique World of a Foreign Service Expert.* London: Doubleday & Company, 1964, p. 251.

17   John Steele Gordon. "Forgotten Viceroy," *American Heritage*, February/March 1992, vol. 43, issue 1.

18   David Phillips. *Educating the Germans: People and Policy in the British Zone of Germany, 1945–1949.* London: Bloomsbury Academic, 2018, p. 117.

19   Richard L. Merritt. *Democracy Imposed: U.S. Occupation Policy and the German Public, 1945–1949.* New Haven, CT: Yale University Press, 1995, p. 273.

20   Earl F. Ziemke. *The U.S. Army in the Occupation of Germany, 1944–1946.* Washington, D.C.: Center of Military History, United States Army, 1990, p. 426.

21 Richard Carwardine and Jay Sexton, eds. *The Global Lincoln*. New York: Oxford University Press, 2011, p. 246.

22 Ibid.

23 Jared Peatman. *The Long Shadow of Lincoln's Gettysburg Address*. Carbondale, IL: Southern Illinois University Press, 2013, p. 148.

MACARTHUR AND THE EMPEROR

1 Douglas MacArthur's radio address, September 2, 1945.

2 Douglas MacArthur. *Reminiscences*. New York: McGraw, 1964, p. 312.

3 Ibid., pp. 281–282.

4 *Foreign Relations of the United States, 1946, The Far East, vol. III*. Washington, D.C.: GPO, 1969, pp. 395–397.

5 William Manchester. *American Caesar: Douglas MacArthur 1880–1964*. New York: Back Bay Books, 2008, p. 10.

6 Ibid.

7 Ibid., p. 479.

8 Geoffrey Perret. *Old Soldiers Never Die: The Life of Douglas MacArthur*. New York: Random House, 1996, pp. 516–517.

9 Richard Carwardine and Jay Sexton, eds. *The Global Lincoln*. New York: Oxford University Press, 2011, p. 226.

10 Ibid., p. 227.

11 "An International Admirer," Smithsonian National Postal Museum website, postalmuseum.si.edu.

12 Emerson O. Bradshaw, Charles E. Shike, and Helen F. Topping, eds. *Kagawa in Lincoln's Land*. New York: J. Henry Carpenter, 1936.

13 Edward Behr. *Hirohito: Behind the Myth*. New York: Villard Books, 1989, 35.

14 Douglas MacArthur. *Reminiscences*. New York: McGraw, 1964, pp. 282–283.

15 Philip R. Piccigallo. *The Japanese On Trial: Allied War Crimes Operations in the East, 1945–1951*. Austin: University of Texas Press, 1979, pp. 263–265.

16 Nadia Schadlow. *War and the Art of Governance: Consolidating Combat Success into Political Victory*. Washington, D.C.: Georgetown University Press, 2017, p. 131.

17 "Japanese Lincoln: Tokyo's Best Actors Give Their Own Version of Drinkwater's Play," *Life Magazine*, April 8, 1946. pp. 77-80.

18 Henry M. Jackson. "Lincoln: Lesson in Leadership," *Congressional Record*. February 28, 1961.

19　Richard Carwardine and Jay Sexton, eds. *The Global Lincoln.* New York: Oxford University Press, 2011.

20　Ibid., p. 230.

"THE GOLDEN RULE FOR WORLD PEACE"

1　Margaret Truman. *Where the Buck Stops: The Personal and Private Writings of Harry S. Truman.* New York: Warner Books, 1989, p. 6.

2　Harry S. Truman address, "Golden Rule for World Peace," October 7, 1945.

3　"Marshall Myths: 'The Most Unsordid Act In History,' "The George C. Marshall Foundation website, March 11, 2016.

4　George C. Marshall, Speech at Harvard University "The Marshall Plan," June 5, 1947.

5　David McCullough. *Truman.* New York: Simon & Schuster, 1992, p. 669.

6　Lawrence S. Kaplan. *The Conversion of Arthur H. Vandenberg.* University Press of Kentucky, 2015, p. 166.

7　Greg Behrman. *The Most Noble Adventure: The Marshall Plan and the Time When America Helped Save Europe.* New York: Free Press, 2007, p. 151.

8　Harry S. Truman, Address of the President to Congress, Recommending Assistance to Greece and Turkey, March 12, 1947.

9　Paul G. Hoffman. *Peace Can Be Won.* Garden City, NY: Doubleday and Company, 1951, pp. 19-20.

10　Ibid.

11　Ibid.

12　*The Economist,* April 20, 1948.

13　Konrad Adenauer, interview by Philip C. Brooks. Harry S. Truman Library, Bonn, Germany, June 10, 1964. Quoted in David Frum, *Trumpocalypse: Restoring American Democracy.* New York: Harper, 2020, p. 243.

14　William Lambers. "How Lincoln Helped to Win the Peace After World War II," *History News Network.* February 8, 2015.

15　Winston Churchill, *A History of the English-Speaking Peoples.* Reprinted in *The Lincoln Anthology,* Harold Holzer, ed. The Library of America, 2009, p. 612.

16　Stephen E. Ambrose. *Citizen Soldiers: The U.S. Army from the Normandy Beaches to the Bulge to the Surrender of Germany June 7, 1944, to May 7, 1945.* New York: Simon & Schuster, pp. 472–473.

17 Henry Kissinger. *Diplomacy*. New York: Simon & Schuster, 1994, p. 425.

CONCLUSION

1 Abraham Lincoln, Address to the New Jersey State Senate. Trenton, New Jersey, February 21, 1861.

2 Winston Churchill. *My Early Life*. New York: Touchstone, 1930, p. 346.

3 Richard White. *The Republic for Which It Stands*. Oxford University Press, 2017, p. 855.

4 Mark L. Bradley. *The Army and Reconstruction, 1865–1877*. Washington, D.C.: Center of Military History, United States Army, 2015, p. 72.

5 Roy Licklider. "The Consequences of Negotiated Settlements in Civil Wars, 1945-1993," *American Political Science Review*, vol. 89, no. 3, September 1995, pp. 681–690. Cited in *Sustaining the Peace After Civil War*.

6 Stability Operations—FM 3-07—Headquarters, Department of the Army, October 2008.

7 Ibid.

8 Gary J. Bass. "What Really Causes Civil War?" *New York Times Magazine*. August 13, 2006.

9 Boutros-Boutros Ghali. *Supplement to an Agenda for Peace*. Position Paper of the Secretary General on the Occasion of the 50th Anniversary of the United Nations, January 3, 1995.

10 Frederick Douglass, Oration in memory of Abraham Lincoln, delivered at the unveiling of the Freedmen's Monument in Memory of Abraham Lincoln, in Lincoln Park, Washington, D.C., April 14, 1876.

11 Barack Obama, Presidential Campaign Announcement, Springfield, Illinois, February 10, 2007.

12 David W. Blight. *Race and Reunion: The Civil War in American Memory*. Cambridge, MA: Belknap Press, 2001, pp. 3-4.

13 Greg Gaffe and Jenna Johnson. "In America, talk turns to something not spoken of for 150 years: Civil War," *Washington Post*, March 2, 2019.

14 William Cummings. "Iowa Rep. Steve King says America is heading toward another civil war," *USA Today*, June 25, 2018.

15 Matt Stieb, "Trump Quotes Ally Who Predicts a 'Civil War Like Fracture' If He Is Impeached," *New York Magazine*, September 30, 2019.

16 Hillary George-Parkin, "Insurrection Merch Shows How Mainstream Extremism Has Become," Vox, January 12, 2021.

17 Maria Cramer. "Confederate Flag an Unnerving Sight in Capitol," *New York Times*, January 9, 2021.

18 David Armitage. *Civil War: A History in Ideas.* Yale University Press, 2017, p. 14.

19 President Ulysses S. Grant, Speech at Annual Reunion of the Army of the Tennessee in Des Moines, Iowa, September 29, 1875.

20 Robert Penn Warren. *The Legacy of the Civil War: Meditations on the Centennial.* New York: Random House, 1961. Reprint, Cambridge, MA: Harvard University Press, 1983, pp. 32, 18.

21 "CONGRATULATING THE PRESIDENT.; A Serenade by the Clubs, and a Speech by Mr. Lincoln," *New York Times*, November 11, 1864.

22 George C. Marshall. "Essentials to Peace" (Nobel lecture), December 11, 1953.

23 John F. Kennedy, Commencement Address at American University, Washington, D.C., June 10, 1963.

24 Michael E. O'Hanlon. "Iraq Without a Plan," *Brookings*, January 1, 2005.

25 Conrad C. Crane and W. Andrew Terrill. "Reconstructing Iraq: insights, challenges, and missions for military forces in a post-conflict scenario," Carlisle Barracks, PA: Strategic Studies Institute, U.S. Army War College, 2003.

26 Abraham Lincoln, Speech at Milwaukee, Wisconsin, September 30, 1859.

27 Mahatma Gandhi, *Indian Opinion*, August 26, 1905.

28 Jörg Nagler. "The Lincoln Image in Germany," *American Studies Journal* 60, 2016.

29 The Martin Luther King, Jr. Research and Education Institute at Stanford University, online document search accessed on June 29, 2021.

30 Nelson Mandela. "Address at HJ Heinz Company Foundation Distinguished Lecture, Pennsylvania," December 6, 1991.

31 John Carlin. "Nelson Mandela: Africa's Lincoln," *ABC News* [Australia], December 5, 2013.

32 Abraham Lincoln, Speech at Springfield, Illinois, October 4, 1854.

Illustration Credits

1. National Archives and Records Administration (NARA)
2. Library of Congress, Prints and Photographs Division, [reproduction number, e.g., LC-USZ62-2578 (b&w film copy neg.)]
3. Library of Congress, Prints and Photographs Division, [reproduction number, LC-USA7-16837 (b&w film copy neg.) LC-USA7-8501 (b&w film copy neg.)]
4. Library of Congress, Prints and Photographs Division, [reproduction number, LC-DIG-ppmsca-19192 (digital file from original) LC-USZ62-7542 (b&w film copy neg.)]
5. Library of Congress, Prints and Photographs Division, [reproduction number, LC-DIG-pga-04994 (digital file from original print) LC-USZ62-1990 (b&w film copy neg.)]
6. Library of Congress, Rare Book and Special Collections Division, Alfred Whital Stern Collection of Lincolniana.
7. Library of Congress, Prints and Photographs Division, [reproduction number, LC-DIG-ppmsca-19199 (digital file from original item) LC-USZ62-92539 (b&w film copy neg.)]
8. Courtesy of the Moorland-Spingarn Research Center, Howard University Archives, Howard University, Washington, D.C.
9. Library of Congress, Prints and Photographs Division, [reproduction number, LC-DIG-ppmsca-69250 (digital file from original, front) LC-DIG-ppmsca-69251 (digital file from original, back)]
10. Library of Congress, Prints and Photographs Division, [reproduction number, LC-DIG-ppmsca-08541 (digital file from original print, recto) LC-DIG-ppmsca-57647 (digital file from original print, verso) LC-USZ62-123372 (b&w film copy neg.)]
11. New York Public Library, Schomburg Center for Research in Black Culture, Photographs and Prints Division

12. Library of Congress, Prints and Photographs Division, [reproduction number, LC-USZ62-75182 (b&w film copy neg.)]
13. Civil war photographs, 1861–1865, Library of Congress, Prints and Photographs Division, [LC-DIG-cwpb-04294 (digital file from original neg.) LC-B8171-7890 (b&w film neg.)]
14. Public domain, photographer unknown.
15. Library of Congress, Prints and Photographs Division, [reproduction number, LC-USZ62-67405 (b&w film copy neg.)]
16. Library of Congress, Rare Book And Special Collections Division, The Alfred Whital Stern Collection of Lincolniana
17. "Part of the Lincoln Financial Foundation Collection, courtesy of the Indiana State Museum."
18. Library of Congress, Prints and Photographs Division, [reproduction number, LC-USZ62-6932 (b&w film copy neg.)]
19. "Chicago History Museum, ICHi-052424."
20. Library of Congress, Prints and Photographs Division, [reproduction number, LC-DIG-ppmsca-59365 (digital file from original item)]
21. Museum of Fine Arts, Houston (courtesy of Bridgeman Images)
22. "Randolph Linsly Simpson African-American Collection. Yale Collection of American Literature, Beinecke Rare Book and Manuscript Library."
23. Library of Congress, Prints and Photographs Division, [reproduction number, LC-DIG-pga-01619 (digital file from original print) LC-USZC2-1720 (color film copy slide) LC-USZ62-10180 (b&w film copy neg.)]
24. Library of Congress, Prints and Photographs Division, [reproduction number, LC-USZ62-128619 (b&w film copy neg.)]
25. Library of Congress, Prints and Photographs Division, [reproduction number, LC-USZC4-14985 (color film copy transparency)]
26. Library of Congress, Prints and Photographs Division, [reproduction number, LC-DIG-ppmsca-18640 (digital file from original item) LC-USZC4-2426 (color film copy transparency) LC-USZ62-117094 (b&w film copy neg.)]
27. "Image from the Collections of The Henry Ford."
28. "Character-Culture-Citizenship Guides" T.G. Nihols Co, Inc. Kansas City. Collection of the Author.
29. Danita Delimont / Alamy Stock Photo. Photographer: Dave Bartruff / DanitaDelimont.com
30. "Punch Cartoon Library / TopFoto"

31. Abraham Lincoln Museum at Lincoln Memorial University, Harrogate, Tennessee
32. Abraham Lincoln Museum at Lincoln Memorial University, Harrogate, Tennessee
33. "United States Holocaust Memorial Museum Collection, Gift of David and Zelda Silberman."
34. "As in 1865—so in 1943"—February 12, 1943—*Philadelphia Record*
35. "United States Army Signal Corps. Harry S. Truman Library."
36. Library of Congress, Prints and Photographs Division, NYWT&S Collection, [reproduction number, LC-DIG-ds-00051 (digital file from original photograph)]
37. Library of Congress, Prints and Photographs Division, NYWT&S Collection, [reproduction number, e.g., LC-USZ62-111645 (b&w film copy neg.)]
38. Alfred Eisenstaedt/The LIFE Picture Collection/Shutterstock.
39. HUPSF Commencement, 1947 (5). Harvard University Archives.
40. Library of Congress, Prints and Photographs Division, NYWT&S Collection, [reproduction number, LC-USZ62-98239 (b&w film copy neg.)]
41. Getty Trust
42. (AP Photo/Markus Schreiber)

Index

About the Author

John Avlon is a senior political analyst and anchor at CNN. He is an award-winning columnist and the author of *Independent Nation*, *Wingnuts*, and *Washington's Farewell*, as well as coeditor of the *Deadline Artists* anthologies. He was the editor in chief and managing director of *The Daily Beast* and served as chief speechwriter for the mayor of New York. Avlon's essay "The Resilient City" was selected to conclude *Empire City: New York Through the Centuries* and won acclaim as "the single best essay written in the wake of 9/11." He lives with his wife, Margaret Hoover, host of *Firing Line* on PBS, and their two children—Jack and Toula Lou—in New York.